Saint Johnny Walker's

How to…
Become A Saint

By
Antonio Salacuri

Saint Johnny Walker's "How to… Become a Saint"

By
Antonio Salacuri

All rights reserved

No part of this publication may be reproduced in any material form, including photocopying or storing it in any medium by electronic means without the written permission of the copyright owner

Warning:
The doing of an unauthorized act in relation to a copyright work may result in both, civil claim for damages AND most certainly a criminal prosecution
In other words…
Don't even think about it

ISBN
978-0-9558556-0-3

Saint Johnny Walker's
"How to… Become a Saint"
Based on a true story
Pro-logos

Hi there… I'm Saint Johnny Walker, (SJW) the author;
And YES, I am a REAL Saint; at least that is what people around my life address me as;
The story in this book is one of a young man, (me) an ordinary person, who knew nothing more than any other person of his age, a young man who in his life knew only how to cook for a living and knew only the odd pint every other day for his entertainment;
But one day, an ordinary day in the middle of November, something out of the ordinary occurred;
And that something turned his life around;
He tried his luck in winning a free winter holiday, and of course he thought his luck had indeed changed when he was informed of the good news;
Little did he know at the time that from that day his entire life will change; little did he know or even imagine what an adventure was actually awaited him; little did he know that he was headed for… "THE" ultimate disaster at first; little did he know he was to go through "hell" and back and not just the once.

I know it's a bit of a tall order for anyone to understand straight away, but reading the story, one would get there; This is a true story of a young man who, though not really a religious person became a Saint;
Yes… "A living Saint" and without realizing it at first, perform miracles, and in doing so, suffered enormously physically and mentally every time; in fact in doing all these miracles, cost him his life a couple of times, but he managed to "come back" and yes, I do explain "how" and of course, how he got that somewhat famous name;
This is a story of "Saint Johnny Walker"

Please note: although this is a true story, the names of people and locations were changed, to; Shall we say…?
            "Protect the innocent"
Also; I feel I must issue a **WARNING**; In reading this brilliant story, it might have an affect on your character, it might change the way you think, and it might change your life;
So, if by any chance you think that the way you think or the way you live is indeed perfect, **do not buy this book;**

                    Happy reading
                Saint Johnny Walker

Saint Johnny Walker's "How to... Become a Saint"

Chapter one

It all started one gloomy and wet afternoon, when I decided to read the newspaper I found in the underground train, heading for home after a straight ten hour work, cooking;
I came across a page with the phrase;
"Would you like a fourteen day winter holiday in Italy, absolutely FREE"?
Free holiday huh?
I mean halloo… who wouldn't?
Mmm I thought, I can just about imagine it, a winter holiday in the sun, what can possibly beat that?
I took the paper with me at home.
I looked out the window, saw the rain drops on the window pain and cried out…
Free holiday huh, Wow…!!!
I can do with some of that;
Well, the first thing that came to mind, as any "normal" person would think was what's the catch?

But what the hell, I had nothing to loose by answering the questions anyway.
So there I was, "hooked" on the idea of a free holiday; followed the page down, and answered all the questions;
I must admit, some of them were odd, some extremely difficult and some of my answers were pure "guess and hope for the best";
Needless to tell you all, I have indeed won that holiday.
All I had to pay was the airport taxes and I had a two weeks holiday in the Mediterranean, in a paradise island;
Oh I could just imagine it, lying under the sun all day breakfast, lunch and dinner all ready for me for a change.
I mean is there a better wish one can think of, especially in the middle of winter?
That particulate moment I was actually seeing the sun out there through the window, even though it was pouring.
A free holiday, in Italy, in the sun, wow!!!
Oh what a day I was having!!!

Two days later, I received the ticket through the post when, I discovered that included in the free holiday was a seven day cruise in a second class cabin, all meals included too;
Oh what?
A holiday within a holiday…?
Wow indeed!!!
Can it get any better I wondered?
I was flying in three days, so naturally through all my excitement I started making all my little preparations;
After all I only had three days to go, and there is a lot to be done; cancelled the milkman and make sure my good friend who lives next door will take care of my cat for two weeks;
These three days that followed for my "departure" I had an amazing discovery, winter days are too long, much longer than summer, even though I knew it was the other way around, every time I looked at my little clock by the side of my bed, somehow I thought it was always the same time, time just wouldn't move;

The times I tested it if it was actually working;
The three days felt more like three weeks.
Needless to say that the last twenty-four hours I had no rest at all, no sleep, was uneasy, packed my suitcase time and time again just to make sure I had everything I needed.
I was going through a rough time, an ordeal I would say;
But, thanks to my friend from next door, I was "easing" down, he was taking my mind to exotic places, the fun I was going to have, the nice hotel, the Mediterranean waters, the cruise, the girls…!!!
Many times I heard him cried out, you lucky so & so, wish I was going with you;
Seeing me like this he was kind enough to stay up and keep me company until the next morning when the cab arrived.
Finally, it was time;
Oh… the adrenaline was so high;
I quickly grabbed my suitcase, say bye to my friend and my cat, and in record time I was in the cab.

The driver was an Indian chap and not at all talkative;
Mind you I was doing all the talking, explaining where I was going and how I won the holiday;
Don't really know if he understood any of all that, but I didn't care really, I was on the move, I was officially on a holiday.
A winter holiday of a lifetime and a free one at that;
Didn't even care of how foggy it was out there, for me it was a nice and beautiful day;
I was actually "living" a few hours ahead of time;
As if the present didn't exist;
Little did I know of what was waiting for me, little did I know I was on my way to… a nightmare or worse even, my nightmare already began;
This "so called" free holiday, would be the reason that changed my entire life.
And I mean change it, big time;
All I know is that I was just a humble chef at a high class as it was known London hotel;

But the events that followed made me or rather forced me to give all that up;
Not only give it up as a chef, but never ever cooked anything for my self either;
My life was changed the day I landed in this Italian island.
I discovered I had or should I say "given" or "Inherited" or even "forced" upon me a "Gift"…!!!
But how or rather the way it was forced upon me this gift no one in this world with the right mind would believe it;
It couldn't have been any harder.
This is a true story that will make you believe the unbelievable.
It will make you think, is it's at all possible?
Things like that simply do not happen.
Unexplainable things;
I mean the "twilight zone" is a child's play;
Incidents that, a "normal" mind cannot easily accept;
This is a story that could easily as some people would say "blow your socks off

Saint Johnny Walker's
"How to... Become a Saint"

Chapter Two
Day one

Here I was at Heathrow airport ready and very much eager to, just go.
As I walked through the sliding doors of the terminal, I noticed something unusual, terminal two was solidly packed with people; nobody was actually talking; instead everyone seamed to be shouting for some reason.
Strangely enough, I sensed there was a "panic" feeling going around.
Trying to "fight" my self through to the counter, I looked at the departure board and guess what? There was a delay on all flights due to fog.
The girl at the counter was desperately trying to reassure the travellers, as she was "bombarded" from everyone and from all sides with questions; as if it was her fault it was foggy;

So I thought the best thing to do is find a chair to sit it out, but no such luck, so I ended up on the floor in a corner, making sure the flight board was in full view. Needles to say I wasn't the only one on the floor, everyone was turning, twisting, trying to stretch, some people around me actually were sleeping.
Ha… can one imagine a massive place like that full of people, and yet no-one to talk to; one could only listen, and all one could hear was the same sentences, over and over again and fro every direction, "we are here more than two hours", "when is this "bloody" fog going to lift", "we will miss our connecting flight" "hope someone will have the decency to inform us", little children saying "mom I want to go toilet";
All that made me murmured, "And I thought I had problems"
Three hours past and the announcement finally came;
 "All flights are cancelled; please refer to your travel agent and bla-bla-bla;

Oh the "rage" in everyone's face
was clear and of course one could
only hear swearing;
Some people were trying
desperately to get to the counter
for more info, as if the weather
is controlled by the girl at the
information desk;
Some took it calmly as I did;
On my way out, I could hear people
actually swearing and I mean
something terrible and yes,
holding little children at the
same time would you believe;
As if it was done deliberately,
some actually demanded their money
back there and them;
I wonder if one can one get the
money back for cases like these or
if there's some kind of
compensation?
And if there is, where does one
turn to after all, my ticket was
free;
I found my self wondering about
that for a while and thought, must
go home and call them;
Got onto the underground and
headed home;
Straight to the newspaper for
their phone number;

Tried desperately to get in touch with the ticket "Donors" maybe they can change the date or something.
To my surprise, they were indeed very helpful, arranged my flight for the next morning, same arrangements and all that, but I will loose one day of the two weeks offered to me.
Well, since I wasn't paying, I couldn't demand anything more could I?
After all beggars can not be choosers can they;
I thanked them and they in turn wished me good luck and happy holiday and that was that.
By now I was so tired;
I actually fell asleep on the couch.
The next thing I knew, I was awakened by a couple of coppers; thinking there's a burglar or something in the flat, my neighbour called them because of the lights being on.
It turned out that my friend was too scared to investigate him self and gave the coppers the key to get in;

I must have dozed off for a good two or maybe three hours; I don't really know.
The next thing I know was, I was on the floor face down, and my hands tied behind my back;
They were asking me who I was, what was I trying to "Nick", they emptied my pockets in record time, searched my entire body for any drugs I suppose, and then they actually allowed me to speak;
I explained the situation and what I went through this morning, but they didn't believe me, so they ask my friend from next door to identify me for them to let me go.
Believe it or not, I actually thanked them for the good job they did and they in turn apologized to me saying "sorry but they had to investigate" and all that;
The whole incident, even though it was a bit "humiliating" made me feel somewhat "safer" if you know what I mean.
I never knew the police can react so quickly.
Mind you, I only hope I will never need them for anything.

As for my friend, he couldn't stop laughing and saying repeatedly how sorry he was.
I suppose I should have foreseen by now that, this so called "free holiday" was not going quite as planned; I mean judging from the days events, well, it was not exactly what I had in mind.
I mean everything was there for me to see, everything was going wrong from the beginning; instead, all I had in mind was the good times that lie ahead of me, the sunshine, the lazing around, the night life, the girls and the cruise that was just waiting there for me; a whole thirteen days of it, nothing anyone will say or do will change that.
This time the flight was at 2am. That meant a quick bite and off to bed for a few hours.
A little after 10 in the evening grabbed my suitcase, said my goodbyes to my cat and my friend next door again, and I headed for the underground.
I know it was a little early, but I was taking no chances, I wanted to… just go;

I checked my self in, got through the checking point and sat down for a coffee; after all, I had about 2 hours to spare.
Finally the big announcement came; That was it; I was on the way to "heaven";
Needless to say I was the first to arrive at gate 5, found my self sitting on the first seat closest to the exit; even though I knew it was still more than half an hour for the flight;
I couldn't stop thinking as I was watching all my fellow travellers coming into the gate, how slow and calm they were.
What is wrong with these people; why are they so slow, they must be the ones responsible for all these delays I'm sure; don't they realise that?
Maybe someone should tell them "get on with it", "Hurry up" or something;
It was 10 minutes before flying time when the girl at the counter announced a 40 minute delay.
I find this "delay" business very stressful because there's nothing

to go with it… they never say why the delay.
One can't help think the worse when hearing that;
Why…? Is there something wrong with the plane?
Is the pilot late?
Maybe he's drunk and cannot fly the plane;
Shit… what if they don't find a replacement?
Maybe they will cancel the flight again.
Oh no, hope not, not again.
And to make things even worse, people started pacing up and down, passing in front of you, and trying to "hide" their worry.
I wonder if they all know that "we" are all going through the same "Ordeal" even though some put a brave smile in their faces;
If you get the courage to ask a ground stewardess the big question "why" the answer is and I think it will always the same;
 "An announcement will be made shortly"
And when it finally comes, 9 out of 10 times is the same; "Due to late arrival of the aircraft";

What a lot of rubbish I would say, the plane was always there, we could all see it through the window.
And if you ask anyone booked on that flight at that particular moment, will tell you the same thing, "Hope for the best"
This and that, the time came for boarding;
Finally I murmured; my troubles are over, from now on is "fun" "fun" and more "fun".
I even tried to get the delay business out of my mind, didn't even care anymore, I was determent to have fun and only fun.
The plane was very big; it had two seats on either side and four in the middle.
My seat was 29E, not a window seat but right smack in the middle.
As I was starting to get comfy in my seat, I see this massive, and I mean really big-fat lady in her late thirties, around 140 kilo, trying to get her fat back side to the seat next to mine.
She had the isle seat but the problem was she couldn't fit, so she was polite enough to ask me if

we can lift the arm-rest that was between us.
Didn't really have a lot of choices, so naturally I obliged; Somehow she managed to sit herself down; the only problem was that a quarter of my thigh was under her, and a lot of "sorry about this" was said as I pulled my self away from under her, and to put you in the picture, I was left with only a three-quarter seat for my self.
I only had about 3-4 minutes to swallow the idea of "half a seat" when another big girl sat on my right side, she was in her late twenties and busty; and I mean "busty" maybe around the 42-44 mark, if you know what I mean;
So, can you imagine the position I found my self in?
She had a good look at me and said;

"Hi, I'm Brenda, I know it's a bit tight but I always imagine during the flight the other end, when we land; after all it's only a three hour flight… so that's the only way to think when in a situation like this.

Well, I suppose she's right, especially when there's no other choice;
During the flight we were served with food and drink.
Now can you imagine, knowing how uncomfortable, narrow and hardly any leg-room between seats because the two ladies due to their size were indeed sitting with legs way apart, thus forcing both my knees to… feel one another, being squeezed by two massive "breasts", one ON and I do mean ON, each of my cheeks?
Would anyone be able to have a bite, or even a drink being in that position?
I just pretended I didn't fancy any and I asked Brenda if she would like anything from my tray and the answer was no; so I turned to the other girl on my left, and the first thing she said was;
"Don't worry, nothing will go wasted";
Three minutes later she exchanged trays with me, and in no time at all she swallowed everything.

It didn't really surprise me looking at her; maybe she needed that more than I did.
Suddenly the unexpected, we hit turbulence, and the sign fasten your seat belt came on.
Even though I never had mine fastened, though I tried finding it, but as you can imagine, that was indeed a bit of a tall order. It was simply impossible to even look for it.
I was so "squashed" I could hardly move, let alone search for the seat belt.
But it didn't really matter; I felt safe enough, I was between two "soft mountains" that gave me a sense of security, if the worst comes to worst, I was probably the only safe person on the plane.
The turbulence was getting even stronger, and the two ladies were leaning towards me.
At last, I was beginning to have fun, and I'm not saying I wasn't scared for a minute or so, but the idea of the two ladies willingly offering their breasts for my protection, made me forget about the possible danger, I felt as if

I had protective pillows against my face.
And what pillows, Wow!!!
Nothing in this world could replace that moment;
I was having the time of my life.
I realised there and then why some people like busty women;
This went on for about 15 minutes or so, and when it stopped, on one hand I was relieved that all was ok, and on the other, well you can understand, my two "pillows" were gone, I really wanted to say to them no, don't go, stay there, I don't mind, really, what is the matter with you, I mean I was there when you needed me, it's not fair.
When the captain announced that we "hit" bad weather but we got permission to climb above it, but for our own safety to keep our seat belts fastened; I simply could not help myself, I murmured "fat chance of that mate" the two ladies must have heard me; because they both gave me "that" look…!!!
Obviously they took it the wrong way.

Slightly embarrassed of the situation, I closed my eyes and pretended I was asleep.
I estimated we had about 2 hours more flying time when we hit turbulence yet again, only this time it was really bad; I could just about see some people crossing them selves; some were actually screaming, some were praying, as for the two ladies? Well, guess what, we were like a sandwich, only I was the ham in the middle…!!!
I felt as if I was the "ham" between two slices of bread and in a toaster;
And the only think in my mind was, least I would die happy.
I wonder how many people would rather be in my position, every time the aircraft shakes as badly as this.
But funny enough, the thought of death didn't really sink in, or even the fact that I could hardly breathe didn't bother me, some people call this seventh heaven, others cloud nine, but I didn't care what, I was enjoying it;

The more the "shaking" the more fun I was having, and that lasted nearly until the end of our trip. And like all good things that come to an end some time, so did this. The captain announced that we will land at a different airport due to bad weather; "apologies for the inconvenience" and all that, he also mentioned the weather forecast saying that the weather was rainy, windy and cold.

"Oh no", I heard a few people say and that included me.

I thought I left all that behind, but hey, I had two weeks to spare, surely the weather will change, everything will go well, think positive I always say.

Finally we landed, about 200 hundred kilometres away from our original destination.

For the two girls the change of airports turned out convenient for them they said; their hotel was in fact on this side of the island. We patiently waited for our luggage, said our goodbyes with the girls, and off they went.

Suddenly I realised I was stranded and a long way from were I was supposed to be;
What does one do in a situation like this?
Stranded in a strange country, and at the wrong end?
I wasn't on one of these "package holidays" so I could not look for a company rep;
I was simply on my own;
I asked a few locals what's the best way to the other end.
Some suggested a taxi, which I found very expensive, and some suggested that I should go by bus.
What an idea, the bus, that way I can actually see the countryside and save some money as it costs one third of the taxi fare, the only bad thing about it was that, it's not a direct route; it will stop in three different towns for a maximum of 15 minutes in each one.
That's not bad, it's only a four hour trip max; they assured me.
It was early morning still and I had all the time in the world.

The idea of a bus trip sounded
great, more like an added bonus
really, a site seeing tour;
By mid-day I should be there,
perfect timing for booking one
self into a hotel;
Of course, being on holiday, one
never thinks of even the slightest
of the slightest "things" that
could or might go wrong;
I mean halloo… what could possibly
go wrong when on holiday…?
Ha… how was I to know what was
waiting for me ahead?
All that positive thinking, was
actually working; it didn't allow
my mind to go anywhere else but
the "extra tour of the country".
I could only think of the scenery
that's ahead and the good times
that awaited me;
Little did I know that I, well we,
the bus and the all the passengers
were heading for a major disaster;
And I mean "MAJOR"

Saint Johnny Walker's
"How to... Become a Saint"

Chapter Three
Day two

So, day two began peacefully enough and with a lot of smiles all around me.
Funny how everybody knows you're a foreigner or tourist to be more precise, received a lot of good mornings or rather "Bon Journo's", a lot of welcome, have a nice stay and all that.
I changed a few ponds for a few million Italian lire, bought myself a few snacks and a couple of drinks for the trip.
I made sure I got on the right bus and off, we were on our way.
Not taking into account the rain and mist, and with everybody genuinely smiling around me with their good-morning sir, bon journo's seniore, and considering what I've been through a day before, somehow, the day didn't feel as gloomy at all.

After about ten kilometres or so the bus suddenly came to a standstill.
This can't be right I thought, we're in the middle of a motorway, surely there are no traffic lights here.
I leaned to my left a bit to get a better look from the driver's windscreen.
But all I could see was a lot of cars and none were moving.
I asked the driver;
   "What's going on?"
He replied;
   "I don't know, visibility is poor, 100-150 yards".
It was indeed impossible to see what was causing the delay.
After a few short conversations on the CB-radio, the driver announced that there was a serious accident, and that there was about six maybe even seven kilometres of traffic tail-back ahead.
In other words there was no alternative but to wait until they clear the wreckage from the road.
Well, what one does until the "all clear"?

I just sat there "killing" snacks and "murdering" drinks;
The accident gave everybody in the bus "the" subject to analyze, and from their behaviour and tone of voice, everyone seemed to have a different opinion as to what could have happen.
Me?
I was just a spectator trying to make some sense in what they were and of course enjoying this unique Italian language; for me it was more like a real live theatre with real people and no actors; and even though I could understand almost nothing, from the way they were behaving I new what they were discussing; in other words, I was enjoying the show.
The driver decided to turn the radio on, I suppose for any news of the accident, all I could hear was a lot of bla-bla from the radio and a lot of arguing between the passengers.
This went on for a good half an hour, when suddenly everyone stopped arguing and pointed their ears to what the radio was saying;

I realized it was news about the accident.
The driver then explain to me that there were seven cars involved and a few people were injured, some serious, and they are clearing the road so with a bit of luck we should be on the move again soon.
About 20 minutes later we were, dead slow but moving.
When we reached the accident point, the bus slowed right down and going from side to side to avoid bits of metal from the road;
And at one point the driver stopped and asked the copper something and of course asses the damage and so did everyone else on the bus.
It was indeed a site;
Piles and piles of twisted metal everywhere;
Needless to say what went on the minute we left that point
As usual, everyone had his/her own opinion as to who was to be blamed and all that bla-bla.
The driver was picking up speed.
Bla-bla and bla-bla in the bus, when the unexpected happened; we heard a "bang" and the driver was

desperately trying to keep the bus on a straight line or bring it to a stop, but with the speed it was travelling, it simply wouldn't obey;
He was fighting with the stirring wheel and we were fighting to stay seated;
The bus was going from one lane to the other, swerving to the left then to the right, everyone in the bus was leaning left then to right, trying to hang on to something, some people fell off their seats, and a couple of bodies flying, yes, flying; blood everywhere, a lot of screaming and everyone panicking.
Finally the bus came to a stop, but upside down;
I was so preoccupied in trying to hang on for my dear life, I didn't see the ditch coming and… I guess the bus overturned a few time, I think.
I'm sure the whole thing took less than a minute, but for me and I'm sure for everyone else it went on for ever.
I don't think any of us can find the right words to fully describe

what, at that particular minute, went through our minds;
I can only describe it as;
  "Quick visit to hell & back"
Suddenly the screaming stopped, I guess because it stopped overturning, we were all on top of each other, pushing and shoving, trying to get free and out of the bus, or whatever was left of it;
Blood everywhere I looked;
I suppose everyone had one thing in mind;
   "Survival"
I somehow pulled free and out a smashed window.
I felt a bit dizzy and sat for a brief moment on a wet rock, when, I heard a few loud screams coming from inside the bus.
I quickly run back to help.
I remember I was pulling and pushing twisted metal pieces so I can free someone.
I also remember the incredible heat coming from the smashed engine or something, terrible smell of diesel and of course flames;

Oh yes; I do remember flames and lots of them in fact; I remember saying to my self;
  "Holly shit the bus is on fire, I must get out of here";
I remember pulling someone out of there;
My mind went blank after that but only for a short time because I think I went back to the wreckage a couple of times to help get people out.
I also remember I went back to the wreckage one last time to make sure everyone was out.
I even remember saying to my self, good everyone was out of there and safe.
A few minutes later the wreckage was completely covert in flames;
I remember looking around or rather checking all the people and saw every one of us was covered in blood, a few had torn cloths and some were suffering from burns.
Up to that point I felt no pain at all; I thought I came out unharmed, or maybe with a few bruises.

Only my jean jacket was torn a bit and burned a little bit at the top and shoulder.
I tried to wipe off the blood from my mouth, when I realised I had a few teeth missing.

"Oh shit" I cried out, that's all I need; and my voice sounded funny, now everyone will laugh at me when I talk; best to keep quiet I thought and not say anything to anyone.
I don't want anybody laughing at me.
I looked around to see if I was needed anywhere then headed for a tree I saw a few yards away.
Sat my self on the ground and eased my back against the tree.
"Ouch" I cried out, that hurt, an electrifying pain on my right side; oh no, I must have a rib or two broken I thought, better take it easy.
With a bit of a struggle, I managed to lay myself flat on the ground and wait it out until help arrived.
For a minute I thought I was actually fighting with someone, and I don't really know how I got

that idea, but my mind was playing a game, I had flashes of fighting with someone and that I was punching him hard on his chest.
I also remember saying, I hope an extra ambulance will come for me as well.
Then my mind started playing tricks on me.
I was actually answering my own questions.
"Halloo" as we say back home, this is not London, do they have ambulance's here?
Sure they do;
Yes but how many?
We will need at least two dozen for sure;
Two dozen?
Shit, what if they don't have that many?
What if there's only two or three?
And what if they're needed elsewhere?
No-no-no, this is a tourist island, they must be prepared for something like this.
Yea, but rules are meant to be broken, yes?
Oh no, what if it's true and they have to make a few trips; shit,

some of us will die from loss of blood.
No-no-no, I refuse to accept that.
This is not the 19th century.
Things like that simply cannot happen.
What if no one reported the accident?
Oh I'm sure the driver informed them over the radio and that there are 40 injured.
What if the radio doesn't work?
Oh the hell with this, I was actually driving my self crazy.
I just could not rest even a minute longer until I got some answers, so, with one hand holding my mouth and the other my side I went in search of the driver.
He was in a bad shape; he was in real trouble but still conscious.
  "Shit, he is a mess", I said to myself.
I asked him if he had managed to call the emergency services, but he was in no condition to speak. However, the guy next to him said, "don't worry my "Angelo" I did, help is coming soon".
Oh that's a relief, help was coming.

A bit more at ease from the news, I went back to my tree, sat down hoping the help will arrive soon. Then it "hit" me, I remembered he said "Angelo" Mmm… it must be the Italian way of what we say "love" What an amazing thing the mind is, I thought;
I remembered that "That minute" or so that took the bus to come to a stop or as one could describe as "visited hell", my whole life flashed before me as if I was watching a documentary.
And all the images were so clear, just like a real film.
I remembered nearly every moment from my entire life.
I saw my parents, brothers, sisters, relatives that I only saw once in my life, all my friends, my cat; even places I visited.
I even saw faces I haven't seen for years and they meant nothing to me!
If I was to sit down and write about all these, it will probably take me a month of Sundays, and I'm sure I will not be able to remember them all, someone will be missing from the list.

I wish it was the other way,
seeing the future instead.
But the mind has a mind of its own
I always say.
Enough time must have passed
because I heard the sirens.
What a sound…!!!
What a lovely sound, music to
ears;
We are saved; we are not going to
die here.
Within minutes, paramedics,
firemen, nurses, policemen, you
name it, they were all there.
All of a sudden, the wilderness
became alive, became too noisy,
there was even a helicopter going
around in circles.
A bunch of people came to my aid
as well and they were asking me
all sorts of questions; all in
Italian, but I shook my head and
they turned to English;
What's your name?
Can you move?
Where does it hurt?
Can you squeeze my hand?
The questions were coming in fast,
one after the other, a lot faster
than I could answer them;

And from the tone of their voices, I sensed the urgency.
They wanted an answer here and now.
Before I could answer one question, I was bombarded with another one.
I didn't want to answer them, how could I, I had no teeth, they will surely laugh at me.
But they kept asking me, over and over again.
What is your name?
Can you hear me?
Then a girl nurse appeared and said; please tell me your name, I'm Maria, what's yours?
I realized silence will get me nowhere, and when an angelic face like this asks you for your name, one simply cannot refuse, but suddenly I felt so tired, I could hardly keep my eyes opened.
I remember whispering; Tony.
And the angel face dressed in a nurse's uniform, said;
   "Hello Johnny"; stay with me now, don't go to sleep.
I just about remember asking my self;
Johnny?

Suddenly I saw this tornado, and it was headed towards us.
A funny shaped one, unlike the ones we all know.
This one wasn't sucking anything.
It was very thin and long, miles and miles long.
I don't know how, but I knew it was coming for me;
Suddenly there I was with nobody around, just me, no angel face called Maria either, I felt abandoned;
Where did everyone go I wondered;
This tornado thing was rite on top of me, pulling me in.
The powerful sucking force this "tube" had was unreal.
I was holding on to a branch from my tree very tight; but the power of this thing was increasing more and more.
My body was in the air.
I was desperately hanging on to the tree branch with whatever little bit of energy I had left.
I could see the branch slowly braking off.
As if the tree wanted to survive too and the only way was to sacrifice one of its branches.

The inevitable happened, I was sucked "in" or should I say "up", still holding the tree branch.
I could see everything getting smaller and smaller.
Suddenly it went quiet, I could only hear some kind of music, or maybe it was singing; I wasn't sure.
I remember seeing a one pure white cloud amongst the black ones and I was right in the middle of it;
I felt as if someone was there holding my hand and that hand that was holding me was very worm;
The strange and wonderful feeling I felt that moment was or is indescribable, I could only describe it as one of "Happiness" if that makes any sense at all;
when, suddenly I felt pain; someone was punching my chest very viciously.
I opened my eyes and, there she was, the angel face dressed in a nurses uniform.
I remember her saying to me; Welcome back Johnny, stays with me now don't go away again.
I don't know what happened next.

I don't remember anything else after that.
I must have fallen asleep or passed out.
When I woke up I found my self in a hospital bed with a collar around my neck, a tube coming out my arm, a lot of bandages around my head, a gadget of some kind to keep my jaw from moving and I was wrapped with some kind of elastic corset from the waste up to my nipples.
The first thing I checked was, my legs, if they're both still there, and of course a few "vital" parts of my body; well, one hears all these stories about foreign hospitals where they put you in, and before you realize, you wake up with a few parts missing, if you know what I mean.
Remember I said how the mind plays tricks on you?
I thought well, if I'm still in one piece, that means the accident happened at the right time, they didn't "need" any body parts at the time.
That's what I call luck.
A nurse came and said to me;

"Hello there Johnny, welcome back, you had us worry for a while, had a nice sleep, you've been sleeping for almost 10 hours";
She went on;
"Don't you worry about anything, you'll be up and running in no time", and off she went.
Ten hours?
Shit, usually I never sleep more than six, who knows what they "forced" into me.
Ten hours huh, that means I have "lost" another day from my holiday, which means I only have twelve to go.
Twelve and a night; I didn't worry about my injuries at all, all I was thinking was the "good" time I was missing out;
I must get out of this bed I thought, must get well ASAP.
I looked around and saw at the end of the ward a metal stand with wheels;
Aha… that's what I need.
I quickly got up, unhooked the bag with the "drip" from the hook above my bed, and off I went;

I didn't care at all about the pain I was in, all I could think and see was that stand.
When I reached it and hooked the drip bag, I realized everyone's eyes were on me, and it didn't take me long to realize why?
I was wearing one of those white hospital robes, that tie at the back and that my back side from top to bottom was completely open for everyone to admire;
I mean who's idea was this to put the straps at the back, he or she must have been either drunk at the time of designing or completely idiots;
What a site that must have been because nearly every one was trying really hard not to laugh out loud.
But I didn't care, all I was thinking was, get well quick and out of here ASAP.
I asked one of the guys to tie a few of the strings for me so I won't be the laughing stock, and I started walking around the ward, pulling the metal stand with the drip.

I suppose it was getting a bit late; that is for hospital standards, because the nurse came in and had a go at me.

"No-no-no, you must stay in bed and rest she said, don't want anything to happen to you, not on my shift."

I couldn't very much argue with her;

In fact I was feeling rather tired anyway;

She was a big girl and from the tone of her voice, very "bossy". She helped me back into bed, gave me "that look", she pointed her finger at me as if to say, don't even think about it, she went around all the patients, turned the lights off, leaving only one by the swinging doors and disappeared.

As I was lying there gathering my thoughts, I felt the need for sleep, probably the walk I did tired me, even though I only did twice the length of the ward.

As I was dozing off, I was saying to myself, tomorrow will be better; I must get out of here, out of this hospital.

Surely, after a good rest, I'll be walking out of here;
I even remember saying to my self, two days lost; surely the third will be a better one;
I mean can it get any worse?
It simply must be a better day for me.
What can possibly go wrong this time?
In fact the last thing I remembered thinking was;
No-no-no, think positive I always say.
I'm sure everything will be great.
After all, I am in a hospital, what can possibly go wrong in here?
Hahaha, how little did I know, of what was to come;

Saint Johnny Walker's
"How to... Become a Saint"

Chapter Four
Day three

Bang; the double door opened and the lights came on, and a very loud and I mean "LOUD" "Bon journo tutti" and then in English "good morning gentlemen", it's a nice day out there, and she started pulling the curtains wide open.
She was so bloody "noisy";
She wanted to make sure we're all awake;
I looked out the window and it was still on the dark side out there.
What's the matter with these people, I thought;
Had a good look at her, I wanted to have a go at her, when I realised it was the same "big" girl from last night.
What?
Was she here all night?
It must have been an easy night for her, it was very quiet.
I certainly didn't hear anything.
A nice day she said?
How could she possibly know that?

It's still bloody dark out there.
I asked what time it was and
someone said a quarter to six.
A quarter to six?
Why did she do that?
Why did she wake us up at this
time in the morning?
Does she think we're going to work
or something?
She should be locked up, torturing
sick people like that.
I felt I was a prisoner during the
Second World War, and that we were
about to be tortured by the
"Gestapo" just like all those
films, where there's a massive
German woman, eager to start her
job and gives you the feeling that
she's enjoying every minute of it,
the only difference being, this
one is dressed in white.
Then the tea lady appeared with
her trolley.
Oh yes…!!!
I wouldn't mind a cup of tea;
She started her round wishing
everyone "bon journo" and giving
to everyone a big mug of tea.
Oh no, she went pass me, giving me
the "sorry look";

I wanted to cry out and say; I want some, please, don't go, please, but couldn't, because of his stupid metal gadget around my mouth.
I couldn't even open my mouth, let alone say something.
It's not fair, why?
Everyone was enjoying his tea except me;
It made me feel so sad, as if the tea was the last thing on earth.
My kingdom for a cup of tea, nothing in this world matters more, TEA…!!!
And in my "sorrow" the unexpected, the unthinkable happened!
A miracle…!!!
The tea lady came back with a mug and a straw for me.
Oh what?
And she didn't even mention anything about my kingdom.
I wanted to kiss her, what a nice lady, the nicest, sweetest, most adorable little person in the world…!!!
Here was a person with a heart.
Here was a person that actually feels what you're going through.

I signalled her with my finger to come closer, she leaned towards me and I whispered in her ear, "gratsie dante"
She in turn nodded, squeezed my hand for a second and said, "Get well soon son", and to my surprise, in English.
I felt as if my own mother was there looking after me.
Oh... I was so grateful and happy!
What a lovely feeling!
What a lovely old lady!
Even though the tea was a bit on the cold side, I thought it was the best tea I had in years.
But my joy lasted but a few minutes, as the cleaning ladies came in; all four of them;
They separated in two pairs and started changing the bed sheets, they were a bit rough on the patients too, because I could hear a lot of ouch, slowly please and much more.
But did they care at all?
"Not on your Nelly" as we Brits say;
They wouldn't give a rat's ass.

All they wanted was to finish their round as quickly as possible;
And of course they had this deep and very serious conversation going between them.
The one was rolling the patient to one side; the other was pushing the sheet from under him, and then rolling the body back towards her as if it was a stiff, for the other one to pull the sheet away. And then it was the same ordeal to replace the dirty sheet with a fresh one.
And throughout the entire process the bla-bla.
I wander what was the subject? Whatever it was it must have been very important because none of them would even listen to the patient's cry for mercy.
Whatever it was, they were so "in" to it, they were not even looking at the "victim" that was going from side to side in between them, as if he was a heavy statue on a table that needed dusting.
Oh no, don't fancy that one bit. I'm not gone be their next victim, best if I get off the bed ASAP and

long before my turn comes, don't really fancy going through that ordeal.
I think the cleaners were happy when they saw me up and out of the bed, because it took them less than a minute or so to do mine.
Looked out the window and saw the sun was up and shining.
Shit… the sun is up, and I'm stuck in here.
That made me more determined for a quick exit from the hospital.
I started pacing around, slow to begin with, but after a few rounds in the ward, my confidence was growing and growing, I wanted to walk everywhere, visit the entire hospital, and go from ward to ward, after all, I am a "resident" here, must know my way around;
But as I was ready to go out the swinging doors, the doctors appeared and one of them said;
   "Everyone to the beds pleases, quickly."
Well, who can say no?
"His Masters Voice"
Of course we all did, suddenly as if we were synchronised, we were all silent; all I could see and

hear was the doctor performing a quick check-up with each patient and asking a few questions from the other doctors, they must have been student doctors gaining experiences.
Oh brilliant!
That's all I need.
I'll be like the others, a guinea pig.
Of course my turn came.
Quick check up, explained to the students what and bla-bla, and said to me;
  "How are "We" feeling today, OK…?"
"We"?
What's this "We" business?
Halloo…!!!
"I" was the one hurting here.
Is he taking the "Mickey" out of me?
Is he adding to my misery?
My only wished I had the courage to say what I really felt like saying; and that is, buzz off or something even worse.
He double checked my jaw, as if he knew what I wanted to ask him and said;

"Too early to say, but I don't think there's permanent damage, we'll know for sure in a few days, as for the ribs, we are a bit lucky here weren't we", looking at me in an ironic way.
"You don't have any broken ones, but there's a few badly bruised, not to worry, take it easy and the bruises will go, all in good time."
He wrote something on the chart, hanged it back to my bed, and off he went to the next guy.
We again?
Too early to tell?
Don't think there's permanent damage?
We'll know in a few days?
What kind of answers are these?
Is this guy for real?
Is he a real doctor?
If he doesn't know, who does?
Or maybe he thinks I have all the time in the world to… spear.
I'm on holiday here and my time is limited.
That was enough to put anybody down.
These doctors, they're all the same, they never give you a

straight answer, as if you don't have the rite to know.
I think there should be a low against that.
But I was not ready to throw in the towel; not just yet.
I simply refuse to allow a two bit doctor, to put me down.
I'll show these people how quickly I can recover.
I'll show them just what I was made of.
I quickly got up and started my exercises, hooked the drip bag on the stand and I took off.
Although some of the nurses had a different idea, I would have none of it.
I gave a few people "the look", placed my finger in front of my mouth indicating to anyone trying to stop me, shut-up, leave me be, out of my way, and I didn't care how they interpreted my behaviour, nothing would stop me doing what I wanted to do.
And it worked, because from then on, no one would dare say anything to me; not any more.
I was the king, silent maybe, but the King nevertheless…!!!

And my kingdom was the hospital.
Who would dare say no to a king?
I was going here there and
everywhere.
I was humming loudly "MMMMM-MMMMM"
to any human obstacle, as if to
say… coming through, out of my
way, from alley to alley, ward
after ward, time and time again.
I've met everyone on that floor,
eight words four on one and four
on the other side of the building;
four ladies and four gents, and in
the middle the reception, two
hundred and forty-five paces going
and two hundred and forty-five
coming.
As for the wards, forty-five one
way and sixty-five the other;
News travels fast I suppose,
because everyone knew I was
British, my name was Johnny and
that I was "The" bus "Hero" for
some reason.
I suppose they call heroes those
who survive crushes here.
I was even given a nickname here.
Everybody was saying hello Johnny
Walker the hero.
The good part about this was or
rather seemed to be a happy one

because who ever I happen to face or rather the minute they were looking at me, there faces were somehow changing and I mean apart from the typical smile, their faces looked happier somewhat;
Ha… Johnny Walker huh… I could not believe how these Italians give someone a nickname;
Well, Johnny because that's what the nurse wrote down and Walker I suppose from my pacing up and down like a yoyo.
Mmm… Johnny Walker huh?
I wish I had a couple of shares in that company.
I don't know how many times I walked up and down but, every time I felt it was quicker and quicker, too bad I didn't have a stop watch to confirm that.
I was so sure that that must be a good sign, so I quickened the pace as much as I could;
I even tried to run but was impossible, because I was also pulling this stupid drip-stand with me.
Do I really need this drip thing I asked myself, don't think so, I feel great.

So off to the girls at the reception, got a piece of paper and a pen;
I asked the girls to remove it for me but the answer was "no chance"
"I don't need it any more please remove it";
Then the sister said;
"Only the doctor can make that decision, not me and certainly not you, do I make myself clear"?
And she went on;
"Its bad enough we allow you to wonder around and pretend we don't see you, any more of that and I personally will tie you to your bed, do you understand young man, and I hope my English are good enough".
Oh shit, here's another "Gestapo" thing.
This one was for real!!!
"Call the doctor please" I wrote.
"All in good time she said, the doctor will come whenever he's ready, now do you mind, we have work to do".
Got the feeling she was a bit pissed off with me; I wonder why, but it didn't surprise me, even in

59

films we see the hospital sisters never smile, they're so serious.
I wonder if they're the same miserable at home.
How do their husbands put up with them; poor guys, feel sorry for them, or maybe none of them are married; I mean who would want to wake up every morning and face that?
Oh I don't care really; I've got my own problems.
This and that comes lunch time, the smell of food was everywhere, I thought I smelled stew and then boiled fish.
Oh good, at least we'll have something to eat.
I quickly went back to my bed and prepared my self for what's to come.
I hope the "chef" has a big gastronomic fantasy.
I was so hungry I thought I could eat a horse.
And a few minutes later, the delivery girls with their trolley arrived and immediately started sharing out.
Fantastic, my timing was perfect;

People say hospital food "stinks"
but I didn't care.
Anything really, after all,
beggars can't be choosers' rite?
I haven't eaten anything since
England, I think.
The girls had a List, what each of
us was allowed to eat,
They were coming closer and
closer.
Oh the aroma was killing me.
I wonder, is it fish or meat?
Does it taste as good as it
smells?
Or maybe chicken, that's it, must
be chicken.
Oh I don't care really, I'll take
anything they offer; I was really
starving; even my stomach was
complaining to me with lots of
noises.
And then the unthinkable happened;
They both went pass me, giving me
that "poor guy" look.
I froze, didn't know what to
think, I nearly had tears in my
eyes, when, the Gestapo sister
appeared with a new drip-bag, gave
me the "bossy" look and said;
   "This is your lunch, enjoy it";
I was stunned.

I could not believe what just happened.
What a bitch!!!
Gestapo is the rite name for her alright.
If that was an Italian joke, I for one was not amused, I wanted to get up, grab her from the neck and squeeze as hard as I could.
I was so hungry I could hear my stomach complaining even with all those noises around me;
It never occurred to me that I could hardly open my mouth, let alone eat proper meals.
I completely forgot that my mouth was swollen and could hardly open it especially with this metal object covering a third of my face.
But hey, could anybody really blame me?
I haven't had a decent meal in three days, and the smell, oh that smell was killing me;
It's not fair, they should have kept me in isolation, and it would have been better, this was pure torture.
I cannot take this any more, must get out of here;

I mean everybody was munching away
except me.
I was ready to pull the sheet off
me, when a nurse came with some
kind of soup for me;
She said it was chicken with
vegetables blended together;
She gave me a thick-ish straw and
wished me "bon-appetito Johnny".
Oh I was so hungry and thankful;
I thought I could easily fall in
love with that girl; she was so
nice and polite.
Even though I was hurting, I
swallowed that soup in record
time, at last I had something warm
in me, and it felt good, even
though it was on the tasteless
side.
It wasn't long before visiting
hours was up, and slowly the ward
was "ours" again.
And of course I was up and about
again.
Somehow, I found the courage to
ask Gestapo for an ice-bag, or ice
cubes and a piece of cloth of some
kind to keep the swelling down,
and to my surprise she said;
    "Yes, that's a good idea.

She asked one of the nurses to get it for me.
Mind you, she still had that mean Gestapo look.
I'm sure she doesn't like me, mmm best to keep avoiding her as much as possible.
The nurse came with the ice bag; I nodded as a thank you gesture and carried on.
Now I had one hand pulling the drip-stand and the other holding the bag over my mouth.
The "ice" idea seamed to be working, the swelling was not as bad anymore, and every so often the nurse was kind enough to replace the ice cubes.
Things were looking good;
I was in and out of the loo checking my face in the mirror.
Must get rid of this collar, it's so uncomfortable.
Is it a good idea?
Maybe it's too early, like the doctor said.
I want to scratch my neck.
I desperately need a shave.
Better ask the Gestapo, oh no, that's a bad idea; remember what happened last time?

She said she would tie me on the bed, and I do believe she would, mustn't push my luck.
No-no she wouldn't do that, would she?
Well, her name's Gestapo, she's liable to do anything.
Better not I suppose.
Best if I leave it on for a while longer, at least until I see a doctor.
That's a bit odd, where are the doctors?
I haven't seen one for ages.
I waited until the Gestapo left the reception and, pen to paper again, asked the nurse;
Where are the doctors?
She said they are in a meeting.
Mmm... meeting huh, that's a good excuse.
I wished I could speak, just to say yea, pull the other one.
Oh well, she wouldn't have understood anyway.
Meeting she said, ha... meeting my ass.
There's never a copper around when you need one as they say.
They should be locked up, deserting us like that.

Carry on I said to my self.
I mean what kind of an answer I was really expecting to get, I suppose any excuse is a good excuse.
As I was doing my "rounds" I got a bit curious.
How many floors in this hospital?
What floor this is?
Are the other floors the same?
Is there's a dental section?
Yes, that's what I need.
Must explore, I must find it.
Are they using old or new technology?
I simply must investigate.
The decision was made, and it wasn't long before I was in the lift.
Aha… I was "stationed" at the third floor; ok, where do I start from?
I think from the ground floor, yes, best to start from the beginning, maybe it will be signposted, yes;
I'll look for signs.
Pressed the "G" and the door began to close slowly.
Yes! I was on the move.
I was going places!

Freedom at last!
Oh, what a feeling!
And there I was, on the ground floor.
Mmm, where do I try first, left or right?
Let's try the left, pretty much the same as my floor.
Ah, a few signs, lets have a look.
Three signs, CASUALTY, PHARMACY, and EXIT, with little arrows pointing.
Not what I was looking for, maybe I better ask.
Found the main entrance reception desk, and wrote on a pad, where is the dental surgery?
The girl said;
  "On the second floor, but there's nobody there now; it opens for patients during the morning only, in the afternoons it's usually closed, unless there's an emergency".
Emergency only?
And what do you call this?
I'm not an emergency case?
I suppose now that I took up "residency" I'm not listed as emergency case any more huh?

Hahaha… so much for my quick exit theory;
Shit, yet another setback.
Oh well, first thing then, better go up to my own floor were everything is familiar.
As I was coming out of the lift, there she was; my biggest fan, the Gestapo…!!!
And did she have a go at me…?
   "Mr Johnny Walker, or should I say Mr Johnny Wonderer, were do you think you are"?
   "Buckingham palace maybe"?
   "Well… let me assure you young man, you are not".
   "You're in my territory now; did you know we looked everywhere for you; just where were you"?
   "Your behaviour is simply unacceptable, the doctors came around and you were nowhere";
   "I hope this was the last time; and who gave you permission to leave this floor"?
Permission… Johnny Walker?
How did she know my nickname?
Johnny Wonderer huh… What next?
Shit man, never in my entire life got into so much trouble as I did

in just one day here, not even in school.
The doctors, I must find one and ask him to remove the collar; I hope they're still around.
I started checking the wards; and there they were, found them.
When I approached the "senior", I thought he was going to have a go at me as well, but no, he was very polite, he removed it and said;
  "By the looks of it tomorrow I'll remove the bit that's holding your jaw as well".
He smiled and asked;
  "Did the sister have a go at you"?
I nodded yes.
  "Don't take it personal, she's a bit on the bossy side; but she's as good as gold, she takes her job very serious; we call her the general"
  "The best advice I can give you is, don't mess with her, and avoid her as much as possible, especially when she's in a bad mood; and yes, what you are doing is great";
I supposed he meant my running around.

"Keep it up and you'll recover in no time".
I thanked him in my own way and left, as for removing the "drip thing" he said maybe tomorrow, we'll see.
Bad mood…?
What?
Did Hitler ever have a good mood day?
Come to think of it, in all the films and documentaries I saw, I've never seen him smiling.
What a miserable bastard he must have been!
I'm not really crazy after all.
I'm not the only person in here to acknowledge the "Hitlerism" in this woman!
How I wanted to tell him, "What general", more like,
"Hilda", the "SS" Gestapo general"
I'll take back what I thought about the doctor this morning, don't know what I was thinking, he's as good as gold, and knows what he's talking about!
If anyone tries to stop me now, I'll just say "hey, the doctor approved" or even better, "I'm under doctors orders"

Now where did I hear that before?
Yes, that's what I'll say; it has a nice ring to it too!
And so I carried on, full of confidence, the doctor was on my side;
SS Gestapo general huh?
She wants war?
By George I'll give her one, let the battle of Britain begin!
Even the smell of food did not do anything to stop me, I was here there and everywhere, I knew that the old lady with the food trolley will get something in the blender for me, I had no worries there.
And there they were, the dinner ladies.
Hang on a minute, these are not the same ladies, where is that good old lady I know?
Do these ones know my condition? Did anyone inform them I'm on "baby" food?
Oh shit, what if they don't, that will mean I'll be on a strict diet till tomorrow.
It's not on; all these running around made me very hungry, must get something in me, maybe when they see me like this, they'll

understand, best to return to my bed.
And there I was, in bed like a good little boy waiting patiently for my baby food.
And miraculously the "baby food" was there for me, they knew all about my condition and they had it ready for me.
They handed it over to me in a funny looking pint glass with the straw.
What the hell is this "gadget"?
I hope it's not one of those the patients piss in?
No, surely not.
They wouldn't do that, do they, would they?
No-no-no, I remember I saw a guy using a pissing thing this morning and it's not the same.
I'm almost sure it was a metal one, a shiny stainless steel one.
Aha… now I know why they call that "Stainless steel" no matter how many times one pisses in them, "They" never leave any stains what!!!
Ha… that was good, I like that; Maybe I can use that as a joke!!!

I was trying not to laugh out loud, I didn't want any one to get the wrong idea, you know, laughing out loud for no reason, which will probably mean I was loosing it to them.
I had my soup "thing", washed it down with lots of water, and off I went again, this time I used only the corridor a few times, this time I had no collar, I could "spy" on my enemy easier, but the Gestapo was nowhere, not even in the back room behind the reception.
Shit; and I was ready for battle, where the hell is she?
I thought a war was declared.
Come out and fight like a "man".
I know; maybe this is one of her strategic plans, to attack me when I least expects it;
Yes, that's it; she will attack me from behind.
I must be on alert at all times, must know what's around me, all 360 degrees at the same time, nothing will be taken for granted.
"Victory" shall be mine…!!!
And when she's finally down, I will sing "Rule Britannia"

And upon my arrival home, Her Majesty the Queen will award me the Medal of Honour for bravery…!!!
Hell, when she hears I defended Great Britain single handed she will probably wait for me at Heathrow airport;
Oh no, what if the flight is a bit delayed, will her majesty wait?
Yes, I'm sure she will.
She'll probably sit at the café and have a cup of tea.
But where on earth is the Gestapo? I had another good look around; she was nowhere to be found; I finally gave up on her, went to the nurse at the reception and whispered in her ear, "where's Gestapo"?
She said "who"?
Oups, "the sister"?
  "She went home", she said.
I thank the girl and left.
I was disappointed, she sneaked away.
My Victory suffered a set back, a small delay; only a 24 hour delay, but delay nevertheless.
Never mind, I'll get her tomorrow.

All this "excitement" made me feel very tired, I felt the need to lay down, but my inner self was saying to me, not yet, do a few rounds more, remember you want a quick recovery.
So I did.
Went around twice more, but I was slowing down, and on my last round one of the nurses helped me to my bed.
She said to me;
   "You must take it easy, go to sleep now, I think you need it".
She tucked me in, said "goodnight Johnny Walker", and left.
Johnny Walker huh, I'm not sure if I like it but I'm beginning to get used to it; I'm very tired; tomorrow will be a nice day I'm sure.
What can possibly go wrong this time?
No-no-no, I don't want even to imagine that something might go wrong, no-no, think positive, everything will be "A OK"
Even though I was knackered, I just could not go to sleep.

I mean I closed my eyes and kept them closed for a while, but it didn't help.
It seemed my mind was on over time.
The sun was shining out there every day since I've been here and I was stuck here, within these walls.
I mean they don't even have a balcony for the patients to sit just for soaking up some sun.
Come to think of it, no hospital in the world has, I wonder why?
Mmm; I think I know why.
The designers or architects never had a day spent in a hospital to know what it feels like.
I think architects should ask patients first.
Suddenly I felt I was drifting.
I knew I was ready for sleep.
As a last day's thought in my mind was the next day.
How good it was going to be for me.
I was thinking only the good things.
Somehow I forced my mind to think only good things;
It must be a better day tomorrow.

I'll even find a way to "destroy" Gestapo;
Maybe it's time people around here should start calling me "General Johnny Walker"
I am almost sure that things will go my way;
Everything will turn up the way I want;
Nothing will go wrong;
Nothing can go wrong;
Hahaha… How little did I know of what was waiting for me the next day;
What was really installed for me was unbelievable…!!!
I don't think, you, yes you, the one who is reading this book now, can, not only imagine but not even in your wildest nightmares could see, guess or imagine what was really waiting for me the very next day;
And if you want to make it more exiting, do not turn the page for a while and think;
What can possibly happen to a patient in a hospital?
Hint?
Let your imagination run wild;

The point is, this could be a little test for you;
I know it is easy for you to just turn to the next page and read all about it but, can you resist, are you strong enough to say to your self, "No I will not turn to read but imagine for a while what could happen to a patient in whilst in a hospital"?
Could you deny your curiosity and not turn the page and put your mind or rather your imagination to work… imagine it all…???
And if the answer to that is indeed yes; how long for;
How long will you resist the temptation…?
All I can tell you (just to help you out a bit) is… think of the unthinkable;
What a test huh…???

Saint Johnny Walker's
"How to... Become a Saint"

Chapter Five

Day Four

Bang the door and the lights on again.
It was the same nurse as yesterday.
 "Bon journo seniori", then in English "good morning gentlemen" and all that, only this time I thought it was even louder, and one by one the curtains were opening.
The same shit but different day I suppose.
Isn't there a different way of waking people up?
Don't they realise that, maybe one of us will get a heart attack.
I must have a word with that girl, but suddenly I remembered the "declared war";
Aha... it's that Gestapo, she must be the "trainer", and she is the one in charge.

I mean even the doctors call her general, yes, that's it, and these girls are following orders, they can't help it.
Orders must be obeyed and all that crap.
The "Hilda-SS-Gestapo-General" was already at work, the war was on, and this was part of her plan.
Yes, that's it; she was testing how strong the enemy was.
But I knew better.
I was not ready to raise the white flag.
Doesn't she realise I'm British?
No one and I mean No One messes with Great Britain.
Has she not read history, never even heard of whoever messes with Great Britain always ends up a loser, does she not know that I am and always will be ready to defend my country and in doing so, I will destroy anyone who dares to even think of messing with us…?
Oh I was ready to defend my country alright.
Duty calls, "For King and Country" and all that.
I was ready for action.
I had my own strategic plans.

No matter what her plans were; I would find a way to face and destroy them.
The Battle of Britain, phase two was about to begin.
My thoughts were interrupted, as the tea ladies came into the ward with their trolley.
Yes, Tea, best ammunition for a British soldier, every cup is like a hand grenade, and when they came around I asked them for a second mug, and they did, they actually left a second mug beside the bed for me.
I wanted to be fully armed for the battle.
The tea was great.
Just what the doctor ordered as we say back home.
I quickly got up, went to the loo, and, on the alert.
The Gestapo might sneak in on me from behind, locked the door and looked in the mirror, the swelling was down.
The ice thing was a good idea after all.
Full of confidence, I was out of the loo looking for trouble.

I was searching and searching, wear could the enemy be.
She was nowhere to be seen.
What sort of strategy is this?
You can't have a battle from a hideout, can you?
I must find her, I will search every inch of this place.
I must find and destroy the Gestapo once and far all.
But the task of finding her was indeed a loosing battle.
She simply disappeared, off the face of the earth.
I know; there must be a secret passage or something, leading to her HQ.
A secret room where she plans her next move, that means I have to wait it out, be on the alert at all times, be on the lookout for any sudden moves.
After all, I'm behind enemy lines.
Maybe I'll try the other floors.
Yes that's it; she's on a different floor, probably recruiting "new blood".
I must find her before she finds me.
I found myself out the lift, and on full alert of course, in case

she comes out firing; the double door of the lift opened slowly and I was ready for her.
I wanted a face to face, a one on one confrontation.
I wanted a "dual" to say the list. But no, no such luck, instead of the Gestapo the doctors came out, they were starting their so called rounds I suppose.
 "Ah… Mr Johnny Walker, you're on the move again I see, feeling better are we"?
There's that "WE" again.
Is this guy taking the Mickey or what?
I mean can one imagine "Posh English" with an Italian accent? Every time I hear this guy talk to me, I really want to laugh and laugh, but due to my condition I tried not to;
 "Did we have a good rest last night"?
I don't know about him, but I slept like a baby.
Didn't have time to finish that thought, when he said;
 "Can we have the pleasure of your company, young sir"?
I knew he was taking the Mickey.

I suppose that was the polite way of saying, get back to your bed ASAP.
Well, one cannot really say no to him, can one?
 "His Masters Voice"
And of course I did.
I was sitting up in bed before they even came to the ward.
Yet another setback, this Gestapo lady was very lucky.
She must have nine lives, every time I'm ready for the kill,
she'll find a way to slip away.
Eventually, my turn came with the doctors;
They checked my eyes, ears and ribs.
   "Best to keep the corset on for a while he said, it will help you a lot, and it also prevents you from any sudden moves, take it off only when having a bath, now let's see that jaw".
   "MMM-MMMM"… he murmured and took the gadget off me.
Oh what a relief.
   "How does it feel Mr Walker" he asked?
Thumbs up from me;
   "Can you move your jaw"?

I tried, but a sudden pain I felt, well, felt more like struck by lightning stopped me.
I didn't need to say anything; he knew I was in agony.
Best to keep it on for a few days more and back it went.
  "Don't you worry Mr Walker, the rate you're healing up, you'll be out of hear in no time at all".
Bet your ass I will mate;
  "And keep up whatever is you're doing, those famous walks of yours, they'll do the world of good for you".
  "And don't forget the ice bag, that's also a good idea you came up with, keep it up".
I pointed to the drip thing in my arm and he said;
  "I already gave orders to remove it as soon as this bag empties" and off he went to the next guy.
So I was rite, I was on schedule for a speedy recovery.
The only thing now was, to concentrate on my jaw.
Why was it hurting so much…???
I mean there was nothing broken according to the doctor, so what was wrong?

It must be a muscle or something, probably bruised badly.
Yes that's it and I know just what to do.
Ice, that's the magic word.
I don't think the ice bag will help, not with this gadget around my jaw.
I must design my own.
Off to the ladies at the reception.
I was looking around, always on alert for the enemy the Gestapo; but she was not at the reception;
That's good, she's not here.
That will give me time to "perfect" my attack.
I quickly wrote on the girls writing pad what I wanted.
To my surprise she obeyed my order, no questions asked.
Aha… she is switching sides, she must have had second thoughts, and she knew what was best for her.
Yes, now I have a co-fighter, another soldier on my side, and best of all she obeys orders.
I quickly rolled the ice cubes in this piece of cloth and started banging it on the wall;
I wanted to crush the cubes;

The girl said;
 "Can I do that for you Mr Johnny Walker"?
She went into the little room and a minute later she comes out with some kind of elastic tube filled with crushed ice.
Ha… it looked like a long and overused condom.
She said;
 "Why didn't you say you wanted crushed ice"?
What an intelligent soldier, she realized what I wanted to do and she came with the answer.
Yes, only the best for British army!!!
I immediately started pushing the "condom thing" between gadget and jaw.
Holy Mother of God, I went through hell.
After a long struggle, it was in place, and I was in agony.
But I wasn't about to let the enemy see that.
And still no Gestapo, where the hell was she?
I asked the girl, where's the sister?
And the answer was;

"She wasn't feeling well, and called in sick".

"Another sister is taking her place, and she's on her way, she should be here in a few minutes". The girl gave me a little writing pad and a pen attached to it and said;

"Keep this with you at all times, I think you need it".
Then said;

"I was thinking of you last night when I went home; it's just a little something from me".
Oh brilliant!!!
I was thankful and obliged, well a bit of everything really.
Now there was a person!!!
A complete stranger, thinking of me all night, what a nice girl, I don't think even your so called best friend would do that, not now days.
Ha… Gestapo sick?
Not feeling well?
That's not on… I thought there was a war on.
Coward's way out more likely, a deserter I would say, even if she is a general.

Sounds to me that she wants to surrender;
She realized she was facing a superior and more intelligent army; more like an impossible task for her.
 "Mission impossible" as we say.
Defeat was inevitable and didn't want to humiliate herself.
Bitch…!!!
She cost me my medal.
The Prime Minister will be more the happier though;
His government saved a couple of pounds.
I wonder how much does a war medal cost.
Oh I don't care really.
 I'm not going to ever "Earn" one anyway.
The time was just after ten, mid-morning.
The drip-bag was still a half full or rather empty or whichever is the correct word, and my jaw was frozen; in fact I started feeling a bit num, well, a bit more than a bit actually.
I hope I will not end up with a frost bite.
Oh I don't know.

I started this and I was determined to finish it.
I hope the new sister will be nice though; I mean she can't be worse than Gestapo, surely not.
Can anyone be worse than that?
Even so, I wish she recovers quickly, if anything to finish this war we started.
I really want to raise the Union Jack and sing "Rule Britannia"…!!!
Since I had no war to fight, my job now was to find the dental department, and if I remember well, the girl downstairs said 2nd floor.
Yes that's what I'll do.
I'll go and see for myself.
Are the dentists here the same as back home?
Do they have the same technology?
Off to the lift and down a floor, and there it was; a big sign on top of swinging doors.
   DENTAL SURGERY
Yes, finally, I found what I was looking for.
There were two benches outside the door, one on each side of the corridor, a lot of miserable

looking people and nearly all of them holding their jaws.
They looked at me in a weird way, probably thinking, look at this clown, dressed only with a "night gown" with a metal gadget around his jaw, pulling another metal thing with him, as if he's ready for an opening act in the circus.
But that didn't put me off, I simply ignored them.
I took the courage to go through the door.
It was a big-ish place the size of the ward I was in, a lot of machinery; divided into small individual sections, and each one had its own dentist and a "moaning" patient in.
A lot of "ouch" was "flying" around from all sides, and at the far side there was a desk, with lots of files on top.
I guess it was the reception.
I approached the guy to explain why I was there.
He spoke to me in Italian and I knew he must have said can I help you, or something along those lines, but I shook my head anyway,

letting him know I didn't understand or speak the lingo.
And then to my surprise he switched to English and said;
   "I know you".
Know me? How can he possibly know me? I've never seen him before in my life, how could he?
And he goes;
   "You must be Johnny Walker, yes"?
This time I looked at him puzzled. And he went on;
   "I knew you were going to pay us a visit, would you like to sit down"?
And he brings a chair for me.
How on earth could he have known I was coming here?
And how does he know my name?
Ha… my name, I mean the Johnny Walker one.
I don't know how I got stuck with that name in the first place, but I was beginning to get used to it. He said;
   "You're the miracle of the year"!!!
   "Everyone's talking about you";
   "We all had you for dead when they first brought you here".

"You're becoming a celebrity, an idol, everyone is admiring you, and how can a person recover so quickly".

"After what you've been through, if that was me, it would probably take three months to come to the stage you're in now, Bravo"!!!

"Did you come here for examination"?

I nodded yes.

"I'm afraid there's nothing I can do for you, not in the condition you're in, wait a few days, when the jaw strap is removed we'll see what we can do, ok"?

He went on;

"I can see your eagerness, you being here confirms that, but as I said, give it a few days".

"I'm aware of your progress at all times and the minute I think you're ready I will sent for you, rest easy, after all I'm your number one fan"!!!

I waved goodbye and left.

Mmm; Idol huh?

Everyone's talking about me?

Number one fan?

A fan club, what!!!

Me, a fan club, whatever next;
Not only I'm a hero back home for
a war that never took place, I
have my own fan club here too.
Fame at last!!!
I'm beginning to like this
Country, I mean really like it,
even though I haven't seen much of
it, yet.
It took these people a couple of
days to recognise a star.
I might decide to stay here, with
stardom like this, and a fan club
to go with it; I can do anything,
what girl can say no to me?
I feel I can move mountains.
I'm the king of the jungle!!!
I'm the captain of the ship!!!
Hail Johnny Walker!!!
Johnny Walker?
Shit.
What am I going to do about that?
Everyone knows me as Johnny
Walker.
I can't go out there with a
different name.
I will loose my fans for sure;
I definitely don't want to do
that, I'm too important for them;
and it makes me feel good.

I better wake up; this is all a
dream and no way near reality.
Then again it must be;
I clearly heard the man say "Idol"
and "Fan Club" and "celebrity".
Shit, I must think of something.
And suddenly it hit me!!!
Oh my God, my own clothes, where
are my cloths?
I was running around so many days
now practically naked and nothing
like that crossed my mind.
How stupid of me.
And my money, where's my money?
Where's my passport?
And the suitcase, where's the
suitcase?
Oh shit, what am I going to do
now, who do I talk to?
What if they show me the exit now
and say that's it, there's nothing
more we can do for you?
Oh… my… God…!!!
I'm not even wearing underwear;
everything is hanging loose down
there.
What am I going to do?
Shit, I'll be arrested for
indecent exposure.
What will my fans think?

I quickly went upstairs to the girl at the reception and wrote on the pad she gave me;
Where are my things?
With the sweetest smile she replied;
   "Don't worry Johnny Walker, it's OK".
I noticed the way she looked at me, her smiling was in such a calm way, she was more like, admiring me; she must be one of my fans I thought.
OK?
What the hell does that mean?
I tried again.
   "Where are my cloths, my suitcase, my passport, and my money"?
She again, very calmly said;
   "It's safe; the police have everything locked in a safe place for you";
   "They wanted to talk to you as well, but we said in a couple of days or so, when you're better".
   "O… O… OK";
What a relief, at least I'll have something to wear.
I don't want to be the laughing stock, especially to my fans.

The police want to talk to me?
Why me?
Maybe it's about the accident.
And what do I know what happened, they should ask the driver.
And why did they take my stuff?
Who gave them permission to do that?
I hope they're not going to charge me storage.
No-no, they don't do that, do they?
I mean what else can it be?
I'm not a criminal and I don't have a criminal record anywhere in the world.
I know, maybe they want to join my fan club, yes, that's it; my fan club is growing by the minute!!!
Oh I am great I am!!!
Rite now I'm the most famous person on the island.
I feel I'm at the peak.
I feel I can now say it.
 "Top of the world ma"
I felt so good I thought I was growing in height as well, a couple of inches an hour; I was on my way to become a "Giant"!!!
The next step is the TV, they will want interviews.

Maybe I'll get an agent; Yes, I'll definitely need one.
I was leaning on the reception counter dreaming away when I felt someone was close to me, very close in fact.
I turned and there she was, the new sister.
O… my… god…!!!
She was HUGE…!!!
She was something else.
And I mean a "mountain of a girl" Straight away she reminded me of the "carry on films" with that big fat blonde nurse, her face was the same too, the only difference was the heir stile; this one's was more like the First World War German helmets, with that metal thing pointing upwards.
She was the female version of Kaiser.
She stood there with her hands on her hips and said;
 "You must be the famous Johnny Walker, yes"?
Oh yes, yet another fan!!!
I was rite; the club is growing by the minute.
I just looked at her.

"Listen to me "little man" she said looking down at me.
"I know your kind, I don't care how famous you are and or why every one here is admiring you; personally I don't give a shit; I'm here to do a job; you better remember one very important thing, I am the one running the show here".
"I don't want you around the girls; they also have a job to do here, I don't want them distracted, unless it's an emergency, I don't want you near the reception; I know your kind, this is not the time or the place for all that, is that clear"?
Holy shit…!!!
We got rid of "Gestapo" and now "Kaiser"
Who's next Stalin or Lenin…?
And what did she meant I know your kind?
I never, for the life of me thought anything like that?
I never tried my luck with the girls; why did she say that to me?
What am I doing wrong here?
I seem to get in trouble all the time.

Come to think of it, some of the girls are indeed gorgeous!!!
I was rite though, this was a clear confirmation.
Hospital "sisters" are some kind of a special breed.
They all look alike!!!
There are all massive and professional "killers"
No wonder the doctors call them generals, they don't want to get on the wrong side of them.
They can't really call them "killers" it will be the end of them, so "generals" instead.
I know exactly what they have to put up with every day.
It's no wonder they disappear all day.
Yes, that's it, there's never a doctor in the hospital no matter where you look, you only see them when they do there "rounds", and now I also now why there's a bunch of student doctors with them.
Yes, that's it, "Human Shields"
Of course, why didn't I think of that before, every time a doctor pays you a visit, he's surrounded with a bunch of white coats;

Perfect defence; 100% full-proof security; every doctor has his own bunch, and the best part of all, these bunches are all volunteer bodyguards.
I looked at the drip bag and it was just about empty; then looked at Kaiser and pointed it out.
She said;
   "In ten minutes, go to your bed and wait, it's nearly lunch time anyway".
Yes, lunch time, I'm starving.
I didn't realise how quick time went by, I was so pre-occupied.
And there I was, sitting up in my bed, and that nice girl at the reception came and pulled that tube out from my arm.
Oh yes, what a relief.
I felt as if I was a prisoner, a member of the chain gang and they finally unlock the chains off.
Freedom at long last, now I can go-go-go…!!!
Nothing can stop me now, what!!!
I can actually have a shower, I must be stinking, I felt as if the last time I had a bath was a year a go.
I must go and have a shower.

I desperately need one.
Quickly got up, ready to go when, the diner ladies came through the doors.
Oh no, I can't go now, I'll miss lunch.
I don't think they'll wait for me, no chance.
I mean not that lunch was something exotic, but it was something, something to keep me going.
Whatever it was on the menu, for me it's the same really; liquidized shit with chicken flavour.
I was beginning to feel like a baby every meal time.
I was actually feeling what a baby was going through; it's no wonder baby's grow so fast, every day the same shit.
They must know that the only way to stop this is to grow as quick as possible.
It was also a bit embarrassing, everybody was eating a "normal" meal except me; everyone had a few visitors around them at that time and all eyes were on me, some were giving me the "sorry' look and

some were desperately trying to hide their amusement, I think; I mean I came to a stage where every time someone was to laugh about something, I use to think it was because of me, I was the cause, I was in other words… the joker or the clown;
And that was no fun at all; in fact, I actually felt what a real clown feels or must feel; I mean can you imagine… halloo, I do mean YOU, as I said before, every time I mention or rather you read the word you… I actually mean you; yes you; the one reading this; so, can you imagine what it feels like having to make everyone laugh every day especially for a living? Ha, I do not think anyone in this world gives a shit what that person feels or even worse, what he or she go through every time just to keep you entertained or amused…???
I don't know if they were laughing at me or not, but I certainly was not amused.
Oh how I miss solid food, a nice juicy steak and chips, yes chips, oh how I miss my chips.

I wish I could order a take away.
The dinner ladies brought my baby food and my straw, and it took me less than five minutes to "drink" it, only because it was tasteless and the quicker one makes that thing called food disappear the better;
My mind was on the shower.
Hang on a minute, in order to have a shower I needed shampoo, soap, towel, underwear, where was I supposed to get all that from?
Oh shit, that means I would have to face Kaiser.
I know; I'll approach one of the girls when she's not there.
Yes, that's what I'll do.
I quickly wrote on my little pad.
   "I need to take a shower urgent stop".
   "Where can I get shampoo and soap stop".
   "I need clean clothes stop".
   "Especially underwear stop".
I folded the "message" and off I went.
This time I had no tube in my arm to think of or a stand to pull, I was free!!!

104

I went pass the reception area pretending I was looking the other way;
Shit, the Kaiser was there.
I got the feeling she did the same thing, pretending she was busy writing.
Shit, how do I do this, how do I give this note to the girl?
I was going from one end of the building to the other and constantly thinking, she must go sometime, I'm sure she will get off that chair sometime; the loo maybe, yes that's it, she will want to use the toilet sooner or later.
But no, she just would not budge, what the hell is she writing all this time, her biography?
I must have spent a good two hours, going up and down, and she was still there.
Oh what is wrong with this woman?
That's it, I have had enough.
I'm not going to take this any more, up to here and no further; that was it; I have made THE decision; I will go there and tell her off, I'm not scared of Kaiser.

I mean who would "dare" say no to a Brit?
I'll show her that British soldiers are fearless.
I went there and just stood at the counter, directly in front of her and she looked as mean as ever.
She looked up and said;
   "Yes young man"?
I handed over the folded paper.
She read it and said;
   "It's about time young man, or did you have the idea that we give "bed-baths" here"?
Then I saw her smiled and said;
   "And what's this about clean clothes"?
   "Where do you think you're going"?
   "Ah… maybe you think you're having a night out"?
Nurse she cried out;
   "Give the young man a clean rope, a towel and some soap".
Then looked at me again and said;
   "You wait here young man".
I did; in fact I froze;
Shit she was scary.
The girl came with all that, neatly folded in a pile.

The Kaiser took it off her and handed it over the counter to me.
   "Wait there" she said.
She comes around the counter and said;
   "Follow me".
Follow her?
Where is she taking me, hell I know where the shower is;
Why is she coming with me?
Oh my god, she's going to drown me; she was well informed from Gestapo and she was taking over, and that means the war was not over yet.
A new general to the battlefield; I have to come up with new strategic ideas and ASAP.
I followed her to the shower room knowing that my end could be close, too close for comfort.
She pushed the shower door open and with her hand pointing, said;
   "In here young man, quickly".
I went pass her dead slow, she grabbed me from the shoulder, stopped me, and closed the door behind her.
Shit man, I was captured; I was a prisoner of war.
This is it, the end is here.

I was dead and there was nothing I could do.
The Kaiser was about to declare victory.
What humiliation.
But it wasn't to be.
No final blow.
She had other plans for me because... suddenly she twisted my body around like I was a little toy and I was really if one would or could see her size comparing to mine; I was no longer facing her, and I was in no condition or position to do anything but wait for the final blow; I was in other words... "Dead meat"
I felt I let England down.
I was devastated.
The only comfort for me, if one can call it comfort was the Kaiser didn't have the courage to finish me off face to face.
Just like a firing squad, they don't shoot you facing them, they blindfold you first.
But instead of the final blow, she started untying the straps from the robe from my back.

Her breasts were huge like two big cannons; I actually felt them resting on both my shoulders.
I was glad she was wearing a bra.
Shit, what's this?
I mean I could not help think…
Door closed, breasts resting on me, and with her hands all over my back…???
Holly shit… I mean… spare the thought, what!!!
Is she going to rape me now?
Shit, that's all I need, yet another humiliation.
For the life of me, I couldn't even imagine what it will be like.
Me and the Kaiser?
HOLLY SHIT, this is not happening, I mean it can't;
I was completely at her mercy.
I think "telepathy" was the rite word that flashed through my head; I'm sure but I think she was thinking the same thing because she said to me;

"Don't get any funny ideas young man, and don't go shy on me either";

"I have seen it all before".

There I was, standing before her, stark naked and completely humiliated.
I bet the Kaiser was having the time of her life.
I quickly went in the shower cubicle and pulled the curtain. She said;
   "I'll be back in a few minutes, there's a button here beside the door, pres it when you're ready, I'll come and tie your back, I don't want you running around half naked exposing your self, this is a hospital you know" and she was gone.
There is a God after all.
I was spared.
I know what it is, she doesn't like easy victories.
She's worse than Gestapo, she wants to torture her prisoners; she likes "playing" with her victims.
OK, Mrs Kaiser, two can play this game.
I'll find a way to get one back at you.
This means war, and not just war, if she thinks I'm going to take this "sitting down"… Well, you

better think twice about that Mrs Kaiser, because you have another thing coming!!!
I quickly had my shower, using only the green bar of soap I was given, just like in war camps.
I wouldn't dare ask for shampoo, she was liable to put me against the wall and shoot me from six paces away.
When I finished, I quickly got into the robe and pres the button like she said.
It took her some time to come which gave me the time to think of my next move.
I must find out what her weak point is, yes, that's it, her weak point.
I must work on that.
The door opened and she was in like lightning.
I looked at her and she said;
   "Come on, turn around".
I was a bit slow to do so.
   "Mr Walker, do you think I have nothing better to do".
   "I don't have all day, come on turn".
As she was tying the straps, she said;

"You've got a nice bottom, but it's not nice to expose it"
Holly shit, I knew it; she really fancies me.
No wonder she said not to expose my self, I know why.
She wants me all to her self.
Come to think of it, she also said earlier what you want the clothes for.
Oh shit, she definitely fancies me.
She couldn't very much do anything in the shower room because everyone at the reception knew she was with me in there.
Probably she'll squeeze me in a corner somewhere and rape me when she sees me walking around, she'll find an excuse to follow me, pull me in a dark room and…
Oh no, I mustn't give her that chance.
Shit, I'm glad I'm in a ward and not in a private room.
I'm sure she was going to pay me a visit during the night.
Imagine me on top of her, or even worse, her on top of me?
Would that be a site or would that be a site!!!

Shit, this is not happening, not to me.
I quickly run away from her, I was thinking my bed, yes, my bed is a safe place; there are too many people there, too many witnesses.
And in record time I was sitting on my bed were I felt safe.
What kind of a war was this?
This is a different ball game.
How do I face this?
I mean this was a war without a front line; this was about "protecting my honour"
What a day I was having, and I thought yesterday was bad.
The only thing that was in my mind was Kaiser; when, the dinner ladies came in; I thought, oh no, baby food again.
Oh well, it's better than a "Kaiser Steak" surely;
Ha-ha... Kaiser Steak...!!!
I like that; it has a nice ring to it.
All the days' excitement made me feel really tired;
I felt the need to lie down.
Take it easy for a change.
I started "drinking" my food, it was really terrible; in fact it

was revolting and felt I wanted to throw up.
I can't eat this?
This is worse than liquidised shit.
What the hell was in it?
Even though I was a professional chef, I could not understand what it contained.
Maybe leftovers, blended all together, and I was the… lucky guy to be served with it, dispose of it, whatever "it"
I felt like I was a dustbin or a disposal unit or at least they were using me as one.
Shit, no wonder people hate hospital food.
Maybe I should go downstairs to the kitchen and show them a thing or two.
I just left it there by the bed side.
I felt my eyes heavy, pulled the covers and turned to one side.
I didn't care that there were visitors still in the ward.
I just wanted to sleep.
My last thoughts were…
What a day huh…?
I nearly got raped.

Surely tomorrow will be better.
What can possibly go wrong tomorrow?
Ha… How little did I know of what was waiting for me?
Yes, I know;
You were waiting to read something really terrible to happen, exiting maybe, or even something un-imaginary right???
Well; hold on to your horses as we say;
It did, and maybe all the above put together;
Trust me;
It really did, the very next day;

Saint Johnny Walker's
"How to... Become a Saint"

Chapter Six
Day Five

I woke up the next morning very early, it was still dark out there, the lights were off and all I could hear was snoring, and not only from one patient, I would say six maybe even seven, they all sounded like a philharmonic symphony orchestra, or to be more precise a <u>"snore-a-phonic" orchestra;</u>
And they were so synchronized!!!
I felt like doing the conducting;
All I have to do is, translate; transform; Trans-something, whatever the rite word is.
I think I'll invent a word or two here; trans-slate all this trans-listening snoring sounds into different sounds, as if each "snore" sounds like a different instrument.
I was THE "Maestro" of course.
Oh this is good!!!
I closed my eyes and my imagination did the rest.

116

I was swinging my arms like a real conductor.
Swinging, waiving, pointing, you name it I was doing it.
Oh, it was the real thing alright.
I was happy!!!
This went on for a while.
Some of my "musicians" were turning to one side and going quiet and others were coming on.
I only had to "adjust"
What a feeling!!!
My very own Symphony Orchestra!!!
Or rather "Snorephony Orchestra"
Fantastic!!!
I must have slept a good ten hours.
I never thought I'll ever say this, but I actually felt tired from sleep.
That was a feeling I never experienced before.
I didn't know whether it was good or bad.
And there she was, bang on time, the human clock.
She never misses a minute, always on time, as if she has a built in Swiss made alarm clock.
The way she pulls those curtains and shouts the famous by now

words; "bon journo tutti" and "good morning gentlemen" and all that.
It's as if she is crying out for help, as if she was saying;
  "I have had enough; I can't take this any more, day in day out always the same shit".
And the worse of it all, she made sure we knew that, she was clearly informing us, it's you, you're the ones I blame, if it wasn't for you lot I was going to be in my bed now.
Yes, that was Mary, the miserable human clock.
And we had no choice but to listen to that "melody" every morning.
Only this time she didn't make me jump with the wake up call, I beat her to it.
I was up long before and I was having the time of my life.
I was already at work with my "orchestra".
The old routine started, with the tea ladies coming in, just as the sun was on the up.
It's another nice day out there.
Shit, another sunny day and I'm stuck in here.

I can't even go out to meet the sun, let alone soak some.
I have no clothes to wear.
I definitely have to do something about that.
Oh shit, it's the Kaiser What?
What the hell is the Kaiser doing here this time in the morning?
Shit, that's all I need now.
I mean first thing in the morning to face the Kaiser what…!!!
I bet she couldn't sleep last night probably thinking of me I'm sure.
I mean what else can it be?
She came in very early, only to have that bit of extra time for figuring out how and where to sneak up on me, push me in a dark corner and rape me.
For the life of me, I could not think of any other reason.
She said in a loud voice "Bon Journo tutti"
She was expecting a reply because she stud there looking at everybody.
Of course everyone said good morning sister.
Well some did anyway.

My self, I just pulled the covers over my head and pretended I was still sleeping.
When suddenly she pulls the covers off me and just stood there at the end of my bed, as cool as only she could possibly be, looking down at me said;
  "Mr Johnny Walker, are you afraid of me or something"?
  "Why are you trying to hide"?
  "You think I didn't see you when I came in"?
  "You're a "Big" man, stop acting like a child".
I remembered the shower, she saw me naked.
Big man?
No, she didn't mean, big as in "Big", no-no.
No, surely she's not going to say that in public, is she?
Oh shit, I'm in trouble.
And I mean "Big" time.
And it wasn't even seven o'clock in the morning yet.
If I was in the army, I could have asked for a transfer, but here?
I wonder, is there another hospital around?
Who do I "plea" to?

I wonder if there's a "customer service"
Come to think of it, I never heard of a customer service in a hospital before either.
After all, I am a customer here, where do I complain?
Now there's an idea.
Maybe I'll suggest it;
The tea ladies came around and one of them said;
  "Bon journo Johnny Walker"
Don't you just love listening to the English language, being spoken with Italian accent?
I nodded and raised my hand as reply.
  "Would you like two cups again"?
I nodded "yes" and she handed one to me and left the other by the bed.
The Kaiser said;
  "Two cups huh"!!!
  "Well, you're a "Big" boy, you need it".
  "You'll need every drop; you have a "Big" day ahead of you".
Shit man, "Big" here, "Big" there...
I think she was trying to tell me it's no use resisting; I think, sooner or later it <u>will</u> happen.

What am I going to do?
I can't even think straight.
I was sipping my tea trying hard to ignore her, with the hope she'll understand that…
I'm NOT interested and go away.
She came around by the side of the bed.
Oh no, she's crazy, she's going to do it here and now, and in front of everyone.
She grabbed my arm and took my pulse, she wrote something on the chart, and said;
   "You're doing well, everything's OK".
   "When you're ready for a shower, you know where to find me".
She hanged the chart at the front of the bed and left.
Bloody hell, what was that?
What just happened?
Is this really happening or I'm imagining things?
Even the guy next to me, who by the way studied in Oxford for four years said;
   "You lucky bastard, she has the "hots" for you".
Oh shit, now I'll be even more famous.

Probably they'll change my name to from Johnny Walker to… oh I don't know "Sex toy" or something.
Shit, I wouldn't like that, I like Johnny Walker better.
Yes, Johnny Walker definitely sounds better.
Would you believe that?
She's actually waiting for me to have a shower?
I'll never have another shower in my life.
Well, at least while I'm still in here.
  "Kaiser, you're in for a big disappointment".
I'll never have another shower.
I'll stink.
Maybe she'll be discussed from my "smelly" body.
Yes, that's the answer.
Keep away from the shower.
And just as I was planning my "great escape" from the Kaiser, it hit me.
I remembered my earlier thoughts that I'm a customer here.
Shit!!!
The bill; who is picking up the bill?
Oh shit, there goes my money.

123

And hospitals usually charge a bloody fortune, they don't mess about.
I wonder, how much do they charge per day here?
Do they charge full board?
Yes but, I'm not really eating myself am I, I only "drink"
Oh no, knowing hospital policies, they'll hit me as hard as they can, they'll probably charge me extra, and they'll have a good excuse too.
I'm pretty sure on my bill it'll say;
   "Extra charge for liquidizing my food" or something along those lines;
And what about Kaisers work?
The extra "loving care" I'm receiving.
Not forgetting VAT.
That VAT thing is a real killer.
Whose idea was this VAT business anyway?
I mean this VAT thing, what is it?
You work very hard to earn some money, the government comes and takes half, and with whatever little money left, you want to buy let's say food, just for survival,

the government says, oh no you
don't, you want to survive, It
will cost you extra, pay VAT.
If you walk in the streets naked,
you'll get arrested for indecent
exposure, so you go and buy a pair
of pants.
Oh no, you want to wear pants, you
have to pay extra VAT.
And "WE" don't say anything.
This is daylight robbery.
And "WE" accept it.
"WE" must be masochists!!!
"WE" must like pain so much that,
we just accept it; you know… it's
a normal thing and all that.
It's part of the system.
It's part of life.
I never in my life heard anyone
complaining about it.
It's no wonder people declare
bankruptcy.
VAT my ass, shit man not me.
I hate even the idea of vat.
I'll declare bankruptcy too.
Yes, that's it, bankruptcy.
That's what I call a good idea!!!
I'll sign something saying I'm
officially bankrupt.

What if the hospital officials say, OK, you will wash the dishes until your bill is paid in full.
Shit, I'll be in the kitchen the rest of my life.
I'll come out an old man.
No, they wouldn't do that.
Or would they?
No, I don't think so, not now days.
Now days they're modernised, they call it community service.
They'll take me to court, and the judge will say;
   "I sentence you to twenty-five years community service and the sentence begins immediately".
Holly shit, that's even worse, I think.
Knowing you're free and yet your not.
What am I going to do?
Looks like I'm in deep shit, and I mean big time.
Deep as in the deep end of the pool and the worse part is or rather feels like even though one knows how to swim, is drowning.
I was just sitting up in my bed, thinking how deep the deep end of

the pool is when visitors started arriving slowly.
I watched them coming in the ward, each one with flowers, fruit, biscuits and drinks, all for their loved ones; as if they're expressing in a silent way their love and at the same time give the patient some comfort;
Some sitting on the patients' beds and some beside; some look happy, some very worried.
The guy in the corner was trying to give his wife courage.
Poor woman, she must be very worried.
That's nice I thought, he was in the sick bed and yet, giving courage at the same time.
As I was watching and studding the people, two ladies came in the ward; two I haven't seen before.
They were also bearing gifts, and a big bunch of flowers each, they looked kind a… lost.
They were clearly looking for someone.
They were looking to the left then right, left and right again as they walked along;

Suddenly they stopped right in front of my bed, and they were both looking at me.
Who are these women?
Why are they looking at me?
I've never seen them before in my life.
I'm the wrong person to ask for information.
I couldn't answer any questions, not with this gadget around my jaw.
They both came beside my bed and one of them said;
  "You are Johnny Walker yes"?
Who are these ladies, what do they want from me?
And how do they know my name?
I had to answer somehow.
Yes, I nodded.
  "We want to say we're sorry we didn't come earlier to see you; we owe you a lot".
  "We feel you're part of our family now".
  "We brought you a few things, we know it's not much but we will be here every day from now on, and if there's anything you want, just tell us".

I took out my little pad and wrote;
Maybe you're mistaking me for someone else.
I'm sorry but I don't know you.
The girl said;
 "No mistake, you're the one who save my brother";
 "You pulled him out of the bus and gave him life".
I wrote me? I gave him life?
 "Yes you, you did" she said.
How did I do that?
 "You gave him mouth to mouth and the rest".
 Me? I wrote again, no-no no, I don't remember anything like that and you must have the wrong guy.
 "No we don't, we spoke with all the survivors and they all said the same thing".
 "You were the sole hero of the accident".
Survivors?
 "Unfortunately the driver was killed, but you saved more than half the people the bus".
 "And we will for ever be in dept, we owe you a lot".
I wrote;

"Listen lady, I'm very thankful you came here with your gifts and all that, but no, I cannot accept them, find the rite guy, or as you put it, the rite hero and give it to him, if he did half of what you say he did, well, he really deserves a medal; personally I would very much like to meet him and shake his hand".
They both shook their heads and smiled;

"Are you sure you have the rite guy here"? I asked again; "I can only remember pulling one person out, and that was with a lot of help from one or two others; I can't even remember their faces either, sorry".
They looked at me, smiled and the younger one said;

"No, no, there's no mistake whatsoever, all forty or so people said the same thing; the hero is the English guy";

"He saved more than half of the injured people".

"You", she said;

"You saved more than twenty five lives".

"And my brother was one of them; people say you gave him mouth to mouth, you breathed air into him".

"People say you were pumping his chest and smacking him"

"You were talking to him at the same time".

"When he finally was breathing you turned him over, face down and everybody saw that".

"My family will be in dept to you for ever".

"God put you on that bus".

"He knew what was going to happen and put you there on purpose".

"You pulled so many people out of the burning bus".

I wrote;

"Something somewhere is wrong.

I don't remember any of all that actually happening; if that was me, I assure you I would remember. Sorry, I don't; maybe you're trying to make me feel better and I thank you for that, but please believe me, it wasn't me".

The girl was reading what I wrote and at the same time she was translating for her mother.

131

The mother smiled and whispered something in her ear.
The girl translated and said;
"Maybe you don't remember now but it will come to you".
The mother wiped off the tears in her eyes, took my hand and kissed it, she said;
"Gracie, thank you, thank you".
I was a bit embarrassed, an old lady to do that?
Then the girl did the same thing. These poor people were looking at me as if I was a "Saint" they were ready and willing to offer me the world.
I didn't know how to react really. I went all shy.
Nothing I said was going to change anything.
What they heard from people, is what happened, and not what I said.
The mother kissed my hand again, and said I will go to see Giorgio for a while.
"Is Giorgio your brother", I asked?
"And where is he, is he OK"?
"Yes", she said; "He is my brother and he's ok now, he is in

intensive care, but the doctors said he's going to be ok; maybe today or tomorrow they will bring him here, in this ward, I'm sure he would want to thank you in person; a few of the other guys are in intensive care as well, but the doctors are saying they too will come out shortly".
And she went on;
   "There's a few with broken legs and they're on the next floor up, as for the ladies you helped, they also want to see you, of course they're in the ladies wards but none on this floor".
   "I found them all, and I talked to each and every one of them; I wanted to know what actually happened".
   "I even visited people, who were not injured bad enough to keep them here and were at their homes, lucky for them they had miner injuries, a few cuts maybe and a few bruises";
   "They also had a lot to say about you".
   "All of them said the same thing; you were in and out of what they described as fireball, and

every time you were coming out of there was with another person in your arms"

"Some said they froze and some were admiring the strength and courage you've shown".

"The last one you pulled out was Giorgio".

"You must have realized he was not breathing, he was dead".

"You brought him back to life"!!!

"You must be an angel" and kissed my hand again.
She went on;

"How is it possible, everyone is asking, in such a shot time, you managed to pull all these people out and with no one to help you"?

"No one would dare go near let alone in that fireball".

"It must be a miracle because you don't have any burns at all, I can see that".

"So, what do you call that"?

"Isn't that a miracle"?

"Some of the survivors you pulled out have quite a few burns on them, one of them serious, about forty per cent of his body".

"They're all in the burns unit and yet, you come out with nothing".
"Isn't this a miracle"?
I was speechless.
I was just listening to the girl, the way she was trying to tell the story to me and at the same time living it; well, at least trying to.
I could not move an inch, the whole story was very interesting, to say the least.
It was like she was reading me a bed time story.
She stopped, wiped the tears off her eyes and said;
"So you see, no matter how many times you deny, you're everyone's hero, you're my hero"!!!
Just then every one in the ward was applauding;
Shit I was embarrassed.
The way this girl was telling the story, must have been loud enough for everyone to hear and I never realised everyone went quiet and just listen; I was so… into it.
I wrote
"Please listen to me, I don't know were you got your information

from, but nothing like this happen; the only thing I remember was pulling only one person out of the wreckage, and I'm not sure even whether it was a man or a woman, and that IS the truth".
I gave her the paper to read.
   "Please" she said after reading it.
   "It's no use denying it any more".
   "No one will believe you".
I simply could not believe that; all that in the story actually happened, especially the fire part, I mean me in the fireball?
Do me a favour.
It's not possible;
I'm scared of fires as it is.
No way, surely I would remember something.
Am I loosing it?
I don't think so.
Oh shit, maybe I'm suffering from Amnesia.
No, I can't be, I remember everything else in my life.
Usually Amnesia means not remembering your name even.
At least that's what we see in films.

And I know my name, I'm Johnny Walker.
Shit, it seems I got stuck with that name for real, and I was beginning to get so use to it and I'm beginning to use it too.
It must have been after nine because the doctors appeared.
   "Can we have the ward for one hour please", they said.
Then a couple of nurses came in asking the visitors out of the ward for a while until the doctors examine the patients.
Soon it was empty from visitors, the girl said to me;
   "I'll see you later" and out she went.
The doctors had their usual round, only this time they spend more time than usual on some patients.
Eventually they came to me.
The head doctor examines me from head to toe.
The usual MMM-MMMM and he took the metal gadget off.
He asked me;
   "Can you move your jaw"?
I did, and it wasn't hurting as much any more.
I whispered to him;

"I don't want it any more".
He said;
"The antibiotics and pain killers we gave you seam to be working well, but its best if we keep this on for another day".
I whispered again to him;
"Please no more".
He said;
"Trust me, you need it and putting it back on he said;
"It's only one day more".
I nodded; thumbs up, and he left.
The next two guys he visited gave them the all clear.
They were going home, lucky bastards.
How I wished he would have said that to me.
I was gone a go straight to the hotel, in the pool, and a one hour hot bath.
Bath?
Shit, the Kaiser, I forgot about the Kaiser.
She's probably waiting for me somewhere.
She'll trap me in a corner somewhere and rape me.
I'll stay in bed, yes, that's what I'll do.

The two guys next door to me were already dressing up and getting ready to go home.
A minute or so after, they both came to me and said their goodbyes.
They shook my hand and wished me good luck.
One of them said;
  "Goodbye Johnny Walker, I heard everything the girl said to you, you are a very brave man, not many people will do what you did, good luck again, it's been nice knowing you", shook my hand again and left.
I must admit, he made me feel really good.
Brave Huh?
That must be a joke;
I'm scared of my own shadow, especially at night.
As soon as they left, the nurse pulled the wards double door wide open to allow the visitors back in.
I was in for a big surprise.
I had about twenty or so visitors.
One by one they were shaking my hand.

Each one was looking at me with admiration.
Each one bearing gifts, leaving them for me beside my bed and each one was holding a bunch of flowers.
And they were all for me.
I realised they wanted to say something to me but didn't know how or even from where to begin.
I could see their eyes checking me from top to bottom.
I wrote in big capital letters;
　"WHO ARE YOU PEOPLE"?
It turned out that they were relatives of the survivors.
They all heard their relative's story of what happen.
Some of the women were kissing my hand, some were really crying.
One of the men took my writing pad and wrote his home address and said;
　"My house is your house, the minute the doctor says you're ok I want you to promise me you will come to my house, you can stay with us for as long as you want, and you can stay for ever if you want".

"You saved my two boys; I will for ever be in your dept,
   I will always owe you".
Then everyone started writing their addresses.
And everyone was saying come to our house; you can stay with us and all that.
I was bombarded with kindness.
And the "thank you(s)" were coming in from all sides.
I just didn't know what hit me first thing in the morning.
All these people, they all came for me.
Looks like my fan club was growing...
I wrote;
   "You have the wrong guy; I don't remember any of what... you think I did".
I showed the pad to this tall man, who I thought his English were near perfect.
He read it and said to all the others;
   "He's also modest".
   "What's with you", he asked me.
   "It's no use denying it; we all know it was you".
One of the women said;

"I heard you can't eat solid meals yet, so I liquidized some fruit for you, I also know about the straw, I brought a boxful of them for you".
Another said;
"We asked the doctor to tell us what we can bring you; anything that will make you feel better" and the woman was actually smiling and said;
"The doctor said he hasn't eaten solid food for nearly a week, by tomorrow we will take the metal jaw-holder off, and he will be able to eat, and as far as I'm concern, he can eat anything he likes";
Oh, My, God… I could do with a juicy steak and lots of sauce.
I know, fish and chips, yea!!!
A big fat long piece of cod!!!
Or maybe English breakfast, a full English breakfast, with lots of chips and a few slices of toast and butter for lunch and to wash it down… a pint of lager!!!
Oh this is living!!!
But instead, I wrote; nothing thanks.

It was too embarrassing to ask for anything.
One by one they shook my hand again, some kissed me carefully on the cheeks, and they all left.
I suppose they wanted to go to their loved ones.
I felt a bit relieved when I saw them go.
After all I couldn't have a conversation with them, and I think they sensed that I wasn't ready for them.
The nurse came and arranged the flowers in vases for me.
It was as if I was in a flower shop.
There were flowers everywhere, and so many different colours.
I felt important.
I felt great!!!
I always use to think, what is the big deal about flowers; waist of money and all that.
But looking at these flowers around me, knowing each bunch had a thank you written on every petal, made me feel I was special, gave me a feeling I never experienced before.

It was indeed a feeling I never knew existed.
I was in a different world, and I knew in each one of those bunches there was a story.
There was a name, a person I saved as they say.
I somehow managed to remember each one of these people's faces before the accident arguing in the bus.
I knew what bunch of flowers was from whom.
With so much love and kindness around me, my confidence was at its peek.
Oh how happy I was.
Suddenly I noticed everyone's eyes were on me, patients and visitors, all eyes looking at me.
Suddenly I was the subject.
A few of the "other" visitors came to shake my hand, wish me the "get well soon" thing, and some reminded me what a brave man I was; some were even sure that I was sent by God.
It made me feel embarrassed.
I felt the need to go out.
I couldn't take this any more, every little move I made everyone's eyes were on me.

I couldn't even scratch my neck that felt so itchy.
I must get out of here.
On my way out of the ward, everyone went silent; all eyes were on me as if I was putting up a show.
What a relief, I was out of there.
So I started my usual walks.
Every person I was passing, he or she would actually stop, make way, and say "Hello Johnny Walker"!!!
And the way they were saying that… full of enthusiasm, full of admiration;
I must have heard that sentence a few hundred times that morning.
Nearly everyone wanted to shake my hand, some were padding me and some were just touching my shoulder.
I must admit, at the beginning it was fun, I was enjoying it; but all of a sudden I was the centre of attraction.
And I mean THE centre.
It didn't matter whether in corridors or even what ward I was walking into just to "escape".
I was the star attraction, the star of the show, and people were

clapping, and in some cases I noticed, I had long and I mean long standing ovations, patients were getting out of their beds, "hello Johnny Walker", "well done Johnny walker".

I mean here I was, the kid from nowhere, suddenly found my self with the biggest fan club in the world; as if I was the biggest Hollywood star.

What a moment that was, I would saver that for ever.

Wherever I went in that hospital, I had the same treatment.

The hospital was my kingdom, I was indeed the king.

What a feeling!!!

Suddenly, the aroma, no matter how good or bad the food is, when the aroma hits you, oh… immediately you feel hungry;

I suppose lunch time was not far. Best to go back to my ward, the dinner ladies will look for me for my usual baby food.

Half way there, I saw the Kaiser about fifty yards ahead.

Oh shit;

Thru all this excitement and my sudden "fame" I completely forgot about the Kaiser.
How do I go pass the reception without attracting her attention?
Shit, it's like going to heaven but I had to pass from hell first.
But I had no choice.
I headed towards the ward, hoping for the best.
Well knowing my luck?
But she wasn't there.
Oh what luck, she was missing from the reception, even though I thought I saw her here.
Were on earth did she disappeared to.
That put a smile in my face, so I carried on.
As I walked thru the wide open door of the ward, I couldn't believe what I saw.
The Kaiser was there, by my bed, probably waiting for me.
I mean what else it can be.
I never heard of "sisters" visiting patients?
Is she going to try something here?
No, there are a lot of people here.

Reluctantly I approached my bed. She was rearranging "my" flowers and she said to me;
"Hi Johnny Walker, I see you're a popular man now".
"I've never seen so many flowers, all for one patient before, these are lovely".
She also said;
"Don't forget your bath this afternoon; I'll be at the reception desk when you're ready, try and make it before three", and off she went.
The Kaiser wasn't giving up; she wanted me here and now.
And she wanted me for the wrong reason.
Well, for me that is.
How was I gone get out of this?
I must think of something.
The dinner ladies came; the usual round, and my usual baby food, this time it had a beefy kind of taste, which wasn't bad actually.
This time I also had a lot of fruit juice that I was given to me this morning from one of the lady visitors I had.

Half an hour or so went by; I could no longer just sit there in my bed, I had to get up and go.
A minute or so after, I was on the move.
But I didn't reach far.
As soon as I was out of the ward, the girl that I was supposed to have saved her brother was there with her mother.
She said;
   "We were coming to visit you, how are you doing OK"?
I nodded OK.
They both seemed happy to see me. She asked me;
   "Is there anything you need"?
I wrote on my pad.
   "No thank you, and thank you again for coming to see me, you don't have to do this".
   "Nonsense, she said, we feel good when we see you".
Again I wrote, you don't owe me anything; please don't feel obliged".
Your brother needs you to be there with him, not with me.
   "We need you" she said.

"You make us feel good and somewhat secure when we're near you".
"OK; go to Giorgio now and wish him well from me".
They both gave me a gentle hug and kissed me on the chicks and left.
I curried on with my walking.
But the Kaiser was looking at me as I went by the desk.
The best thing I thought is to go to a different floor.
When I reached the lift area, I saw so many people there;
I just couldn't go near them, they already had turned towards me, I suppose they were expecting me to go up or down with them.
I decided not to.
Instead I looked towards the stairs.
"Yes, I'll go down by stairs".
As I was going down, I could here everybody whispering to each other, "That's Johnny Walker".
"Hello Johnny Walker" here, "Hello Johnny Walker" there.
Wherever I was turning it was the same.
What am I going to do?
I thought being famous was fun.

I had not even a minute to my
self.
This is very frustrating, best if
I turn back and to my bed, at
least there I'm more at ease.
Half way down the staircase, I
suddenly stopped and turned to go
back.
And that's when it happened, it
had to happen.
Someone behind me coming down the
stairs couldn't stop in time, and
he pushed the one in front of him,
he in turn pushed me and I fell
backwards pushing a woman down
with me and the next thing I know,
we were bunched up on the floor on
the middle landing.
I was hurt, my metal gadget that
was holding my jaw was off and a
few of my toes were hurting.
Almost immediately people started
helping each other up.
Suddenly I felt the need of
oxygen.
I had difficulty in breathing.
I heard a lot of shouting for
help.
I was in agony.
A few nurses came and cleared the
landing, and within a minute or so

I could only see a few doctors around me, and the questions started again.
Where does it heart and all that.
I was very carefully transferred onto a stretcher and I was on my way to the X-ray room.
No… No… No… This is not happening.
I cannot believe what just happened.
How stupid of me, the entire fault was mine.
I was the one who, out of the blue decided to turn back, I didn't give anyone a chance.
I hope everyone's ok.
It took about twenty minutes of X-raying.
The doctor examines the negatives and from his face expressions I knew the news was going to be bad.
It turned out that the damage was; three toes broken, a twisted ankle and two badly bruised ribs.
The good news was about my jaw, even though my metal gadget came off, was in tacked.
Well, that's a relief.
Off to another room were the plasterer was.
He was actually waiting for me.

He said;
 "Hi there Johnny Walker, you escape from me last time didn't you"?
 "Not this time though, you're mine now".
Who the hell is this joker?
He started working on my foot immediately.
He must have been very good in what he was doing, or maybe it was those pills they gave me, but I felt no pain while he was plastering my foot.
When it was all over he said;
 "It is best to stay in bed for a few days, if you must go, take it very easy, and try not to put a lot of weight on this foot".
This and that, he personally wheeled me back to my ward and helped me to my bed.
All of the way there, I could hear everyone was asking, what happened to Johnny Walker?
I was the star attraction yet again.
Johnny Walker was the main subject.
The name Johnny Walker was in everyone's mouth;

I was glad the hospital didn't issue newspapers;
I would have made the front page day in and day out.
He helped me on the bed and said;
  "Remember, take it easy".
The next couple of hours were unreal, unbelievable.
The human traffic and the chaos that was in this ward;
Where did all these people come from?
It seams the entire hospital, residents and visitors came to see for themselves, they came to asses the damage.
Everyone was wishing me quick recovery, some of them in writing, on the cast.
Within minutes the plaster around my foot was covered in all sorts of colours.
There was a long queue of people, all of them waiting patiently for a chance to shake my hand and wish me well.
Just like queuing up for a season ticket of some kind;
This went on until dinner time when, the Kaiser came in.

She was sending people back were they came from.
Actually she was saying to everyone, enough for today, come back tomorrow.
He'll still be here tomorrow and all that.
She actually ordered a nurse to stand guard by the door, and turn people back.
Then she came over to me.
Oh shit, I was in trouble again.
I saw "that" look of hers.
She said;
   "See what you've done"?
   "You have created extra work for us".
Oh shit, I knew it;
   "This used to be a nice and quiet hospital for sick people, what are we going to do with you"?
   "I suppose you're not to be blamed for all this chaos huh"?
   "And another thing, you missed your bath, I was waiting for you and instead you went and broke your leg".
Yes…!!!
I'm sure she meant I escaped from her "jaws".
Yes, now she will have to give up.

Her fantasies will stop here.
No more harassment; no more embarrassing moments.
Yes…!!! Ha, Ha… I got you by the "balls" Kaiser.
And there was nothing she could do, or at least that's what I thought.
Little did I know what she had in mind for me the next day?
On her way out the ward she stopped and turned around.
She looked at me and shook her head; as if she was telling me… you just wait; there and then I knew; I knew the Kaisers mind will think of something to get back at me; I was indeed sure of that;
She was already planning tomorrow's attack.
But no matter how hard I tried to figure out what, I just came out with nothing, no answers.
I'm not really a religious person, but I do remember saying, "God help me".
The dinner ladies came and gone, my usual baby food was as usual the same shit, but with all the day's events, excitements and the

chaos; I was feeling kind a peckish anyway.
Little at a time, I actually "drunk" all my food;
I was tired;
I really felt exhausted.
I fell asleep sitting up.
The nurse came and covered me with the blanket.
For a minute or so, I thought it was Kaiser and I jumped.
The girl said;
   "Its OK Johnny Walker, it's only me", as if she knew the whole story.
As if she knew I was "living" a nightmare.
I thanked the girl and the only thing on my mind was… tomorrow;
Tomorrow it's gone be a better day I'm sure.
Well, especially after today?
What can possibly go wrong?
What can happen to me lying in bed all day?
Hahaha… How little did I know of what was waiting for me;
What was to come…!!!
And let me assure you, what actually happened to me today was nothing; and trust me when I say

nothing to what was waiting for me the very next day;
As I was dosing on and off, I felt somewhat uneasy;
For the life of me, I felt so tired I could not think why;
The only thing that was in my mind was tomorrow for some reason; somehow, I knew that tomorrow will not be an easy day for me, even though I said or rather convinced my self not to leave my bed; the uneasiness I was going through was enough to somewhat convince me otherwise, enough to know something really terrible was waiting to happen, and that something, somehow was waiting for me; but, come what may, I had to deal with whether I like it or not;
Well, all I can tell you now about tomorrow is that amongst other events, that was the day I discovered the truth about THE GIFT I Possessed;

Saint Johnny Walker's "How to... Become a Saint"

Chapter Seven
Day Six

Day six began just like the day before.
I woke up before everyone else.
My orchestra was there and practising, only difference was, there were a couple of instruments missing from my right.
It was the two that were discharged yesterday.
But it didn't matter much because there was enough noise to cover the absentees.
I pulled myself up to a sitting position and although the pain from my leg was still there it didn't really bother me that much.
After all, I had a whole orchestra to conduct.
I couldn't let my musicians down;
So I took one of my famous straws and started waiving.
I was having the time of my life;
I was actually daydreaming during the performance.

I was in the famous Royal Albert Hall, and there were one million people watching me perform; when, the big nurse came thru the door and spoiled it all.
Her timing, as usual was terrible.
The usual, "bon journo tutti, good morning gentlemen, it's a nice day out there" and all that crap.
Come to think of it, after the morning wake up call, she actually disappears, is that really all she does?
Imagine, if someone was to ask her, what do you do for a living?
I wonder what the answer will be.
 "I pull the curtains wide open and then disappear"
  Or, "I am a curtain puller"
Oh that one made me smile;
I wonder what the salary is for a job like that.
Would they give a job like this to a man?
Would any man do it?
And of course the tea ladies appeared, bang on time.
The best moments of the entire morning are when we see these ladies come through the doors.

They have this smile when they offer you the tea.
One gets the feeling that they are offering their love as well, as if they are giving you the mug and instead of tea, it's full of kindness; one gets the feeling they're telling you in a silent way, I know what you're going through, don't worry, everything will go well, drink up, you'll feel better, and believe me one does feel like that.
They are the two kindest ladies I know.
I never once saw these ladies with a long face, even though they must cut their sleep short for us to have hot tea at this time in the morning.
They deserve every penny they get and much more.
And I bet you nobody thinks of them as "humans".
I noticed the patients don't even look at them;
They get ignored something terrible.
I wish they'll make me head of this hospital, they'll be the first to get a raise.

I mean, how would any of us feel if they don't turn up for work one day?
Can anyone imagine their morning without tea?
It's like saying imagine the world without music.
It's totally unthinkable.
I asked one of the nurses for a pain killer and she said only if the doctor approves.
Of course I knew that, but I was trying my luck anyway.
I tried to move my leg a bit, but the pain was really bad.
I was desperate; I had to pay a visit the loo.
I straggled a lot to get up, but manage it ok;
I walked to the loo with the help of co-residents.
I could not believe the weight of the cast.
I felt as if someone put pieces of iron in with the plaster, to punish me for wanting to use the stairs.
I was in real agony.
I wanted to cry out help or something; but who could help me?

We came out of the ward, and
headed for the toilets.
And the unthinkable happened.
The Kaiser was there, she saw us
and came running.
She was there next to me in a
flash.
She took over from the guys and
said to them;
It's ok, I've got him and you can
go now.
Oh shit, I knew it.
I remembered the way she looked at
me last night.
The clear message she sent me when
she looked at me and shook her
head.
This was her chance;
I was helplessly at her mercy.
She lifted me up and into her
arms.
I could not believe the strength
she had;
Oh, you are big and heavy she
said.
There's that BIG again.
I felt like a little baby that was
about to breast fed.
She took me to the toilet, very
gently put me down and said; would
you like any help?

I shook my head.
I'll be out side the door, call me when you're done.
Oh how I wanted to stay in there with the door locked all day, but the toilet is not really a nice place to spend ones entire day in.
The minute I opened the door to come out, she said;
   "You took your time, but never mind anything for you".
   "After all, you are Johnny Walker"!!!
She picked me up again like before and, carried me all the way, back to my bed.
Anything for you?
I am Johnny Walker?
What the hell is going on?
Suddenly I became that important?
These people think I'm some kind of a celebrity or something.
The minute this gadget comes out, I'll straiten things out.
I'm not the famous Johnny Walker they all think I am.
I'm just a simple, ordinary bloke that lives in a one bedroom flat in London's Hampstead;

The doctor said he'll take it off today; let's hope he keeps his word.
The Kaiser was all smiles today, she said;
"Try and rest your foot, don't put any weight on it, in other words stay in bed, at least today, you must give your ankle a chance to heal properly".
"Please Mr Walker, do that", and off she went.
Did she say please?
Am I hearing things?
I don't believe it, there's hope for her yet.
The Kaiser is getting soft, it's unbelievable.
Miracles do happen after all.
Two new patients were brought in; they took up residency next to me. One was really in a bad condition, one leg in plaster all the way to his bum, his one arm in plaster all the way to his shoulder, the other heavily bandaged, and his body was in a corset, just like mine was, only longer.
As for his head, one could hardly recognise him, he was bandaged

everywhere, only his eyes and a little of his mouth were showing.
The other guy was not as bad; he only had both his legs in plaster, that's all.
Ha, that's all, what the hell am I saying.
As if it's not enough.
Poor guys, they must have been involved in a serious accident, ha, don't I know what they're going through.
Then the linen ladies appeared.
Oh no, they will want to change my bed sheets, I must get up before my turn comes.
One of the nurses came in the ward with two crutches, she said; I have a present for you.
She saw me trying to get up and offered to help.
 "Don't worry Johnny Walker, these crutches will help you a lot, I would recommend you use them every time you're moving around, but my advice is give your foot a few days rest before you start your famous walks".
I went half way around the ward, just to get use to them.

They're very uncomfortable and my armpits were starting to hurt, shit; imagine walking with these things for a long period.
I don't think I can do it.
I only used them for a couple of minutes and I felt exhausted.
I must go back to my bed.
The minute my bed was ready, I was in it in a flash.
Oh what a relief, I felt as if I run the London marathon.
Then the doctors, it was there turn.
The usual thing; from patient to patient, questions and answers, from patients and students.
It's funny, listening to the doctors every day doing the same thing, one gets to know what each patient is suffering from, and knows what the next question will be; it's as if the doctor has the questions written down, and in the same order.

"Good morning Mr… how are we feeling this morning"?

"MMM-MMMM, let's see now, does it still hurt"?

"Don't worry, everything will be fine".

It's like reading a story book over and over again.
Then your turn comes.
I mean I could have easily said to him; "don't bother with the questions, I know them by heart".
And he goes;
   "Ah… Mr Walker".
   "Our most famous patient, Mr Johnny Walker"
I mean I ask you; wasn't he expecting me to be there…?
   "Let's see now, how are we today"?
   "Maybe this, and he points to my foot will slow you down a little bit".
You got that right mate.
   "You gave us a bit of a shock yesterday Mr Walker didn't you"?
   "How's the jaw"?
   "Does it heart still"?
And he takes the gadget off.
   "Try and move your jaw".
Even though it was hurting a bit I said;
   "Its ok, I don't need it any more.
He said;
   "Yes I agree".

168

I asked him for some pain killers,
my foot and ribs where hurting and
I desperately need them.
He said;
   "Yes I will but, you must take
it easy for a while".
That was that and off to the next
guy.
I don't know what he could have
offered him apart from a few words
of comfort;
His entire body looked to be in a
real mess.
And that's exactly what he did.
He said to him;
   "Bon journo Giorgio, come stay?
(How are you to you and me);
I mean I ask you;
What the hell kind a question is
that; can't he see…?
   "Don't worry Giorgio; I see
everything is coming along fine";
   "Give it little time and you'll
be up and about".
Of course that was all in Italian;
I mean I'm not known for my
Italian but that much I knew, hell
I heard that time and time again
in there, I got to know that
sentence by heart;

The same thing more or less said to the next guy with the two broken legs.
The minute the doctors finished their round and left, the nurse came with a little trolley with everyone's medicine.
I took my pain killers quickly, with the hope they'll take effect as quick.
Then the nurse opened the door for visitors.
It's funny how quick the place was transformed.
The one minute it was peaceful and quiet and the next total chaos.
It's as if from a quiet monastery into a football crowd in the space of a few seconds.
I looked at my flowers and thought ha, there are no more flowers left in the island; they brought them all to me yesterday.
People were coming in the ward at an alarming rate.
Apart from the patient's relatives, people were coming in to see me, people I never saw before in my life, and each one bearing flowers and gifts, drinks, chocolates, biscuits, books for me

to read, cuddly toys as if I was a kid, you name it and I do mean you name it, it was given to me.
I must have shook hands with dozens and dozens of people,
Hugs and kisses, well wishes and lots and lots of well wishing cards; in fact, the gifts were so many; people didn't know where to leave them.
A couple of nurses came for help, they were throwing yesterdays flowers away from the vases and replace them with new, they were stacking up the biscuits the chocolates and all the other gifts.
I had enough of everything to open my self a shop.
Hell, I don't think sweet shops have as many.
I had to put a stop to this.
But how can one stop anyone wanting to wish you well, not to mention the polite side of things.
I mean can one imagine, being in a sick bed in a foreign hospital, no relatives or so called friends to pay one a visit and express their concern or even a typical "hello" thing just out of curiosity to see

if you're going to "make it" till tomorrow, and instead of being grateful for having visitors, even if they are complete strangers, reject them all…?
I mean these people were indeed genuine and yes, they could have easily wouldn't have bothered, but they didn't; they were there and they were there for me and me alone, and allow me to inform you that, there's nothing in this world better to make one feel better when in a sick bed;
Suddenly I saw the answer; it was there in front of me.
And I mean "The Kaiser";
Oh I never thought I'll be so glad to see her.
Yes, would you believe the Kaiser is my savvier I thought?
I called her towards me using my index finger.
She came and I whispered in her ear; "help"
Oh she was quick;
She understood what I was going through.
And immediately she said to everyone;

"No more please, he needs to rest now, come back in the afternoon or tomorrow, thank you".
And she started diverting the human traffic out of the ward.
She pulled the mobile partition and surrounded my area.
I heard her saying to the nurses that I wasn't to be disturbed by anyone.
Peace at last!!!
I always wanted to be rich and famous, but this is ridicules;
Is this the price of stardom?
Who needs it?
No, it is not a good idea at all.
From now on, I will concentrate on the rich part only.
What's the point if you're rich and cannot enjoy it?
No, no, no.
Best is the rich without the famous.
The Kaiser came back and asked me;
 "What are we going to do with all these flowers"?
 "Did you see how many bunches are on the floor"?
 "We don't have enough vases to put them in for you".
I said;

"Distribute them all to the ladies wards or wherever you think is best".
And that was enough for her, she called two nurses over and they started picking all the flowers and taking them to the ladies across the other side of the hospital.
That was good, now there was enough room for me to get out of the bed at least.
And then an unexpected event was about to take place.
The Kaiser came again and said;
  "You have a visitor".
I said;
  "I thought we finished with all that";
  "This one I allowed" she said.
  "He is a member of parliament".
  "He came especially to see you".
An MP, to see me; why and what on earth for?
  "And he brought you a gift, a gift I'm sure you'll like".
In he comes with the usual flowers and a few carrier bags with the usual goodies, chocolates biscuits etc;

An MP came to see me, I wonder why?
I couldn't get over it, he came especially for me?
I really wonder why, I'm not going to run for presidency.
Oh I don't know about that, maybe I will make a good president.
Or a prime minister!
I'll be a great PM!
He introduced himself to me and said;
   "You saved my nephew; and from what I heard, if it wasn't for your bravery, he was going to be burned alive and I wanted to thank you in person".
   "I also heard about your little accident yesterday and thought you mite need this".
He pushes the partition to one side and, aha…!!!
There was the most beautiful thing I ever saw.
It was a wheelchair, the latest model, buttery operated, with full extras, a folding little table on one side, compartments on the other, hell it even had rear view mirrors.
Wow…!!!

That was the most useful gift of all.
My own transport!
That means I won't be stuck to my bed any more.
That means I'll be on the move again without using my legs.
That means I don't have to take it easy like everyone says.
I have found my freedom again.
I said;
  "Can I try it"?
He said smiling;
  "It's yours; you do whatever you like with it".
There I was, on this wonderful piece of technology.
I put my hand on the joy stick and… lift-off…!!!
Left… right… forward… reverse… it was brilliant…!!!
I felt as if I was in one of these go-carts.
Oh what joy!!!
I was so happy!!!
In fact I can't remember ever being happier.
I must have said thank you to the MP maybe a dozen times.
He looked very pleased as well, I could see it in his face.

He in turn thanked me for saving his nephew and said;
  "If there's anything and I mean anything else I can do for you, call me" and he gives me a card, with his personal number on.
He whispered in my ear;
  "Please keep this to yourself, not many people know this number".
He shook my hand, thank me again, wished me a quick recovery and off he went.
Oh what!!!
What a day I was having!
My own transport!
Freedom...!!!
Now I don't need the Kaiser for the use of the loo;
Oh shit, I hope she won't be pissed off.
I was just admiring my new set of wheels.
And it didn't take me long to master it either.
I was going from corner to corner.
I was pulling in between two beds and breaking the last moment, everyone was cheering and having fun too;

It made me even happier seeing my fellow "sufferers" joining in the fun I was having.
What a lovely bunch they all are.
Everyone was shearing my joy.
I was acting like a little kid.
Hell, I was a little kid.
I mean every time I was breaking and reversing they were cheering me saying "ole" "ole"…!!!
Man, I was happy, and the best part was, I felt no pain at all, both my feet were resting on the foot rest, so I had no worries there.
Oh what a gift!!!
One of the nurses came over and said;

"Mr Johnny Walker, did you know that in the ten years I am working in this hospital, it is the very first time I hear patients laughing and having so much fun"
But it wasn't enough for me, the showing off in the ward just wasn't enough, I wanted to exhibit my new set of wheels to everyone.
I was in and out of every ward on that floor.

Ladies and gents wards, I wanted everyone to see, and to admire my perfect driving.
All through my excitement, I nearly crushed a few times, and I nearly knocked a few people down. It was only luck that prevented a major disaster from happening.
When, suddenly there she was, out of nowhere, the Kaiser was standing in the middle of the corridor, legs apart, hands on her hips blocking my path.
Oh shit, why did she have to spoil it all?
I knew straight away I was in trouble yet again;
I approached her slowing down, I thought she looked a lot bigger somehow, a lot taller and the way she stud there!
The closer to her I was getting, the bigger she looked.
I knew she was a big girl but, I never realised how big.
She seemed or rather looked gigantic!!!
I wonder, is it because I was sitting?
And that look she had, oh I knew that look.

I was indeed in trouble again.

"Mr Johnny Walker"

Shit, here it comes.

"You are becoming a nuisance".

"You will cause an accident".

"This is a hospital, not a racing track".

"Do I make my self clear"?

"Any more of this and I'll take the wheelchair away from you, is that understood"?

I mean could I really argue with her, she was right for one and not forgetting that I was dealing with "The Kaiser"

So I lowered my enthusiasm and said in a low tone;

"Yes sister, I'm sorry".

I mean who in the rite mind would dare argue with the Kaiser?

And anyway, she added;

"Its lunch time, better go to your ward or you'll miss it.

I was so busy with my "Rolls-Royce", I didn't realise the time, the diner ladies were actually there and handing out grub.

We were having some kind of roast beef with boiled potato and veggies.

Aha… this time they didn't have to liquidise it for me.
No more baby food;
Solid food what…!!!
Yes…!!!
I didn't care what it would taste like, the only thing that mattered was, the solid bit.
I parked next to my bed, opened the folding little table from the side of my machine and waited.
That kind lady served me with the usual smile she had.
She said;
   "Good, now you can eat proper food".
I felt the urge to hug and kiss the nice old lady.
I put the breaks on and stood up.
I stretched my hands out for her so I could cuddle her and she was more than willing in responding to my call, in fact I got the feeling she really wanted me to give her "That hug";
I hugged her a bit tight, actually her hugging me was really tight and for a good thirty seconds too, I felt there was some kind of heat coming from her body, or was it coming out mine, I don't really

know which, kiss her on both cheeks, and thanked her a couple of times.
Even though all these days I was there not one person ever called herby or mentioned her name, after hugging her, I knew it;
It was indeed puzzling as to how I knew that and to be sure I was right, I asked her;
   "Mama, is your name Anna"?
I noticed she had tears in her eyes.
She also hugged me back again, this time even tighter.
I felt something weird; I felt that heat again between us, only this time it was more intense and yes, it was indeed coming out of her and yes, I felt that my body was indeed sucking it all in.
I have never experienced anything like this before and my first reaction was… pulling my body away from her; I noticed her face was one of happiness and somewhat more on the bright side;
She said;
   "No-no, thank you for giving me the biggest and most wonderful gift in the world";

"You are an angel".
I said what gift?
And she told me something very weird!!!
She said something to me that puzzled me, and I mean puzzled me big time.
She said;
"You were sent here on purpose, you performed a few miracles, but your job is not finished yet".
"You have THE gift"…!!!
"You will find yourself in places where you will perform miracles".
"You will know where you will be needed and go there".
"God sent you back here".
"And I want to hug you again, please can I"?
She just didn't wait for an answer, her arms were around me and she was squeezing and squeezing, saying at the same time over and over again thank you, thank you.
When she finally let go, she looked at me and burst into tears, happy tears I would say.
She knelt before me and kissed my hand as if I was a priest.

I said;
"What are you doing mamma Anna"? She said;
"I know; I saw it all in my dream".
"But it wasn't a dream, it was a vision"…!!!
"You died in that accident and God sent you back";
"You already performed two miracles".
"The first was the bus and all those lives you saved".
"The second was me, you just saved mine, I don't need to tell you how you did, you will know all in good time".
"Just carry on the way you are". She kissed my hand again, crossed herself and walked away.
I was left there wondering, frozen more like;
In fact, the entire ward patients and non patients and even the staff were in the same boat as I was; everyone had the same puzzled look on their faces;
What the hell just happened here?
What just hit me?
What is this nice old lady talking about?

I think this old lady is loosing it, she must be.
I mean OK; I can accept the bus thing, only because everybody says so, but her life?
How?
Maybe because nobody takes any notice of her and I did?
I think she's far gone poor thing.
With all these roomers going around, she must have imagined herself injured in the bus as well.
Yea, that's probably it.
Poor old lady;
I noticed, everyone around me was staring and some crossing them selves;
They all saw and heard the old lady;
I just looked down at my food as if nothing has happened; I mean I realised that that will put an end to this… charade;
My food was getting a bit cold so I just dived in.
At last; solid food;
I know I had three half teeth missing on one side, but I could still chew well from the other.

I enjoyed that; even though it was unsalted, it was great.
The old lady's words were still on my mind.
Is she really crazy?
What if she's not?
God sent me back?
Back from where?
I'm not even a religious man, well, not really.
No, that's impossible.
What am I saying?
Am I loosing it now?
No, I must stop thinking about it.
The old lady just saw a dream that's all.
She's just confused.
Let's see now, where shall I go now?
I don't really fancy all these people coming in to see me.
I think most of them come, out of curiosity anyway.
I know; with all these chocolates and biscuits I have, I'll take some to the children's ward.
Yes, the best idea I had all day.
I hanged two carrier bags on each side of my wheelchair and a couple on my lap.
I was out of there like a flash.

People were asking me;
  "Where are you going with all that"?
I didn't bother answering, I just went.
On the way to the lift I asked the Kaiser;
  "What floor are the children,
and she said the fifth.
She also said;
  "That's a very nice thing what you're doing".
  "I'm proud of you Johnny Walker".
Proud of me? the Kaiser?
I knew it;
The mighty Kaiser is getting soft on me.
I don't even know if that's really a good thing.
In no time at all I was in the lift going up.
All these millions of times I used a lift and although I always see the metal plate were the buttons are, I never actually realise there was a mistake.
And come to think of it, no matter what country you're in or what country the lift was manufactured

in and brought there, they all have the same mistake.
   MAXIMUM LOAD 450 KILOS
   6 PERSONS
I mean halloo; Persons…???
There's no such word I think.
I always thought one is a person, two are people.
Oh I don't know maybe they're rite and I'm wrong.
And this lift, I mean talk about slow motion, and it stops on every bloody floor whether it's full of people or empty.
At last the 5th floor.
It was like rush hour in London's Oxford Street.
My God there are so many people.
Do they all have sick children here?
The minute I came out of the lift, another weird thing happened.
As if by magic or something, everyone stood still.
As if I pointed the remote control at them and pressed freeze.
I mean some people were on their knees crossing themselves as I passed them.

They cleared a path for me still
looking at me in a most peculiar
way.
I didn't know what to make out of
this.
What is it with these people?
Oh I think this island produces
weird people for sure;
Oh I don't care really;
I came here for the kids and the
kids I will see.
I went straight to the reception
to ask if it was ok.
The sister and all the nurses came
around from the back of the
counter and surrounded me.
They wanted to meat me and shake
hands with me.
The first one was the sister.
I had the idea that all sisters
are huge, but this one was petite;
They all knew who I was.
Well what can I say; my "fame"
reached the fifth floor?
The sister looked very happy with
my presents.
She said;
  "It's not often we get famous
people visiting us".

I asked her if I can give her the bags with the goodies for the kids, and she replied;
  "Why don't you do that your self, I'll come with you and introduce you to them, they knew you were coming; we already informed them of your visit".
  "They all know Uncle Johnny is coming to see them".
  "We have about sixty children here and they're all waiting to see you, it's been three days now, and every day they ask for you".
  "Where's Uncle Johnny"?
  "Is he coming to see us today"?
  "The answer we were giving was, if you're good and take your medicine he will come".
  "Needles to say it's been the easiest three days for us".
  "We owe you a lot already, thank you".
I was stunned!!!
I said;
  "How on earth could you have known that I was coming"?
  "I didn't know I was until ten minutes ago".

Now how the hell did they know I was coming, that really puzzled me;
How is it possible to know that? What is going on here?
I mean what…???
Is this a dream?
I asked the sister;
   "Would you pinch me a little please I want to wake up".
She smiled and said;
   "No, it's not a dream; you're here because God sent you here".
I said;
   "God didn't send me here, he couldn't have".
   "He never said anything to me".
   "I don't think He needs to" she said.
   "Please come with me" she said and I followed.
We went into the first ward and… surprise-surprise, almost immediately there was a total silence;
I could see the surprise look on the parents, as if they didn't believe I was there.
As for the kids, the silence lasted less than ten seconds.

So I wheeled my self from bed to bed, kid to kid.
I was handing out a few goodies to each one.
What's your name, how are you, are you a good boy, are you a good girl and all that, over and over again.
Then the next ward, then the next; I must have received hundreds of hugs and kisses.
The genuine love these children shown towards me were really unreal, or should I say indescribable.
As if I was Papa Noel, or father Xmas.
Mind you, I was happier than the kids were, especially when I was hugged.
Oh I could jump for joy!!!
What a feeling!!!
I promised them all, if they were good and take there medicine I'll come and see them again, this time with a special gift.
By the time I went down to my floor and my ward, the people were queuing up again and waiting patiently to see me, shake hands and leave for me their presents.

Not to mention the well wishing cards and flowers.
At least half the ward was filled with all sorts of goods;
Every one of the patients was glad to offer me their little cabinet and all the space that goes with it next to their beds.
The bagfuls were coming in non stop.
I was really embarrassed at one time, because I got so use to this, I actually offered my hand to someone for him to kiss it.
As if I was a King and he was a loyal subject.
But I came to my senses quick and pretended I was stretching my arms.
The Kaiser appeared as if she knew I needed help.
She did what she had to do and put a stop to this.
The only thing I heard was tomorrow.
Oh, she is good, by George she is.
She knew precisely when to appear.
It was a little after four still, but felt really tired.
What an exhausting day, and it's not over yet.

It's still a long time before visitors leave.
I turned around and… my God…!!! What am I going to do with all these things, not to mention how embarrassing it was;
There was no room for anyone to sit, every little space there was, it was taken; all these bags…!!!
I wheeled my self to the reception and to The Kaiser.
I said to her;
   "Please, please, and please again".
   "Is there some way we can give all that to a home or something"?
She said;
   "Yes, Johnny Walker"
I already arranged for a school bus to take some of it; there are three homes not far from here, one for orphans, one for children with special needs and one for homeless families.
I asked;
   "Did you say already arranged it"?
She said "yes".
   "And how did you know I was going to offer"?
She stopped me and said;

"Yes I knew, and don't ask me again how".
I mean I was talking to the Kaiser, who in the rite mind will want to argue with her.
And in no time at all, two guys appeared and with the help of two nurses they were rearranging the goods in the bags;
A lot of visitors joint in as well, clipping a card with a name of a child written on it and carrying them downstairs to the bus.
Four hundred and fifty five carrier bags in total;
I felt a bit guilty.
All these people working hard because of me I thought.
I asked the guys if they can take a few more bags, but they said;
   "Sorry, there's no more room, maybe tomorrow or a day after".
I went back to the Kaiser;
I said to her;
   "There's a lot more, what are we going to do with all these bags"?
She said;
   "Enough excitement for today";
   "I want you in your bed in less than five minutes";

195

"I'll come around for your injection".
"What injection I said, I no nothing about any injection".
Well she said;
"You don't but I do, so off you go".
Oh… Shit.
I knew it, just when everything was going well for a change, she had to spoil it all.
Shit…!!!
"Come on young man, I haven't all day, I want to go home".
Well, no choice really.
Kaisers orders, they must be obeyed.
It's like "His Masters Voice" thing.
And of course back to my bed I went and waited.
She came over with a nurse wheeling a long-ish trolley with warm water in a plastic mini tub, towels and I don't know what else.
"Time for your bath" she said.
The nurse wheeled over the partition thing and there I was, in bed, secluded in a cubicle, with the Kaiser ready for action.

That was the moment she was waiting for; she knew she would get me sooner or later.
I bet she was thinking about this all day.
Injection my foot;
What a clever excuse to get me in bed.
She bent towards me and whispered in my ear.
Get undressed.
What?
   "Do you want me to shout so everyone will hear"?
   "Get undressed now".
Shit, what an embarrassing moment.
I did but dead slow.
She unclipped my corset thing and gently "unwrapped" me.
Now lay back and enjoy.
Oh………… shit………!!!
She'll do it, here and now, there's no stopping her.
I was completely naked in front of her.
I was desperately trying to hide my sensitive parts.
But she would have none of that.
She pulled my hand up and over my head.

I was at her mercy, at her disposal;
She could do anything she wanted with me.
   "Come now Mr Walker, you're a big boy now, don't be shy;
   Remember, I've seen it all before".
The only thing I could say to her after that was;
   "Please be gentle with me".
And she started sponging away.
She knew where it mite hurt me and she was ever so gentle,
Especially when she came to… my private parts or should say "sensitive parts";
She turned me over ever so gently and sponged away.
Well, what can I say, I enjoyed that enormously.
Man… she was good…!!!
For a big person like her, she had such a gentle touch.
I felt wonderful.
I said;
   "Thank you sister" and she replied;
   "I'm not finished with you yet young man".

She pushed me to one side and before I knew what, I felt the needle in my bum.
Ouch...!!!
After that wonderful sponge bath she gave me, she goes and spoils it all.
She said;
  "That's it, that wasn't that bad was it"?
She helped me sit up and wrapped me with the corset again.
She then helped me wear a fresh robe, off the bed and onto my wheels.
I asked her what was in that injection and she replied;
  "Pain killer and something to help you sleep".
I thanked her and she said;
  "Goodnight, I'm going home now; my shift is up".
The dinner ladies came and we had some kind of tasteless chicken with veg.
I mean who can really eat something as tasteless as this?
I really wonder; does the chef ever taste any of this shit?
I mean really.
Maybe he's not a real chef.

I must go down there one day and see him.
I hope he won't be offended if I give him a few tips.
I had as much food as a mouse can put away within the space of ten minutes.
I took my diary and started writing the days events.
I even named my dairy "Pal"
Hi there pal;
What a day huh, full of surprises, shocks, adventure.
I wonder what's in store for me tomorrow.
Surely it must be a quiet day.
Shit man, I deserve a quiet day.
It's been "Hectic" all week.
I will program it tomorrow.
Make sure everything will go smoothly.
Oh I'm so tired.
I was injected with something, and whatever that was, it's taking effect on me now;
I can't keep my eyes open;
What did the Kaiser put in that injection?
I climbed up to my bed.
I remember thinking;

I hope I won't get into any
trouble tomorrow.
I mean what can go wrong?
Yes, tomorrow I'll be as good as
gold.
Maybe I'll stay in bed all day.
Maybe that way nothing can go
wrong;
Yes… bed;
Bed and only bed, all day.
I do hope whatever was in that
injection will last long, long
enough for me to sleep for hours
and hours;
I mean what can possibly go wrong
if I'm all day in bed?
Hahaha…
How little did I know;

***Saint Johnny Walker's
"How to… Become a Saint"***

Chapter Eight
Day Seven

Bang that door again.
Shit, it's the human clock…!!!
I don't know how she does it but she has this technique to bang that door so loud, as if she's banging two metal pieces together, and yet, I never saw her holding anything.
Today's banging noise made me jump up; just like the first morning.
I felt like a little kid locked up in a dark room and just as I was beginning to get use to it she comes and traumatises me with her sudden scary bang.
Shit, what was in that injection the Kaiser gave me?
I must have slept a good twelve hours.
Oh no, I missed my symphony.
I felt as if I let my people down. The Royal Albert Hall was packed with people and all waiting for me to perform.
Only I didn't turn up.

What will my fans think of me now?
The usual "bon journo tutti" and
"good morning gentlemen" and all
that usual crap;
The curtains wide open;
  "It's a nice day out there";
The usual performance;
And of course the disappearing
act;
I know I was only about a week
there but, that morning I felt as
if I took up a permanent residency
in there, and this lady's
performance every day was
beginning to annoy me;
Then the tea ladies;
Seeing them so early in the
morning, one gets the feeling
they're there just for you,
especially when there's this huge
smile that comes with it;
One tends to forget all about
Marias performance a few minutes
earlier, the "anger" just
disappears;
Yes, the nice tea lady with all
that gibberish about me saving her
life.
I will ask her again, although I
know she's loosing it, but I still

want to know how I helped save her life.
I wonder what a fantastic story she'll come up with.
I hope she still remembers that dream.
As usual she comes around with my two mugs.
I asked her;
   I said "please "mamma" do you remember the dream you said you've experienced"?
She said;
   "No one can ever forget a dream like that".
   "And how did I help save your life"?
   "You said one day you will tell me, remember"?
She said;
   "You will find out how yourself, when the rite time comes, I'm not allowed to tell you, not just yet".
Ha… I knew it was all gibberish.
I knew it all along.
She's definitely loosing it.
Poor old lady and I like her very much.
It wasn't long before the doctors came and gone.

The usual questions and of course the usual answers.
The time was passing quietly until visitors were eventually allowed in and of course the usual chaos in the ward.
People were coming from here there and everywhere.
This is getting ridicules.
I mean how long is this situation going to go on?
I must find a solution.
Flowers and flowers, bags full of little gifts, drinks, tins, bottles, cakes, cuddly toys;
As for the queue, it was getting longer and longer.
What the hell am I going to do?
How can I stop this?
I mean I can't really come out and say "Buzz Off" to everyone can I?
Or I have had enough with you lot.
I mean these people come to see me, pay their respects.
I don't really know why, but they do anyway.
They all look up to me.
These are good people.
But I don't want to take advantage of their good nature.

There I was yet again shaking hands with all these people, people I've never seen before and accepting their presents.
But my mind was elsewhere.
And it "hit" me, all of a sudden I knew how.
I think I found the answer.
Yes… what a brilliant idea!!!
I quickly pressed the button that was hanging over my bed for help.
Within seconds the Kaiser came to my rescue.
She asked the people to stand back a bit and said;
  "Good morning Mr Walker what can I do for you"?
I said;
  "Do something for a little peace and quiet; I have something good and very important to tell you".
The Kaiser immediately asked everyone to go.
She found a good excuse and sends them away.
When she came back I asked her;
  "What is the hospital lucking"?
  "I know all hospitals in the world need some kind of a machine or something yes"?
She said;

"Yes, rite now we need a kidney dialysis machine, but it costs a fortune; we cannot afford a new one".
I said;
"Sister, do you see all these people coming for me with all these gifts"?
"Find a way to inform them that; I will not accept any more gifts; whatever they would have spent on gifts we'll take it in money to pay for the machine".
"What do you think"?
OH… the Kaisers face…!!!
I mean I thought I saw it lit up.
She said;
"You must be what people say you are".
"You are an angel"!!!
No-no-no I said.
"I just want to put an end to this chaos that's all".
She said;
"Well, I hear and now I know and confirm".
She bends down and gives me two kisses what!!!
The Kaiser, whatever next?

Within an hour or so there were posters everywhere saying just that.

"Whoever wishes to visit "Saint Johnny Walker" instead of gifts please contribute for a kidney dialysis machine, however big or small the donation is, is very gratefully and lovingly accepted".
Just before the posters went up, Kaiser arranged for me to be moved from the ward to a private room. Well, more like a hotel suite really.
I asked;

"Who's paying for this, I don't think my insurance will cover me for all this".
The Kaiser said;

"Let me worry about that".

"You just concentrate on getting well".
I mean there was a private bath with mirrors, private loo, colourful curtains, a big table, a few nice chairs, fridge, and 21 inch telly.
Oh this is living!!!
They also brought in a huge see-through square box for the

contributions, and the guys set it rite in front of my bed.
People were queuing outside my door waiting to come in, the bags were still in there hands.
I suppose they already have bought and they wanted to leave them there for me anyway.
It didn't take long for the room to fill up with flowers, cuddly toys and carrier bags.
As for the box, even though it was only a few minutes "operational" it was no longer transparent, at least halfway up.
The rate that was going, I think we'll reach the target in record time.
Now I didn't mind the visitors, in fact I was very pleased, the more the better.
The more I was seeing the box getting filled, the more pleased I was.
It was lunch time and the Kaiser asked the people to come back later or tomorrow.
She asked me;
 "What do you fancy eating"?
Oh my world!!!
 "I have a choice now"?

"Well, you're not Johnny Walker any more".

"Now everybody knows you as Saint Johnny Walker, and that includes me".

What…???

She went on;

"I was a non believer, but now"?

"Why now" I asked.

"What did I do to change all that"?

"Is it because of the money box"?

"Although I must admit it was a great idea of mine, but any one could have thought of it".

She said;

"No it's not the box like you said, it's a few thinks that happened during your stay here".

"What could have possibly happened here like you said for you to call me that; the only thing I know is that I was a bit, well…? "Nutty" running around, being always in your way, I was always in trouble; create more work for you, after all, you said that yourself".

"Please tell me, I'm really curious".

And she goes;

"OK Saint Johnny, now that we're alone I'll tell you".

"Ever since your arrival, everyone here and I must admit, I don't know why, but we all began to have this weird feeling; we all knew something was going to happen; no one knew what this something was; the only thing we could imagine was maybe the government will make a few changes, maybe a few more staff, or a few more doctors; there were roomers also of a pay increase, but nothing of all that;
I wasn't on this floor when you first came in, but don't think I didn't know of your arrival".

"As you can imagine when there's an accident with so many injured we are all on alert".

"I happened to be on duty and was called down to casualty".

"We asked all the injured what happened, how did the accident happen and all the rest, and they all said the same thing".

"Thanks to the English guy, he saved all of us".

"And they were all asking, and I do mean all of them, if you were ok"?

"We all wanted to see who this English guy every one was asking about is"?

"Even though all these people said the same thing, we just couldn't believe you did what you did".

"Simply because you had no burns whatsoever on you".
And she went on;

"At the beginning we all thought you were a just crazy Englishman who could not sit still, I even heard one male nurse describe you as English "Hooligan" and that we should keep an eye on you".

"But after a few days we all changed our thoughts about you, we even changed the way we were looking at you; you saved all those people from sure death; you were going in and out of the fireball and pulled them out, every last one of them; and they all confirm that story".

"Surely they didn't make it up".

"In fact the last one you brought out said to me when I asked him";
He said;
"I was on fire and my legs were stuck somewhere; I could not move and I was really on fire, I knew I was going to die, I knew there was no hope, but suddenly comes the Englishman, I saw him, and he was glowing"!!!

"He put his arms around me and the fire was no way near me any more, he pulled a heavy piece of metal off of my legs, he pulled me out, made sure I'm ok and he went under a tree and collapsed".
She went on;
"That was your first, what I then called some kind of trick".

2nd... "Most of the people you saved suffered burns, and yet, no burns on you, not even your clothes".

3rd... "Everyone you saved swears it was you that pulled them out, and every time they were seeing you going back in the fireball without any hesitation";

"Everyone swears it's true, and I assure you, I spoke to each and every one of them my self to confirm that";

"Everyone said you were sort of glowing and that you had some kind of what looked like a shield around you protecting you from burning"!!!

4th… "A couple of days a go, you hugged Anna, the tea lady you call mamma".

"Well let me tell you a bit about our Anna".

"She's a volunteer worker in this hospital; she is suffering from cancer, or should say was, the doctors gave her six months to a year".

"She wanted to work so she wouldn't go crazy".

"The minute you gave her the tight hug she felt it all, she was telling me she felt some kind of heat going through her body, she then went for a check up and guess what, there was no trace of any cancer whatsoever".

"Even the doctors are puzzled";

"They did test after test on her to make sure there's no mistake".

5th... "Yesterday, you went to the fifth floor yes"?

"We had about sixty children up on the fifth".

"Well this morning we only have twenty or so".

"The forty or so children went home".

"After they came in contact or something with you, whatever they were suffering from it was gone".

"Doctors checked them this morning and, nothing, absolutely nothing wrong with them".

"Today and I'm saying, so far, the box, do you think it just happened? If so; why doesn't it happen to anyone else in here"? I'm doing this job twenty odd years and I've never seen anything like it".

"How did you know we need a dialysis machine"?

"How comes you and only you came up with the idea"?

"Why do you think all these people want to come and see you, touch you or shake your hand"?

"Do you really think they're all crazy"?

"It seems that from the day you set foot in this island, things just happen around you".

"For some, unexplained, but for many and including me, well… more like miracles".

"And from what I've seen and heard, some will do anything you ask from them".

"And the best part is that you make people happy when they see you, especially now with your wheelchair running around".

"And who knows what's to come still".

"Now, "St Johnny", if you don't mind I have some work to go to".

"Well, what is it going to be"?

"The food, what do you fancy eating"?

"Oh, I don't know I'll leave it up to you, surprise me".

She gave me a big smile and off she went.

WOW…!!!

What was all that?

It sounded to me more like a lecture than... oh I don't know, something;

St Johnny?

Cancer healer?

Half the kids are cured?
What the hell is all this?
What a lot of gibberish.
I mean who in the rite mind will
believe any of that.
Angels… Miracles… Healer… The
"Gift"!!!
I mean, come on;
At this day and age?
The gift…!!!
What gift?
I wish I had a gift like that.
Ha… I'll be a millionaire in
record time.
I'll be in all the papers.
The fastest self made millionaire
in recorded history.
The kid with the "Midas" touches…!
People in this island are crazy.
They have a great sense of
imagination I'll give them that.
Maybe it's something to do with
the island;
Just like some of these weird
films we see;
Oh these people must be watching
too much television.
They should write story books.
Well, one thing came out good from
this incredible story.
At least the service has improved.

I mean who would believe the sister will transform from Kaiser to Mother Teresa?
I only wish the Gestapo was here to see this.
I wonder if the Gestapo was going to "break" like the Kaiser.
Now there's a task.
Yes, my next "miracle" should be Gestapo.
I must find a way to break her too.
While all these things were going through my mind, a few more people came in the room and left a few things and some money in the box.
The Kaiser or should I say Mother Teresa came with the biggest portion of cod and chips I ever saw.
 "Holly Mother of God sister";
 "Where on earth did you manage to get this from"?
She said proudly;
 "For me nothing is impossible".
I said;
 "How much did it cost you"?
 "Surely from what I've seen so far in here the chef knows five things to cook only and this is not one of them".

"Don't tell me you asked the chef downstairs to prepare this, because I won't believe you".
"A big portion like this"?
"In London this big a portion will cost half a day's wages".
She said;
"Not only I didn't pay for it, but the person who sent it also sent money for the box".
And she pushes the money through the opening.
"Who is this guy"?
"You will meet him one day; he will come to visit you".
"He heard all about you and he wants to meet you".
"Well, why not, after all, he paid for it";
"I can't refuse him, can I"?
The minute she was out the door, I just could not help my self, I dived in.
The aroma of the English fish & chips was tormenting me.
And whoever this guy is who send this, must have read my mind, because I found a smaller wrapping with small sachets of salt and vinegar would you believe!!!
What!!!

Salt…!!!
This is what I call a miracle.
Now there's a guy that knows what a patient feels like in here.
He must have spent a "vacation" here just like me.
I mean how else would the Kaiser know him?
Oh…!!! Fish & chips!!!
A taste of England!!!
I was munching away like a pig.
It was a moment of truth, a moment to saver.
I never thought I could finish it all.
But man, was I wrong.
I swallowed it all and probably in record time too;
I realised it was a bit more than, too much, but I couldn't stop, it was so delicious.
I mean after so long without fish and chips, who would stop?
Who can actually say no, no more, enough?
The only thing I needed was something to wash it down with.
I press the buzzard and Mother Teresa came.
I said;

"All I need now is a pint of beer, can I have one"?
The reply I got was in a rough-ish voice;
"Don't push it".
I guess it was a bit too early to rename her Mother Teresa after all.
Kaiser it is then.
So I settled for a cola or something fizzy.
"That's no problem" she said;
"You have in your fridge a few different kinds of tins; you can help yourself any time you want".
She asked;
"Are you ready for visitors"?
"There's a big queue out the door".
Oh shit, I forgot.
This means there's no more running around with my wheels.
"Can I have a couple of hours for my self maybe in the afternoon" I asked.
She replied;
"What do you mean a couple of hours"?
"Another hour or so and that's it for the day".

"Don't forget you're a patient here, and like every one else you need rest, you're still a sick man".

"So, if you're up to it I'll allow people to come in".

"And don't worry; I do know when to stop it for today".

"And if you feel at any time it's to much for you press the buzzer".

The door opened wide and the first to come in were six patients in their pyjamas.
They all came in together.
They were accompanied by three nurses.
I noticed they were all heavily bandaged and all but one had broken arms.
One of the nurses said;

"Hello St Johnny Walker, these are six of the people you saved, and she introduced them one by one".

"We are from the burns unit".
I noticed two of them were actually crying.
The nurse said;

"They all wanted to come and thank you personally, even though

we said not yet, but they insisted".
My God, these people deserve a medal.
They can hardly stand straight and yet they came here to see me, and I'm just sitting here in comfort; I felt guilty so I got up and shook hands with them.
They looked so pleased, so happy, and they kept repeating thank you, thank you.
In their faces one could see something different; they looked like they were stunned.
They just looked and looked at me in some weird way, as if they wanted answers or something.
I got the feeling they wanted me to say something, but what can one say?
I mean what answer I could come up with.
After all, they knew what actually happened and I didn't.
The only thing I said to them was;
  "Get well quick guys and feel free to come and see me anytime you feel like, I want you to come; I have a lot of questions that need answers too".

They shook my hand again, said a few times thank you yet again and left.
The poor guys, I can only imagine what or how it is under those bandages.
I can only imagine the pain.
They must be very brave.
I think I am a coward;
I couldn't go through with all that;
I hate to even imagine what is like.
The minute they walked out, the relatives of all six came in, all in one go.
Mothers, fathers, grandmas, grandpas, brothers, sisters, wives, kids, you name it, they were all there.
I don't know how many they were, I can only say the room was not big enough for all to come in at the same time.
Hugs, kisses, handshakes, presents, gifts of all sizes, cuddly toys, money in the box, big smiles, prayers and lots of tears from nearly everyone;
The room was getting smaller and smaller with all the gifts.

A few of the women were on their knees praying and trying to kiss my feet.
I would have none of that and was pushing them back.
The situation was getting out of hand because they were insisting in having it their way and they wouldn't go; they just wanted to stay there.
I kept saying, "OK, enough go now".
I kept saying "what I did was nothing, you don't owe me anything, please go";
But it was no use; they just would not listen.
The more I was straggling to get free from them the more they were resisting.
The situation was not beginning to get out of hand but was.
Some women were holding my hand and kissing it, others wanted to do the same… some I noticed were trying to get closer to me from the back but couldn't.
The people in front wouldn't move.
Everyone seemed to push everyone.
It made me feel a bit panicky.

I felt millions of hands touching me and one of my sleeves was torn;
For a moment there I could not breathe;
I was straggling for oxygen;
I wanted to buzz for the Kaiser but could not;
The situation became hysterical.
I was in trouble;
I really felt they were going to kill me, suffocate me;
Kaiser must have heard it all because she was there in a flash;
She came to my rescue yet again.
She cleared the room in no time.
Oh what a relief.
All of a sudden I felt really knackered.
I felt I was going to collapsed.
I got out of the wheelchair in order to lie in bed and bang, I felt the floor came up to my head hitting me hard;
I was gone…
I must have collapsed, I was out.
When I came to, I was in bed and the Kaiser was trying to bring me around.
I said;
　"What happened"?
She said;

"You passed out and fell on the floor".
"How are you feeling"?
"And how long was I out for"?
"Three minutes".
I said;
"Oh, that's not bad, but my fingers hurt".
She took my left hand and gently checked my fingers.
She said;
"This doesn't look good to me".
She picked me up and onto my wheelchair;
"We're going for an X-ray" she said and she wheeled me there.
And of course the result was two broken fingers.
I mean it had to happen; didn't it?
Back to the "plasterer"
The minute the guy saw me in the room he said;
"Well bless my soul".
"Hello St Johnny Walker, back so soon"?
"What is it this time"?
I felt a bit embarrassed.
I wanted to hide my face.
I felt like a little kid that's always in trouble; the bad boy at

school that gets sent to the principal; I felt like I was the real "Dennis the Menace"
I'm glad the Kaiser explained to him what happened.
She's always there when I need her, always to the rescue.
She was becoming a very important person in my life.
It didn't take long for the plasterer to start his yap-yap, and bla-bla.
He actually apologized for his earlier remark.

   "News travels fast St Johnny Walker" he said.

   "The entire hospital knows about you".

   "People talk about you everywhere".

   "It seems you're the only subject in every conversation, everybody analyzes the miracles that happen ever since your arrival here'.

   "How do you feel about all that"?

   "Please tell me, I really want to know, how do you do it"?
I got the feeling he wanted me to pass over the "technique" so he

will do the same or take over my job when I leave the hospital or something.
And he was a bit pushy too.
He was saying;
  "The minute you touch or hug someone";
  "What is the procedure"?
  "That's "THE" moment yes"?
  "Do you pray"?
  "What words do you say"?
  "And the most important, how do you know who needs and deserves to be cured";
  "Some people don't deserve anything in my opinion".
That wasn't very nice what he just said.
It's amazing how some people think!
I thought all people deserve at least a second chance in life if not a third or a fourth for that matter.
He wasn't a very nice man, I think.
And he wanted answers here and now.
Answers I didn't have.
Answers I was searching for, my self.

But the guy wouldn't take no for an answer.
He just wouldn't accept the fact that I didn't know.
If it wasn't for Kaiser being there, I think he was going to choke the answers out of me.
Even the Kaiser noticed he was delaying the process of what he was supposed to do.
She actually said;
  "Come on doctor, we haven't all day".
Doctor?
Is this guy a real doctor?
I thought he was just a plasterer.
What kind of a doctor will use words like some deserve and some don't?
I was rite, he is a bad man.
I don't really like him.
Eventually he wrapt my two fingers with this wet net thing and all around my thumb, covering nearly all my hand, and started plastering it.
The whole thing took about twenty minutes or so.
I thanked him and we left.
She wheeled me back to my room and said;

"No more visitors for you today".
"I want you to rest, and I mean rest".
"I'll be back in a few minutes".
And that she did, she came back with a couple of painkillers.
I quickly swallowed them.
She repeated;
"I want you to rest now".
"You still have a couple of hours before dinner time, I suggest you use for rest".
That gave me the chance to write the days events in my diary, and… in total peace and quiet.
I was so into my writing, I didn't realise the time
It was indeed dinner time.
The Kaiser came in and asked what would like for dinner.
I asked;
"What do you recommend"?
She said;
"After all that lunch, I think something light".
"And I have it ready for you".
"The nurse will bring it in a few minutes".
She said;

"I'll be signing off duty in a few minutes, please no more excitements, OK"?

"OK, sister, I'll turn in after diner".

She added;

"Don't think I don't know what goes on here in the hospital when I'm not here in person".

"When I say rest, I mean rest, OK"?

"After dinner, take these pills, they will help ease the pain and help you sleep".

"I'll see you in the morning, hopefully in one piece".

"Goodnight Saint Johnny Walker" and off she went.

Two minutes later the night nurse came with my dinner.

She was new; at least I've never seen her before.

She said;

"Orders from the sister, only fruit salad for you, "sorry"

She stood there looking at me.

I knew she wanted to say something but was a bit shy and embarrassed. I asked instead;

"What's up, why do you look at me like that"?

She said;
  "I'm sorry, but I heard all these stories".
  "I wanted to see you in person".
  "I want to ask something but I'm embarrassed to do so".
  "What is it"?
She said;
  "Can I touch you"?
  "Just for a minute"
What the hell, everybody else does.
  "Yes", I said.
And she puts her hand on my shoulder a bit reluctantly.
Her hand was shaking, and she was blushing.
The minute she touched me I sensed she had someone very close to her in big trouble.
I didn't know who that someone was.
I didn't know how I knew either.
I grabbed her hand and squeezed it a little.
What happened after that will puzzle me the rest of my life.
I remember closing my eyes for a few seconds and carried on squeezing her hand.

I was in a different world that minute.

I actually heard a little girl's voice calling me; she was crying and calling my name, Johnny Walker.
I opened my eyes and said.
"Who is Isabella"?
She said;
"Oh-my-God";
"How could you know her name"?
I repeated;
"Who is Isabella"?
She pulled her hand away and in a trembling voice said;
"Isabella is my sisters little daughter, about a week ago she was not feeling well and they thought maybe she's coming down with a cold or something; two days later her condition worsened, so they took her to the doctors, he said, she has ear infection and it's far gone, she needs to go to a hospital immediately".

"The doctors here have her in intensive care";
"They said she has maybe less than 10% of puling through".
"The infection is affecting her brains".

And with tears in her eyes said;
"She's only four".
I said;
"I need to see her right now"
"The sister said you are to be resting".
"I don't want to get into trouble with her, she's very strict; you don't know her, if something doesn't go her way, we all get the blame".
Ha… she's telling me about the Kaiser.
And I nearly said that to her.
I just said;
"Never mind about the sister, I'll tell her you tried to stop me".
She said;
"But even if we go up you won't be able to go in the intensive care".
"Don't waist time I said, let's go".
Five minutes later we were there.
I said to the head nurse;
"I wanted to go in and see her".
She refused;
"No one goes in that room".
"I will" I said.

She was having none of it, no matter what I was saying.
I actually raised my voice, and I was getting louder and louder, and still the answer was no…no…no.
Then, from all these shouting a doctor appeared, then another, and another.
It didn't take long for the reception area to fill up with white coats, doctors, nurses, visitors, you name it.
Everybody had his or her opinion, whether I should go in or not.
There was a bit of a chaos all around me there, until I saw this woman coming towards us.
Somehow I knew she was the mother of the little girl.
She came near me and said;
   "You must be Saint Johnny Walker" shook my hand, gave me a hug and whispered in my ear;
   "Thank you for coming to us, my prayers are answered".
She said loudly;
   "He is going in and no one will stop him".
A minute later I was in dressed like a doctor ready for surgery.
There she was; a little angel.

I'm not a doctor but I could see clearly she was in a terrible condition; she was like half dead and humming.
I went closer and sat on her bed beside her.
Her eyes were opening and closing as if they had a mind of their own, it was clear that she had no control of them.
She had a greenish-white colour.
I picked her up and in my arms.
She felt so cold, more frozen like.
I just squeezed her in my arms and said;
   "Isabella, wake up darling, look who came to see you, come darling look, its uncle Johnny".
I have a big teddy for you, look.
I looked at the nurse and she knew immediately.
She rushed down to my room and brought the biggest one.
I felt I needed a good fifteen minutes with her.
I said;
   "Please everyone, give us some room and quiet please".
Everyone pulled back.

I kept holding her in my arms squeezing a little and repeating over and over again.

"Come darling, wake up, its uncle Johnny, there's a big teddy bear here and wants a big hug".
And a few minutes later I felt it. The "Heat"…!!!
There was some kind of heat between us, some kind of energy;
I don't know whether it was coming out of me and into her or from her to me.
She was no longer frozen, and her green colour was gone.
I could see rosy cheeks and her natural colour was coming back slowly.
I kept repeating those words, and suddenly I felt her little hands squeezing me, harder and harder.
Suddenly, she looked at me straight in the eyes and said;

"Hello"!!!
And in English would you believe? I replied;

"Hello Isabella, how are you darling, are you feeling better now"?
She just jumped away from my arms and started jumping on the bed,

she was full of life, she was so happy.
I mean she was acting as if there was never anything wrong with her. Her behaviour was just like any healthy child of four should be; Suddenly she stopped the jumping and said;
   "Where's my teddy bear"?
The nurse handed it over to me and I gave it over to her.
She immediately hugged and kissed it.
I said;
   "Poor bear; he has no name, would you like to give the bear a name?
   Think of a nice name for the bear".
The name she came up with was more of a puzzle and amazement to everyone.
She said;
   "I will call him "St Johnny""
What…!!!
How could she have come up with a name like that?
There was no way she could have known.

No person in that room could believe what the little girl just said.
The moment she said St Johnny, I heard everyone behind me saying; What…?
As if synchronised;
Isabella hugged me again and again, and again.
She whispered in my ear "thank you".
I mean she's only four, and speaks to me in English?
The satisfaction and the happiness I felt was clear for all so see.
As for her mother, she just stood there with her mouth wide open, probably thinking how on earth Isabella could speak English, how quickly she recovered and God knows what else.
Everyone else in that room was just speechless, and that included the doctors.
I saw some people on their knees praying.
Suddenly I felt very tired.
I could hardly hang on to my senses.
I was about to collapse.

Luckily, the nurse was there and grabbed me.
She helped me onto my wheelchair and I managed to say;
"Take me to my room please".
On our way out of the intensive care unit I saw people praying on their knees, I could hear them saying;
"It's a miracle".
They were all stretching their hands to touch me.
I had no energy left in me.
I gave it all.
I can't even remember the journey to my room.
The girl helped me to my bed, and gave me fruit juice.
She sat beside me on the bed waving something to cool me down.
I was perspiring something terrible.
She wouldn't go anywhere until she was sure I was ok.
I don't know how long after, but I started feeling good again, all my senses were back.
And I felt hungry, I mean real hungry.
I felt I could eat a horse.

It seamed I needed to get back all
the energy I lost.
I remembered the fruit salad.
I asked the nurse where the fruit
salad was.
She brought the tray and onto my
lap.
And what a fruit salad that was,
more like a feast, it had
everything in it.
And what inviting colours?
The more I was looking at it the
more hungry I was;
After I finished it all, I thanked
the girl and picked up my diary.
Obviously I had more to write.
The girl just didn't know how to
thank me.
She was in a world of her own.
Her body was there, but her soul?
She was in a Trans;
As if someone hypnotised her; she
was gone.
I wanted to snap her out of it.
I said to her;
  "HALLOO… wake up girl".
She somehow came to, and said;
  "Yes, yes St Johnny Walker, what
can I do for you, anything,
anything, and I mean anything".

I must have heard her saying a million times thank you.
She was saying, well, she tried…
   "What you did was… what just happened in there"…
Oh she was indeed lost.
Finally she comes out with the rite question;
   "Isabella is ok now yes"?
   "I did see her jumping on the bed yes"?
   "Please tell me";
Poor girl, she was indeed so confused;
I mean she knew I was going to do something, whatever that something was, but by the looks of things, she never expected it to be a full recovery in a matter of minutes;
I said;
   "Yes, she is perfectly healthy";
She went hysterical.
I thought the only way to stop her was to say I'm tired and want to sleep.
I said:
   "Please; I'm tired; I desperately need rest and sleep".
She was still in a state of shock somewhat.
She said;

"Goodnight Saint Johnny Walker"
and left;
I wrote a few more lines in my
diary, felt my eyes heavy and
turned the lights out.
I remember thinking what a day
that was.
What an eventful day.
But I did it again didn't I?
This time I broke my fingers.
What a nightmare that was.
I mean what kind of people are in
the world.
Didn't they see me straggle to
breathe?
Didn't they see I was in trouble?
I mean what the hell were they
trying to do, kill me?
I mean even the six guys that came
before them didn't behave like
their relatives, and they needed
my help.
Mmm… maybe "hooliganism" is an
Italian word after all.
Or at least where it all started
from;
The "motherland" of hooliganism;
Well, if that was in Germany I
would have call it "fatherland"
Isn't it funny, the Germans are
the only ones in the world they

call their country Fatherland, I
wonder why?
Maybe I'll ask a German why?
And I hope he knows the right
answer, not just, well, we want to
be different;
I mean it reminded me of the
football fans, or should I say
football gangs clashing.
I must put an end to this somehow.
I must find a way to have at least
one pleasant day in here.
I think I deserve one.
I desperately need an "injury
free" day;
I mean, if God loves me enough or
even trusts me enough to give a
wonderful gift like that, why the
injuries, why the pain, why the
suffering?
What have I done wrong in my life
to deserve this?
Surely there must be another way;
Why the pain and injuries for Him
to let me know of these gifts?
Maybe He thinks I am probably too
young to understand the impotence
of the whole thing;
Then again if this is indeed all
true, who am I to argue the point?

And even if I really wanted to argue, who do I argue with?
Maybe this is "one of His mysterious ways"
I remember looking up and saying; "Please God; if you are there and can hear me, please, please, please; "No more injuries"
Oh I do hope He is there and can hear me;
Surely tomorrow will be a better day.
I mean what can possibly go wrong again?
Hahaha… How little did I know…!!

Saint Johnny Walker's "How to... Become a Saint"

Chapter Nine
Day Eight

The next morning I heard someone knocking on the door.
I quickly covered my body with the blanket and said;
   "Yes, come in".
And surprise-surprise...!!!
It was the Kaiser with Gestapo; what...!!!
I could not believe it.
What a site huh?
First thing in the morning to see that!!!
Only the Kaiser was in uniform.
They both said;
   "Good morning Saint Johnny Walker".
I replied;
   "Good morning sisters".
   "Are you both on duty"?
Gestapo said;
   "No, I'll be in tomorrow, but I simply had to see you today, I wanted to give you a hug".

"Why on earth would you do that I said; all this time you were here you didn't and now you do"? She said;
  "We all heard of your "gift"
  "We simply didn't believe all we heard; well, some of us did anyway; some of us thought it was some kind of a trick you pulled; then there's was Anna, the tea lady, then the kids, and then last night, if that wasn't a miracle I don't know what a miracle is". And she just hugged me and kissed me time and time again.
  "It's no wonder people call you a Saint now".
  "It's no longer Johnny Walker; from now on I'll call you Saint Johnny too".
Then the Kaiser took over.
  "I thought I left strict orders for you to rest, yes"? I said;
  "Sorry sister".
  "Sorry my foot" she said. Holly shit; I never heard her talking like that before;
  "Next time I give an order you obey, is that understood"?
  "Yes sister".

"Sorry Huh, people just don't listen to us anymore";

"But I'll tell you something Saint Johnny Walker, this is one time I'm glad you disobeyed my orders last night; what you did last night was… was… was… oh how I wish I was there to witness it my self".

"Why did you waited for me to go and then perform"?

The door opened and it was Anna the tea lady, full of smiles as usual, she brought me my usual two mugs of tea and a few home made cookies.

She whispered good morning in my ear as she hugged me.

She was hugging me for a good two to three minutes.

I had to say;

"Mamma; my tea is getting cold" for her to let go.

She said;

"Thank you for giving me life and a special thank you for the little girl, she kissed both my cheeks and my hand".

I saw her wiping off a tear, and as she was leaving she turned to the sisters and said;

"You wouldn't believe me would you"?

"I saw all this in my dreams".

"I knew God sent him back for a reason, he has a job to do here, he's on a mission, and I also know what else he is going to do before he leaves this hospital".

The smile she gave to both the sisters was one of satisfaction I would say.

I mean I was speechless;

The sisters were too;

We all looked at each other, as if the one was waiting for the other to say something.

Gestapo looked at me and said;

"It's true, she did";

"She came to me and said that the English boy is sent here by God".

"Remember the morning you hugged her"?

"Half an hour or so before, she was telling us all downstairs, as she was preparing the tea, she saw you in her dreams and said;

"He will cure me today, he will hug me and my body will be cured, I know… I saw it in my dream last night and she was insisting it

250

will happen, she knew it will; she knew exactly what was about to take place".

"But of course, we all knew miracles don't happen".

"But we didn't want to spoil her hopes".

"I tried to put it in another way to her, so she won't be disappointed if her dream doesn't come true".

"But she would have none of it".

"We all thought she was loosing it, she was getting worse and I thought this is it, it's affecting her brains, in other words we were loosing her, and that her time was up".

"I remember clearly, I actually said that to the other ladies; I was not in a good mood after that, my mind was on how is Anna doing and the nurses were informing me every five minutes".

"Then she came out of the ward full of life".

"She knew what just took place, she felt the heat between you two; she felt the energy leaving your body and into hers".

"But who would believe her".

"As soon as she finished her job she came to me and said;

"I'm ready for any test you like; call a doctor for a check up; I'll prove to you that there's nothing wrong any more; it's all gone, the cancer is gone; gone I'm telling you; and she was jumping for joy".

"I must admit, I thought we really lost her; I remember saying to my self, poor Anna, its bad enough she's suffering from cancer and now this".

"I arranged an emergency test for her, and of course you know the rest".
She added;

"What was I to think at that particular minute"?

"I saw the tests results my self and I still had my doubts, no way, there's no way in the world I would believe all that, even though I had the test results in my hands; this is some kind of a trick I thought and it's not a funny one; that's why I was a bit strict with you; my thoughts were… maybe he can trick a few people but not me and I really wanted to have a go at you; I wanted to tell you, it's not a nice thing what you're doing, especially on a nice old lady like our Anna".

"But seeing Anna so happy and how joyful she was, I went down to the doctor to double check the results".

"The doctor confirmed it, and he said; I run the tests three times, in fact he said he asked a few other doctors to double check everything over and over again too; the doctors compared all the records, of all Anna's previous tests… there was no doubt about it";

"Every little wrong thing was gone"…!!!

"They even had the X-ray machine tested".

"There was no doubt about it, Anna was cured".

"In fact, her entire body is now one of a twenty year old!

"All doctors and professors are puzzled; I mean things like these just don't happen.

"How is it possible; I just wouldn't accept it; I was convinced there was some kind of a

253

trick; I was sure you're a "trick" specialist; I just refused to accept anything else";

"But last night, what you did last night in front of so many people".

"Did you know that the little girl was actually dying"?

"The doctors were expecting her to pass away in a day or two at the most"?

"In fact they were amazed how she was still holding on".

"I am now convinced".

"You were sent here by God Himself.

"You "Sir" are indeed an Angel; you are, Saint Johnny Walker"
She went on and on.
Of course I know different; I felt I had to tell them the truth.
I said;

"Listen to me ladies; first of all I'm not an angel; second, I wasn't sent here by anybody let alone God Himself; I'm here because I was in that bus that had an accident; and my name is not Johnny Walker".
Kaiser stopped me and said;

254

"We don't need any other name, Johnny Walker is plenty enough for us; we know what name your passport says; the police came to ask you a few questions a few days a go and we said you're not ready for them yet; we know all about you; as far as we know, and that goes for everyone in the hospital you're Saint Johnny Walker; and you cannot change that, no matter what you say or do".
Kaiser went out the door but immediately came back in.
She said;
 "There's chaos out there, I've never seen anything like it, there's thousands of people out there".
 "Oh no I said, please do something; I don't feel I'm up to it, I feel very weak after last night, please".
The two ladies picked the money box and placed it out the door; they arranged a security guy from downstairs to stand guard with strict orders.
No one is allowed in except members of staff.
Gestapo came back in and said;

"We decided to move the money box downstairs so people won't have to come up here for donations, which will allow us to do our job better, don't forget, there's a lot of other sick people here".
I suggested getting a few more money boxes and having them placed on every floor.
Why not take advantage of the situation.
She agreed and said;
 "I'll arrange it".
I don't know what or how, but I felt really weak, I could hardly hold the tea mug;
I felt the need of sleep.
My hand was shaking and my eyes felt heavy.
I think I was running a fever.
She pressed the buzzer and Kaiser came in.
They were whispering to each other and one of them went for the doctor.
The other was trying to cool me down with a wet sponge all over my face.
Three doctors no less examine me, I remember one saying;

"Back on the drip"
He said to me;
"You're very weak and dehydrated, you must rest, I'll give you something to relax, and don't fight it, just relax; you must take it easy".
He went on;
"We are all stunned by what you have achieved here, although as scientists we will argue with all these, and as much as we don't want to admit it, we all admire what you did; please Saint Johnny Walker; we need you alive".
"No more miracles, not today at least";
"Just rest, and that's an order; can you do that"?
I said;
"Ok doc, I will".
I heard him saying to the sister.
"Strictly no visitors"
There I was again all wired up.
I remember thinking of his words;
"We need me alive"?
Shit, whatever is wrong with me must be something serious;
And it didn't take long before I was out.

I woke up about three hours later from a lot of shouting outside my door;
The security guy was desperately trying to prevent people entering my room.
From the pushing and shoving the door opened halfway and I could see people pushing each other, trying to get in, asking questions very loudly, flashlights from cameras, real panic out there.
Some of the questions these people "threw" at me were,
  "Are you really a saint"?
  "Did God give you a mission"?
  "Do you have a list"?
  "Who's next on the list"?
  "How many more on the list"?
  "Why don't you answer any of the questions"?
  "Is your name really Saint Johnny Walker"?
  "Don't you think we have a rite to know"?
Bloody chaos if that's the rite word out there.
Who were these people?
They must have been reporters.
One of them managed to throw me a newspaper.

I took the paper and placed it under the pillow.
I was pressing and pressing the buzzer.
I desperately needed rescuing, or at least more help for the guard outside;
I thought if they go pass the security guy, I've had it.
I don't really know how long this battle went on but a few more security boys came and pushed these hooligans away.
Kaiser came in.
She said;
  "I'm sorry about that".
  "We didn't know last nights events made the papers".
  "These reporters don't care about anything".
  "All they want is to get the story from you, and if you can perform a miracle or two for them to witness".
  "I promise you this will not happen again".
  "Please try and forget the whole incident and try to rest; remember what the doctor said; rest and only rest".

I felt a bit peck-ish and I asked her;
"What time is it"?
"Just after eleven, lunch is not far away".
"By the way" she added;
"The guy from the restaurant sent his regards and offered lunch and dinner on him every day for you, so we're expecting a delivery for you".
"Oh you're so lucky, she went on, he never once did that for me"?
It was clear that she was trying to take my mind off the incident that just took place.
She took my pulse and temperature and left.
The minute she left I took the paper from under my pillow.
I unfolded it and there, the top half of the front page was the little girl's picture.
The headline
"She came back from the dead"
"Saved by a mystery angel"
And in small letters, see page two.
As I turned to page two, a folded note fell out.

260

I put it to one side.
I wanted to read about the little girl first.
It described in full detail what took place in the intensive care last night.
It was clear to me that someone must have made some money from this paper.
Now day's papers pay a lot of money for a good story.
That made me sick.
I unfolded the note and read.
   "Hi I'm ……… I'm from ……… news paper"
   Bla-bla-bla… And bla-bla-bla"… He was willing or rather his paper was willing to offer me a check for any amount I liked if I could perform a miracle in front of a few chosen people and of course, a few cameras.
The way the words were written, gave me the feeling he was really taking the Mickey at the same time; I really wanted to ring this bastard's neck.
I remembered what the doctor said, "Rest"…
The only thing I could say was;
   "What an asshole"

I just threw everything in the bin.
I got out of bed and sat on my wheelchair, unhooked the drip bag and hooked it high on the chair.
I wanted to use the loo outside as my one was packed with cuddly toys;
Two of the guards escorted me there;
By the looks of things, I had personal bodyguards now;
All the time I spent in there I couldn't help thinking that;
things are getting out of hand here.
How did I manage to get in so much trouble and that I seem to go deeper and deeper.
What really happened the last five or six days?
How did I get involved in all of this?
I just want to go home.
I miss my one bedroom flat in London; the underground; the Double Decker busses and my fellow Britt's.
They don't disturb you; they leave you in piece.
They mind there own business.

Oh how I miss all that;
Even the miserable weather is better than all this;
I returned to my room with all those things in my mind.
The sun was shining out there and I was stuck in here.
I approached the window to get a little fresh air.
I pulled the net curtains and... what my eyes were seeing was indescribable!!!
There were hundreds and hundreds of people standing there in the parking area directly under my window, under the scorching sun and in that heat;
They all had a lit candle in their hands and they were all looking up towards my window.
The minute they saw me they all started praying.
Nearly all were crossing themselves.
Some were actually hysterical; they were pointing at me and screaming.
I saw two of them collapsing.
I felt a bit odd, didn't know what to do.
Do I wave at them?

Do I say something to them?
Just then the Kaiser walked in with the delivery.
She left it on the table and said;
  "Keep away from the window Saint Johnny Walker, these people will never go home now".
  "They're all here to see you".
  "They all want to come and see you, touch you".
  "Best to keep away from the window";
  "Come now, your lunch is here".
  "Let's see what Giuseppe prepared for you".
She unwrapped and unwrapped.
The biggest T-bone steak he could find in all of the country, mush potato, boiled veggies and salad.
I mean is this living or is it living!!!
On her way out she said;
  "Remember, away from the window".
Oh I was really enjoying that steak.
The only thing in my mind was; Halloo… T-bone without wine…? Unthinkable!!!

All this presents, all these bags
with all sorts of goodies and yet,
not a drop of wine.
No one, out of all these people
ever thought maybe I would have
liked a drop of that every now and
then?
Oh well, its cola again I suppose.
The T-bone must have been really
big because I just couldn't eat
more than a quarter.
Suddenly I felt dizzy, I could not
see clear, everything around me
was moving.
I felt part of me was missing;
I remember checking my body.
I was sure something was missing
and I didn't know what.
I was loosing control of my self.
I felt pins and needles somewhere
on me and my left arm went num.
I remember reaching for the
buzzard.
I don't know if I did or not.
All I remember was the sudden pain
and that I was falling weird.
I woke up three hours later, or I
think I did, and with a head
heavier than my body.

Two doctors, Kaiser and two nurses were there looking over me anxiously;
There were wires all over my body and they were all connected to this machine.
I sensed the seriousness of the situation.
I tried to say something but couldn't.
I could here the doctor saying to me;
  "Stay with me now".
  "Don't go to sleep".
His voice sounded weaker and weaker, sounded as if he was walking away from me.
And then nothing, I couldn't hear him any more.
They were all gone.
I felt a terrible and painful shock on my chest.
I wanted to cry out and say you're hurting me but something was blocking my voice being heard.
I felt as if the air I was breathing was forced back into me somehow;
I was chocking;
What were these people doing to me?

They're trying to kill me;
They won't let me breath;
I wanted so much to breath;
I jumped up and took a big and heavy breath.
I noticed everyone was looking at me.
The doctor said;
  "Welcome back Saint Johnny Walker".
  "Why are you in a hurry to leave us"?
  "We thought you were gone again".
  "Stay with us, we need you around".
What the hell is he talking about?
I'm not going anywhere.
He was the one trying to kill me.
I wanted to breathe and he was blocking my breathing pipe;
Maybe his trying to cover himself;
Ha… I'm in a hurry to go my ass.
What are all these wires for?
  "Are you electrocuting me"?
  "What have I done to you"?
  "I promise I'll stay in my room; I won't go out again; no more torture… Please".
They were all smiling and looked happy.

"He's definitely back" the doctor said.
"Just relax he said and everything will be ok".
I asked him not to give me anything to sleep.
I wanted answers.
What happened?
Was I out?
How long for?
The doctor said;
"The sister will explain to you everything".
They all left the room except Kaiser.
She then told me the whole story.
She said;
"You had a stroke".
A stroke?
Yes she said; "a stroke".
"Bullshit, you were experimenting on me; you can't get any volunteers and here I was; the perfect victim, a foreigner; If he dies, no one will say anything; no one will even claim his body; a stroke my ass, of all excuses"!!!
I mean how could I?
I'm not even twenty seven yet.
She said;
"Cool it St Johnny".

"I'm serious, a heart attack, from pure exhaustion".

"It seems the energy you sacrificed for Isabella was far too much, it caused you to collapse and you're heart had nothing left to keep it pumping".

"You were a bit lucky; the guard outside the door heard you when you fell off the wheelchair".

"What time is it" I asked?
She said;

"It's nearly eight".
Oh shit I said.

"Did I miss diner"?

"I'm starving".

Ha-ha she laughed out loud.

"You're defiantly back".

"What a fright you gave us".

"You were actually gone for nearly three minutes; the doctor was really fighting to bring you back; he had to give you three electroshocks to bring you around".

I said;

"Hang on a minute";

"How comes you're still here"?

"You didn't go home yet"?

"Are you on a double shift"?
She said;

"No I'm not on a double shift, but I couldn't go, I wanted to make sure you're ok first".
She laughed again and said;
"Don't try and move any of the wires; I'll be back with some dinner".
I asked her if she would dine with me since she was here all this time.
I was sure she was hungry as well.
She said she was not allowed, but I insisted and she accepted.
She said;
"Only because I'm officially off duty"
The time it took her to come back with the food, I used it to write the days events in my favourite diary.
Ha… hard attack my ass.
I mean how many twenty seven year olds get hard attacks huh?
What if she's telling the truth?
Shit, that means no more exciting life for me.
This is the end of my youth?
I'm not a young man any more?
I will have to get use to… a middle age man from now on?

I suppose this means I have to slow down.
No more running.
Only walking...!!!
Ha-ha... I have to live up to my name!!!
"Johnny Walker"...!!!
I wonder; is that how he got his name?
"Johnny Walker"...???
Shit, I am loosing it.
I'm not Johnny Walker.
I'm getting so use to it, if someone was to call me by my real name I would somewhat be wondering if it's me.
I noticed my hand was a bit weak.
I could hardly hold the pen straight.
I had to stop for a little break before finishing a sentence.
I felt so tired.
My eyes felt heavy and just about to close when the door opened.
The Kaiser came back with dinner.
She said; "Everything ok"?
"Yes" I replied.
She arranged the food on the table with the wheels and said;
"Pasta with chicken, OK"?

I was so knackered I didn't answer, I just couldn't.
I couldn't even pick the spoon, my hand was so weak.
Kaiser saw enough to realise how tired I was.
She started feeding me.
I could only manage a few spoonfuls and said;
   "Enough; don't want any more"
   "I'm tired I want to sleep".
I remember seeing her clearing the table and wheeling it back to the corner, said "Goodnight Saint Johnny Walker" and left;
As I was dozing off, all I could remember was what a day I had;
I mean what a day.
It seams something must go wrong every day in this place.
As if someone or some-thing is causing it on purpose.
Maybe it's not the hospital, maybe it's me.
Something must go wrong for me every day.
Or maybe it's the island.
Whatever it was, "It" wanted me to stay here.
I must try to put an end to this, no more exciting days for me;

after all I'm a middle aged man now.
Tomorrow I'll stay all day in bed;
I would not move a muscle.
Surely nothing will go wrong.
I must think positive.
I mean being in bed all day, what can possibly go wrong?
Ha… How little did I know……?

Saint Johnny Walker's
"How to… Become a Saint"

Chapter Ten
Day Nine

I woke up the next morning with the worst hangover ever recorded.
I put my hand on my head to… somehow ease the pain, and realised I had bandages all around it.
   "What the hell" I cried out; Where they experimenting on my head all night while I was asleep?
No way, surely I would have woken up.
My chest was hurting something terrible and I had two massive bruises; more like footprints I would say.
It must be from the electroshock they were saying yesterday.
I guess it must be true then, I did have a stroke.
Shit, Oh shit, they said I was "gone"
Gone for three minutes the Kaiser said.
Holly shit, imagine waking up and think of "your own death".

Shit, what a morning start, remembering ones own death.
Well, I could safely say, not many people can do that.
Mind you, it has a nice ring to it.
If someone was to ask me;
  "How was your morning"?
I wonder what the reaction will be when he or she will hear, "oh nothing special, just remembering my death"…!!!
Ha-ha… they'll probably think you belong in a nut house.
Got out of bed slowly and off to the bathroom.
I wanted to see and inspect the damage.
I couldn't work out what could have happen to my head and it was bandaged.
I also realised when I looked at my teeth that, last time I brushed them was a hundred years ago.
I need a tooth brush, ASAP.
I heard the door opened while I was "admiring" my self and shouted;
  "I'll be out in a minute".
Surprise-surprise, it was Gestapo;

"Good morning Saint Johnny".
  "Good morning sister I replied".
  And would you believe she asked;
  "How's your morning"?
Ha…!!!
I knew this question will pop up sooner or later.
I said;
  "I've spent it remembering my death"!!!
She was a bit stunned with what I said;
She just stood there looking at me.
I could see clearly she was a bit puzzled.
I think she was trying to sass me out.
Am I serious or what?
She said;
  "Don't think about that".
  "You don't want to go through that again, do you"?
  "Put the experience behind you".
  "It's passed history".
  "What happened last night is not what's ahead of you; you must think of nice things or nice places instead; take it easy and try to relax as much as possible;

"Do I need this drip thing sister, I don't want it".
"You do need it" she replied.
"By the way sister, what happened and you bandaged my head"?
"You don't remember"?
"No, all I know is that it's killing me".
"When the security boy found you, you were in a pool of blood on the floor".
"You hit your head falling".
"You needed six stitches".
Mmm... six stitches huh; what a nice souvenir to take back home with me;
The tea lady knocked the door and came in.
Gestapo said;
"I'll get you something to ease the pain; I'll be back in a minute".
Anna, the lovely old tea lady came to me with tears in her eyes and gave me a hug, kissed me a few times and said;
"I came in last night after I heard what happened, I was praying all night for you".
"Please get well".

"God is on your side and protects you".
"God doesn't abandon his angels, always remember that".
She went on;
"I know what I'm saying, believe me, I saw it all; I know what's going to happen next".
"Yes that's rite, you predicted a few things, I remember".
"What's next mamma"?
She said;
"I'm not allowed to say".
"All I can tell you is; you'll know what, when the time comes, you'll know when, where and why you'll be needed, and you will act accordingly".
"There's a bit more work for you before you leave the island";
As usual she left two mugs, kisses and hugs me;
Stood there looking at me for a few seconds, kisses my hand and said;
"I must go now; my boys are waiting for their tea".
"Bye for know".
A minute or so later Gestapo came with pain killers and to my surprise, Kaiser was with her.

Kaiser said;

"Good morning Saint Johnny".

"I can't stay long I only came to see how you're doing; is everything ok"?

"Thank you for coming to see me sister, I do appreciate this, are you on duty as well"?

"Yes, I'm up on the fifth with the children".

"By the way, they all know somehow that you had an accident and that when you're better you'll visit them".

"They're all waiting for you and with your presents".

"Just like Xmas with Santa".

"Of course we said to them you're visiting other sick children in a different hospital and that you will come to see then as soon as you can".

"And I'm only telling you this because it will give you something nice to occupy your mind with".

"The children are not as sick as Isabella was, so not to worry and no visiting the fifth unless sister here ok's it".
That was nice of her I thought.
She came down to see me.

Me!!!
Soon after, a dozen doctors came in and of course I was the major subject of the day.
The chief doctor asked me how I was and all that.
He also said;
   "You never sis to amaze me; yesterday you came back from the dead, and today"?
   "I mean look at you".
He turns to his students asked their opinion about this and that, some answers were the rite ones and some not.
He then asked one of the girl students to change the bandages on my head.
She gladly said yes and sat beside me on the bed.
Her hands were very soft and she was ever so gentle.
I felt as if she was massaging my head.
I must say I was enjoying that!!!
She must have done this sort of thing before because the chief said;
   "Well done, excellent job, I couldn't have done it better my self".

Needless to say that, that sounded like music to my ears.
I asked the doctor when they are going to take this off of me and pointed to that heavy cast thing on my leg.
 "Too soon" he said.
 "I feel I don't need it any more" I said.
 "I know my foot is healed, I can feel it".
He said;
 "No, it's far too early; you probably need a good three weeks more".
I insisted that it was really ok and that I wanted it off, but he would have none of it.
I said;
 "Can I talk to you in private"?
He said yes of course.
He asked all the students out.
I said;
 "Now that we're alone; I really want this thing out".
He was trying to explain to me, but this and but that and no broken bone heals in only two or three days.
I said in a loud voice;
 "Are you giving me an argument"?

"Are you forgetting who I am"?
"Do you really think I don't know"?
"I'm telling you it's healed".
"Take me for X-rays if you like, there are no objections".
The guy was lost.
He didn't know what to make out of all this.
He must have thought, well… I am Saint Johnny Walker, and what I say goes.
He was confused and was in two minds; I saw it clearly in his face.
He was just looking at me for a minute or so trying hard to psychoanalyse me first, before making a decision.
Eventually said;
"Ok; I will order the X-rays and you better be rite;
"If you're wrong it will make me look… oh I don't even want to think about it".
That was a clear message to me that he was more curious than convinced.
I said;

"Don't worry doc, I know what I'm saying; just, trust me on this".
He left and Gestapo came in.
She said;
"Did you know you're getting more and more popular"?
There are thousands of people out there waiting to see you and touch you, people with all sorts of problems; people come from all over the island for a chance to just see you; some came just to give whatever money they can afford for our cause".
"I call this another one of your miracles".
"We put out there ten big money boxes and they're already all full I think".
"It looks like we're not only buying the dialysis machine but a lot of other things the hospital needs".
"And if this carries on the way it does, a few other hospitals will be fully equipped as well".
"I can't thank you enough for all this".
"The hospital owes you; the patients owe you".

"The management of the hospital decided to bring one by one the boxes in and replace them with empty ones".

"They are counting the money as we speak".

"There are ten people in the manager's office counting away".

"We will never be able to thank you enough".

"Now, are you ready for X-rays"? Onto my wheelchair and off we went.
To my relief, and I'm sure the doctor's too, the X-ray results were on my favour.
They showed nothing wrong.
It made me think.
How comes everything that happens to me, all those so called accidents, heal so quickly?
People say I have "the gift" and all that;
Mmm; maybe they're right after all.
And I must admit I'm beginning to accept it, but I didn't realise it works on me too.
The doctor who ordered the X-rays was called to examine and discus the findings.

He said to me;
 "You were rite, everything is healed, even your ribs, I just cannot believe it".
 "I'm thirty plus years a doctor and I've never seen anything like it".
 "Are you for real"?
 "Who are you"?
 "What's more important, what are you"?
 "Are you human"?
 "I know we all call you Saint Johnny Walker but, now I'm beginning to believe it my self".
 "I mean all those miracles, and now this".
 "You must have some kind of special powers".
 "I for one cannot explain it".
 "I wouldn't have believed it if someone would have told me; I still don't believe it; it's just eeee… just eeee… well… you never sis to amaze us all!!!
And he went on;
 "We have to study you; you are a great subject".
 "It will be the greatest challenge for us".
I said;

"Yea rite, that's all I need doc, to become a Guiney pig".
"Rite then, we'll take the cast off but you will go for physiotherapy ok"?
"Ok, no problem, that will give me a chance to come out of that room I'm in, my private prison".
They removed it and I felt as if I was released or rather separated from the chain gang.
Just like the chain gang films; Freedom at last!!!
Gestapo then puts a big towel over my head and starts pushing the wheel chair.
She said;
"You need to be covered in order to hide you from all these people, you do understand".
"After all, we're not ready for any more excitements, not yet anyway".
On the way there I realised the corridors were packed,
I could just about see their feet.
Eventually we got there.
The 'physic' was a gorgeous blond in her late twenties.
My God she was gorgeous!!!
Oh yes, a real beauty alright!!!

I wonder if she's spoken for.
I must try my luck here.
She's worth the try.
What if she rejects me, I'll be embarrassed.
The fist thing she said was;
   "Hello Saint Johnny Walker, I'm Susanna".
   "I heard all about you".
   "Did you know you're the most famous person in the world"?
   "I knew about your foot and knew you'll be paying me a visit, but not as soon as this".
   "I'm happy for you".
   "Let's see now".
She helped me out of the chair.
Ha… as if I needed any help, but I was playing my part anyway, and onto a thick-ish mat on the floor.
She grabbed hold my foot ever so gently.
She was turning it a bit to the left then to the right, up and down and at the same time asking if any pain at all.
She then took this little flat round metal gadget and started rubbing it all over my foot.
It felt great.
Oh I was enjoying that!!!

Gestapo said;
  "I'll be back in an hour or so".
I nearly said to her don't bother.
She left and I was alone with the most beautiful girl in the world.
This is my chance.
I must, I simply must say something to her.
She was so beautiful I couldn't take my eyes of her.
The desire I felt that minute was indescribable.
I decided there and then she was the one for me.
Imagine waking up every morning and seeing an angel like this.
I mean who would say no.
I even had a frightening thought of marrying this girl.
She's perfect.
It took me a good ten minutes to finally say to her.
  "Are you married"?
She said;
  "Not yet".
Not yet?
What the hell does that mean?
  "Are you engaged"?
Again the answer was "not yet".
I mean was she playing with me?
Was she having fun with me?

She's not very talkative.
  "Boyfriend"?
  "No, I don't have time".
  "I love my job and I spend all my time here".
I said;
  "What if a nice young man asks you for a relationship"?
  "Thanks but no thanks; that will be my answer"
Well, that takes care of that.
There goes my dream.
She said;
  "Just relax and let me do my work".
Well, I guess it's the polite way of saying shut up.
I better do what she says.
Who knows what she's capable of?
I mean what a conversation killer huh…?
She was working on my foot a good half an hour more when Gestapo came for me.
  "Ready Saint Johnny; it's nearly lunch time".
I got up and thought I was flying.
I felt great.
As if I had a brand new leg.
I said to Gestapo;
  "I can walk".

She said no.
Susanna, the physiotherapist said;
  "Give your foot a chance to heal properly".
  "Rest it as much as possible today and I'll see you tomorrow sometime in the morning, if you think you need me";
I thanked her and off we went.
Gestapo knew another way up, away from the crowd.
We went through the kitchen and the staffs lift.
I saw the kitchen staff hard at work and the aroma of what was on the stove was, oh… a real killer.
I saw some of the staff just stood still when they realised who I was, one of them was pointing at me with his mouth wide open, as if he saw a ghost and was trying to inform everybody but could not say anything from the shock.
When out of the lift and on the way to my room, a few people must have recognised me and immediately I was surrounded; every one was touching me and I was bombarded yet again with all these stupid questions.

And from what I understood they all wanted me to cure someone close to them; as if I was God or something.
I mean if it was just the one or two, maybe, just maybe, I would have have an attempt that is; and even then, there are no guarantees of success; I mean I don't know if I would have succeeded or not, but so many?
I would need two lifetimes to just visit them all, let alone the time I would need to spend with each.
Gestapo was physically pushing people away.
I saw a few nurses there too as was the security boys.
Everybody was pushing and pushing.
I felt millions of hands touching me.
The towel that was supposed to cover my head was gone; I saw it torn to pieces; it seemed everyone wanted it or at least a piece of it;
Lots of hands were pulling my robe and some managed to tear off a few of pieces and believe me when I tell you, lots of my skin went with those pieces;

Lots of screaming, hysterical scenes, shouting all over, Chaos everywhere;
Pure hooliganism at its best…!!!
If it wasn't for the security boys I think I would have been in pieces.
They were going to lynch me for sure;
In fact; another couple of minutes there and I would have been completely naked to say the least;
When finally I was back in my room, the first thing I did was looked in the mirror.
The hospital robe I was wearing was torn something terrible and I had scratches on my shoulders, my neck and chest; I even had a few on my legs.
I felt as if I was wounded in a real battle.
Gestapo came back with a new robe for me to wear.
She also brought surgical spirit and started cleaning my wounds.
I said to her;
   "While you're at it can you remove the bandages from my head, they're torn and I don't need them

any more anyway; I want to have a proper shower".
She did;
She had a good look at the head wound and said;
   "I'll cover the stitches with a piece of waterproof plasterer".
By the time I finished my shower my food arrived.
This time it was chicken curry with rice.
And what a portion, and as for the taste… out of this world…!!!
It was fantastic, I really enjoyed it.
I must meet this guy.
I owe him, big time.
I must have needed that shower badly.
Suddenly I felt great;
It felt like I was busking in the sun, it was wonderful;
Fresh out of the shower, belly full, no chains around my leg, nothing to remind me I had plaster on my hand; and I didn't need any more the corset either;
I felt like a new man.
Oh isn't life wonderful!!!
I was ready for a quick exit from the hospital.

I wanted to go to the reception and tell Gestapo;
"I am out of here";
I opened slightly the door and saw all those people.
Oh shit, I can't do that.
I press the buzzer and a nurse came in.
"Yes Saint Johnny" she said, "what can I do for you"?
"Where's Gestapo" I said.
She said "who"?
Oups…
Oh never mind, where's the sister?
"She's a bit busy with some paper work, but if it's urgent I'll call her".
"No-no I'll see her later" I said and she left.
I turned the telly on and aha!!!
News in English what!!!
All that bla-bla-bla but nothing about England;
What's the matter with these people?
Is it possible?
Nothing happened in England?
Suddenly I missed home.
Oh how I miss London.
I miss my cat.

I hope the guy next door is feeding her ok.
Shit, what if his not?
What if he let the cat out and was run over by a car?
I'll kill the bastard.
There was a knock on the door and I said;
  "Yes, come in".
Surprise-surprise, it was the police.
I completely forgot about them.
Two coppers came in.
One of them, said;
  "Hello, we're from the police".
I nearly said no shit!!!
I mean halloo… they were in uniform, come on…
I mean do I look that stupid?
Maybe they think I'm blind or something.
One of them, the sergeant said;
  "Are you the famous Saint Johnny Walker"?
I mean what kind of a question is that?
He was holding my passport and looking at the page with my photo and all the info he was seeking was rite there.
I said;

"No, I am who my passport says I am".

"Its ok, we know all about you and what you did during your stay here".

"We brought you your stuff".
Oh Great!!!
Now I can wear my own clothes.

"It's about time" I said.

"Why the delay"?

"Sorry" he said; but we were given strict orders you were not to be disturbed".

"We got the all clear about an hour a go".

"Would you please check all your things just to make sure nothings missing"?

"OK… Where is it"?
He asked the other copper to bring it in.
My suitcase wasn't even opened but half burned; the clothes I was wearing at the time of the accident were in a bag, my shoes in another and the rest in another.
I opened the last one and saw my wallet, with my entire life savings still there, my credit cards, loose change, my sunglasses

half burned too; the key of my suitcase still with dried blood stains on it, and my huge mobile phone, slightly damaged and also covered in blood.
I immediately tried the phone but no chance.
Even if it wasn't damaged it would need buttery charging anyway.
I unlocked the suitcase and had a quick check.
I couldn't remember what I have actually packed before I left home.
I suppose everything was there even though burned and I signed for everything.
The sergeant was asking me questions about the accident and the other copper was writing everything said down.
I don't think I gave them any information they didn't already know.
We thanked each other and he shook hands with me.
The other copper offered his hand for a handshake as well.
The moment I took his hand I felt something wrong.
I felt weird.

Instead of shaking his hand, for some reason I was squeezing it hard.
I remember I used my other hand to signal him to be quiet and grabbed hold of his hand with both of mine.
I don't know exactly how long for, but I went into a different world, I was travelling, I wasn't there.
I remember being in this mans house.
I knew his family, his wife Joanna, his son Pedro, and his daughter Christina.
I was actually in his house talking to the family and as we were talking, his wife Joanna changed colour.
She became yellow-ish, then blue-ish, and then she was gone, she just disappeared;
I couldn't see her any more.
I was looking for her, I knew something's wrong.
And then blank.
I was on the floor.
I think I fainted.
When I came to, I was in bed, the sister was there trying all sorts of things to bring me around.

The two coppers were standing in the corner and in a state of shock.
I jumped up and looked at the copper.
I could hear the sister saying "take it easy, relax, it's ok, you just fainted;
   "Yes, you fainted, yet again".
I pushed her hand away and started dressing up.
The sister was saying;
   "Where do you think you're going"?
I said;
   "I have a job to do".
She kept insisting "you're too weak for all that again; can't it wait for tomorrow or something"?
She was trying hard the woman.
But I would have none of it.
I said;
   "I must go with this man to his home".
I looked at him and said;
   "You must take me to your family NOW".
The guy was in a real shock.
He couldn't move a muscle.
He said;
   "My house why"?

I thought it would be quicker and a lot easier if I describe a few things to him.
I said;
  "Your wife is Joanna and you have a son Pedro and a daughter Christina;
  "Your house is yellow colour with brown windows".
  "You have a big veranda outside your kitchen with a big table and six chairs, all green".
  "Rite now your family is sitting there with a few guests and they're all having coffee".
  "Did I say enough to convince you I'm not crazy"?
I quickly got dressed and said to the sister;
  "Arrange an ambulance to follow the police car, now sister, please".
She looked at me as if she wanted a few answers first.
I remember saying to her.
  "Trust me".
The two coppers were still in shock.
I shouted at them saying;
  "Snap out of it, and shook them".

300

"Quickly now please".

"Take me to your house now".

The sergeant looked at the sister with a question mark written all over his face.

She said to him;

"What are you waiting for"?

"You heard the Saint; take us to your house now.

I said to the sister;

"Clear the path for us".

"Quickly now, I don't have time to waist.

She followed orders to the letter. Within minutes we were on the move.

I was with the coppers in front in the police car and the ambulance behind with a nurse and the sister.

All thru the journey both coppers were very quiet, still in a state of shock I suppose.

They didn't know what to say or even think.

They didn't know what to make out of all this.

They didn't know what they'll find or expect to find at the other end.

Speeding, blue lights, sirens, the works!!!
The adrenaline was at its highest; and I mean it reached the very top!!!
Fifteen minutes or so later we arrived.
We quickly got out of the car and headed for the gate, I saw Gestapo with the nurse running towards us.
He opened the front door and we all rushed in.
They were all shocked to see us like that.
Family and friends were asking THE question.
 "What's happening"?
No one knew the answer but me.
I said;
 "Everyone quiet please".
But the big question was still in the air.
So I ordered them to shut up with a loud scream and in Italian…
 "Soupido"
The shock was even bigger for them.
The sister said;
 "It's OK… He knows what he's doing".

Joanna, his wife was looking at her husband in a puzzled way as if she was asking him in a silent way who is this guy, and why is he ordering us to be quiet?
I approached his wife and said.
  "You must be Joanna yes"?
She nodded yes.
I said to her;
  "Just trust me ok"?
I looked at the husband and he gave the ok.
I hugged her a bit tight.
That went on a good fifteen seconds.
I felt nothing.
I then turned towards little Pedro who was next to the mother.
I hugged him tight; poor kid; he was a bit shy and was blushing.
Nothing wrong there either.
Then I looked at Christina.
I went close to her and said;
  "Hi Christina, can I have a hug"?
The father nodded and she did.
It only took me a few seconds to realise there was indeed something wrong.

She must have felt something as well because she was squeezing harder and harder.
I felt a bit drowsy and I pulled away from her.
I remembered what happened last time with Isabella, where I went into this motion and nearly cost me my life.
I said to the mother;
   "Joanna please trust me on this, Christina is a very sick girl; she needs to go for a general check up, and I mean right now".
What do you mean sick?
   "No, she's ok, she's a good athlete, and she's only fifteen".
   "What are you saying"?
   "She never complained about anything like that".
I replied in a rough-ish voice;
   "Are you giving me an argument"?
   "You must trust me, after all, what has she got to loose"?
Both father and mother were looking at each other.
They didn't know what to make out of all this.
The mother began to shake;
I shouted;
   "Halloo"…!!!

"No time to waist here, into the ambulance quickly";
The sister took Christina's hand and into the ambulance together, the mother followed them and off they went.
I tried to say something to the father but he was gone; he was like a zombie.
I turned to the sergeant and said;
   "Can we go back to the hospital now"?
   "Yes, of course" he said.
He was more curious than everyone else;
He was witnessing something totally new.
He looked eager to find out what next.
Upon our arrival, we sneaked in from the back and the kitchen.
I knew my way around there.
In our rush to go up to my room, I don't know what really happened but I collided with someone and whatever he was holding was all over me.
All I now is that it was hot, and I mean burning hot.

It must have been a pot of soup, because I was soaked in burning liquid.
I was in agony.
Within minutes I was in the emergency and nurses were trying to undress me as gently as possible.
I wanted to scream from the pain but I thought what good that will do; after all I was supposed to be Saint Johnny Walker.
I felt as if I had to keep up appearances.
I could here the nurses murmuring "its Saint Johnny…
   Yes it's him"!!!
All this time it took the doctor and nurses to, well… patch me up, I was thinking.
I must stop this.
Every time I shake hands with someone I get these "illusions" these weird feelings, these visions and I end up getting hurt.
Last time it nearly cost my life with a stroke.
Now I'm probably dying from burns.
No-no-no…
I must stop the contact with people.

I knew it, it's this hospital.
Every day something will go wrong;
but why only me; I don't remember
anybody saying I had an accident
in the hospital, ever.
How long is this going to go on?
I'm not very happy about this at
all.
There must be a way out.
And I must find it quickly.
The way things are going I'll
never come out of here.
It feels like I got "sentenced to
hospital" for life.
Oh I can see him now, the judge.
Instead of life in prison he'll
say…
 "Saint Johnny Walker, I sentence
you to life in hospital"
And may the "force" be with you.
Ha…!!! "The Force"
Maybe it's not a gift I possess.
Maybe it is a force.
No… I mean if it was a force,
people would call me Look
Skywalker not Johnny Walker.
Come to think of it, if people
knew I actually walked in space,
they would have named me the
"Skywalker" for sure

Shit, I think I watch too much television.
It took about an hour or so to finish patching me up.
Onto a stretcher with wheels and with Gestapo leading the way, we headed for my room.
Gestapo covert me from top to bottom with a white sheet as if they were wheeling a stiff, so no one will recognise me.
Ha, that's what I call "Undercover job".
All the corridors we went thru I could hear people saying; Jesus a dead man, and others, oh my God he's dead, poor guy.
Oh how I wanted to play a little joke on them.
I wanted to jump up and scare a few.
Oh I really wanted to do that.
I could actually imagine the seen too!!!
I would scare the shit out of them, I'm sure.
And I nearly did too, I mean I was so tempted to do that, just to have some fun at least, but I remembered that these Italians do

308

not mess about, I convinced my self I would end up being a stiff;
I remembered how these people react when they see me.
I still bear the scars from their scratches.
They behave like savages.
They will lynch me given half the chance.
As if they've never seen a man before.
Just like in the jungle when they capture a white man and they see him as white meat.
Ha... I just made up a joke;
What if someone is captured in his car instead of on foot in the jungle, what would they call it, "tin food" hahaha...
I mean I was trying hard to get my mind off the pain;
Finally the sheet comes off me and they transferred me to my bed.
I must say I felt soar all over.
Gestapo shook her head and said to me;
   "What are we going to do with you"?
   "You've done it again".
   "Tell me something" she said;
   "Do you like pain"?

"I think you must do".

"I wonder she said; if there's a part of your body you haven't injured yet since you've been here"?

"You're the first and only patient we ever had that needs mending up in different parts of the body, every single day"; every day we have to call a different specialist to mend you up".

"You are the only person in history who comes to the hospital just to get injured";

"That must be a record of some kind";

"On the other hand the things you do";

"The miracles you perform";

"What can one say about "them"?

"What can I say about you"?

"You leave every one of us speechless every day".

"If it wasn't for the miracles I personally would have chained you on the bed".

"I wonder if you can perform a miracle without injuring yourself in the process".

"Anyway, I'll get you something for the pain" and off she went.

310

A few minutes later the sergeant came in and asked me.
 "Are you ok"?
I said;
 "So long as I breathe, I hope"…!!!
 "Toom Spiro Spero" as it's written in Latin.
It took the guy a few minutes to understand what I just said because he went quiet on me.
After a longish time he said;
 "I like that".
 "So long as I breathe, I hope"…!!!
I think I'll use that from now on, thanks.
I asked him;
 "Any news of Christina"?
He said;
 "No she's still in the general check up room".
 "Family and friends are there waiting".
The guy was looking at me constantly.
He made me feel guilty somehow.
I got the feeling he was about to say something nasty.
He had "that look".

I thought it's best if I start a conversation.
  "What's it like being a policeman"?
He replied;
  "A policeman"?
  "I'll answer you in two words".
  "Like shit".
  "Why do it then"?
  "Some of us because we know nothing else";
  "Some because of family tradition;
  "And some because we think it's a secure job".
  "Very rare you will here a different reason".
  "Maybe one or two new guys will say they want to change the world".
  "You, what do you do apart from miracles, for a living"?
  "I'm a chef".
  "Oh, that's nice".
  "Maybe you'll give me a few recipes for my wife".
  "Yea, maybe" I said.
And just then Gestapo came in.
  "You'll never guess who is outside" she said.

"Oh no, don't tell me, it's the Prime Minister" I said.
"You wish" she said.
"It's Christina's family".
"The asked if they can see you".
"They were informed of your little mishap".
"Cover your self with the sheets" she said.
When the family came in, I saw the father still I a state of shock, the mother crying her eyes out, the boy puzzled; uncles, aunties, cousins and I don't know who else was there; nearly all had tears in their eyes.
Everyone just stood there looking at me;
No one would say anything.
They were all looking at me in a weird way.
The only one that was a bit different was Gestapo.
She had a bit of a smile in her face.
I new the news were good, but wasn't absolutely sure what.
I said;
"What; is Christina well"?
"Is she ok"?

I could see the sister was dying to tell me but decided is best if the family does.
I asked the mother;
 "Joanna say something, talk to me".
She wiped the tears off and said;
 "How did you know"?
 "Know what for Christ sake"?
 "The results shown a tiny little hole in her heart and she had internal bleeding";
 And she went on;
 "I don't understand";
 "The only complains she ever had, were stomach pains and we thought it was from her period";
 "I even said to her it's normal";
 "It's a natural thing with girls";
 "The doctors downstairs said she could have died any day, any hour or even any minute".
 "They put her thru surgery straight away".
 "She's stable now and doctors said she'll be ok".
 "And all thanks to you".
 "I want to kiss you and hug you for ever".

I said;
 "Please don't do that; I'm already in pain".
 "Yes, we heard of your accident, are you ok"?
 "Don't worry about me" I said;
 "I always come out on top".
 "I'll be ok in a day or two".
She asked;
 "Is there anything we can do for you"?
Yes I said;
 "Collect money for the hospital from all your friends, and all you people do the same and pointed at everyone in the room.
I looked at the girl's father and said;
 "You can do the same with all the police stations".
 "The hospital need equipment, machines and I don't know what else; please help for a better life; that's the only thing I want in return; help the hospital to help the needy; if you feel you owe me something, that is how I want you to repay me".
 They looked at me in a way I could not describe.

They didn't expect a lecture like this;
This short but straight to the point lecture I gave them, they realised that the hospital is not just four walls and a few heroes working in them.
They need the rite equipment too.
They all agreed to help and were more than pleased to do so.
The mother and father came closer to me and he shook my hand, still in a state of shock and whispered thank you;
The mother said;
The minute you feel better we all want you to come and stay with us.
We have an extra room; you can stay as long as you want; even for ever if you like.
We owe you so much.
Christina is alive now thanks to you; thank you… thank you… thank you".
She kisses my hand three or four times and, thanked me over and over again.
Now I know why people in here call you Saint Johnny Walker.
I looked at Gestapo and she knew what I wanted from her.

She said to everybody;
   "Thank you all for the visit but now he needs a rest, it's time for his medicine and injection; go home now please".
When they all left I said;
Injection?
   "No, I just said that she said to make people go quicker".
   "Thanks I said for understanding what I wanted when I looked at you".
   "Ha… I know you like I know the back of my hand by now".
   "I even know what you think when I see you straight in the eyes".
Can she really do that?
Oh shit, I hope she never finds out I nicknamed her Gestapo.
I must never see her straight in the eyes, ever.
One never knows.
I mean anything's possible.
Look what I discovered I could do.
A nurse came in and brought dinner.
She said;
   "The usual delivery for Saint Johnny Walker"
The room was already filled with the aroma.

It smelled fishy.
Aha… Fish all-sorts what…!!!
Brilliant!!!
Just what I would order in a restaurant;
The entire sea fruit collection, one can ever imagine.
What a feast!!!
I mean a real feast!!!
There was fried calamari, grilled cattle fish, octopus in tomato sauce, mussels in vinegar, giant grilled mussels, big Mediterranean prawns all pealed with garlic sauce, a piece of cod cooked in butter, lots of chips, a piece of grilled salmon, smoked salmon, tuna salad, special fried rice, lobster already sliced and ready to eat, prawn crackers, the works.
WOW…!!!
I wonder if the sea produces anything else.
There is a God after all and he's looking after me.
I said to Gestapo;
  "All I need now is a pint of draft beer; even if it's out of a can.
Oh I could murder a pint now.

"Is there any chance of that happening"?
Even though I knew I was pushing it she said;
"You know I can't do that, alcohol is not allowed in here but, I'll see what I can do for you and that is for two reasons, the first being, apart from the burns, you're perfectly healthy for one, and the second, well the second is I want to buy you a beer, you deserve it, what I witnessed today was, well you know; and believe me; the minute I go home I'll have one with my husband too; I'll raise my glass and say here's to Saint Johnny Walker".
I started eating like a pig, as if there was no tomorrow.
Ten minutes later she came with a couple of large cans.
"Promise me, only the one today, the other one is for tomorrow, and keep it wrapt; I'll put it in the fridge for you".
"Bon-Appetito" she said and I'll see you tomorrow".
"Bona Note" sister I said and "Gracie mille".

"E… You speak Italian now E"…!!! She said;
"I cannot thank you enough; you have made my day like you British say".
Oh what a wonderful thing life this is; I mean this is real living!!!
The most expensive food and a beer to wash it down; hat next huh… I mean what can beet that;
I know; I'll have the other can as well.
I'll just say I drank it in the morning.
No, I better not, I promised her I wouldn't.
I was eating and eating;
I thought no one could finish all that food, but I did believe it or not;
I finished it all!!!
I stuffed my self.
It was so good I just could not stop.
I turned the telly on but nothing of interest, so I turned it off again.
I got out of bed and started walking around the room.

After all that food I felt I needed the walk.
After a while I sat down and started writing in my diary the day's events.
Another day gone;
And what a day that was.
And yes, I did it again.
I managed to get injured yet again.
I mean I couldn't have managed it even if I planned it.
What is it about this place?
I'm beginning to accept the possible fact I'm not to leave this place at all.
But why do I have to get injured every day.
If God wanted me to stay here for a while, why did He give me the power to heal my self quickly every time?
I mean He wants me to heal quickly and then punishes me with yet another injury;
Why...???
That's not fair.
I haven't done anything wrong in my life.
I'm a law abiding citizen.

I even pay my taxes to the full,
so why I'm I getting punished?
Well, maybe one day I'll come face
to face with Him and ask Him why;
oh, and PS:
I must make it a priority to meet
this Giuseppe guy;
I must thank him for everything he
sends for me; what a nice man.
I feel a bit tired so I'll turn
in; even though I wanted to have a
quick shower before bed but I was
all patched up.
Another day full of excitements
and of course injuries yet again;
Surely, surely tomorrow will be
better;
I mean what can go wrong again?
Nothing, I'm sure of that.
Tomorrow will be a perfect day.
Nothing will go wrong.
I feel it.
I'll be ever so careful so, no
more injuries.
No more untoward surprises.
Ha… How little did I know…!!!

Saint Johnny Walker's "How to… Become a Saint"

Chapter Eleven
Day Ten

I woke up the next morning very early, still pitch black out there.
I was still feeling soar from the burns on my body.
I got up and straight to the mirror in the bathroom.
I wanted to assess the damage first hand.
 "Holly shit" I cried out;
What a horrible and ugly site to see first thing.
There were little bubbles on my chest full of liquid.
 "Shit";
Am I going to look like this from now on?
I hope not.
I mean I looked as if I was suffering from leprosy.
What if these bubbles never go?
What if the bubbles go and leave behind marks.
Black horrible marks;
Yaks…!!!

It's like being "branded" for the rest of my life.
Shit, I'll never be able to go swimming ever again.
Nobody will call me "Saint Johnny" again.
More like "Branded Johnny" from now on.
No-no I must think positive.
I know; the magic ice cubes;
Yes, that's it.
The ice cubes will do the job just like they did with my jaw.
Oh yes, oh I am great I am…!!!
I mean who else would have thought of the magic cubes?
Only the great Saint Johnny Walker of course!!!
Maybe I'll go to the reception and ask the night nurse for some of these "magic cubes".
Yes, that sounds like a good idea.
Surely no one will be awake this time in the morning so I should be safe.
I opened the door slightly and had a good look from the gap.
It was as quiet as a graveyard is, at this time in the morning.

I opened the door wide and saw a security guy sleeping on the chair outside my door.
Very quietly I went passed him and to the reception.
The girl was reading something and she nearly had a heart attack when she saw me standing rite on top of her at the other side of the counter.
I whispered; "SH... quiet".
She said;
   "Saint Johnny, what are you doing here"?
   "Why aren't you in bed; is there a problem"?
   "No... No problem, I just need lots of ice cubes, and if you can crush half of them for me please".
She said;
   "Certainly, anything for you";
She came back a few minutes later and she brought a plastic bag with crushed ice and a plastic container filled with crushed ice and said;
   "Put this in the little freezer for later, just empty the bag when it melts and stuff it with ice again".

I thanked her and back I went to my room.
The security guy was still asleep and I was ever so quiet.
Ha… security!!!
I mean anyone could just walk in and murder everyone in here and this guy will still be slipping.
Very carefully I started removing a few of the bandages on my chest.
Some of them were stuck on my skin as if they were glued on with super glue.
I wanted to scream as loud as I can as I was pulling them.
I must admit I changed my mind a few times but was determent to get rid of them.
I was in agony…!!!
   "What a way to start your day Saint Johnny" I whispered.
It must have taken me a long time to remove them all.
I remember the very last patch; I decided to remove it in one quick pull.
I nearly fainted for the pain.
I sat on the "throne" the loo and did two jobs at the same time.

Doing my business from one end and cooling down my wounds on the other.
Oh what a relief and I mean from both ends…!!!
Hahaha… that's what I call a double pleasure what!!!
And then I came up with this brilliant idea.
I decided to have a cold shower.
Quickly I went into the shower cubicle and turn the cold water on.
OH… MY… GOD… The water was bloody freezing.
I mean there's cold water and there's cold water;
And this was neither;
It was bloody freezing; it was like melted ice;
I just stood there under the running water for s few minutes.
There was a metal pipe on the wall designed for the disable.
I was holding on to that in case I fall from trembling.
My whole body was shaking.
I was frozen.
I thought if I stay here another minute or so they will find me in the middle of this giant ice cube.

And for a brief moment I was actually visualising it.
Mmm; that mite not be such a bad idea, I thought
I'll leave a big note for everyone to read,
   "Do not break the ice until the year 2277"
WOW…!!!
Saint Johnny Walker in the 23rd century…!!!
I wonder what it would be like.
One thing for sure, I'll be the oldest "young" man on earth!!!
Oh I don't know really; the way technology is progressing, or maybe "rushing" is a better word;
On the other hand, who in the rite mind would volunteer to be frozen for two hundred years?
I came out of the shower shivering.
I quickly dried my self all over except my chest.
I wouldn't dare even touch any part there.
I got dressed and left my shirt undone.
I put the blanket around me and sat on my wheelchair.

I noticed some of the bubbles had burst already.
Aha… maybe I'll burst the rest too.
I started squeezing them; dead slow at first but since I was getting nowhere I was squeezing harder and harder.
I couldn't use force as my hands were num from the cold and shaking so much.
I had no control over them.
As if they had a mind of their own.
The bubbles were bursting a lot easier than I thought they would.
I felt a little relief every time each one was shedding all that liquid.
It wasn't long before I had no bubble left to burst, but I had patches of wrinkled skin on me.
More like empty little bags.
They ware just "hanging" there.
My chest looked like one of a hundred year old.
So, clever me… I decided to pull and remove some of wrinkled skin away.
I picked the bigger one to start with.

I was sort of pulling slowly from the opening, from were the liquid come out from.
But when I accidentally touched behind the wrinkled skin in the middle of the patch on my chest, I let out a very loud scream.
I couldn't help it, it hurt me so much.
It was so loud the security guy was awakened and rushed through the door.
He said;
  "Are you ok sir"?
I said;
  "Yes, go back to sleep".
I know, I shouldn't have said that, but at the time I didn't know what I was saying.
I push the skin back to cover the patch and pressed the ice bag on my chest.
I wasn't so cold any more apart from my frozen chest.
Oh I could do with a cup of tea now.
I could hear noises out the door.
I heard movements out there.
People must be getting up.

Suddenly I missed Maria, the night nurse with her "special" wake up call in the ward;
I miss that… human clock would you believe;
   "Bon journo tutti" and then turning it to English, "good morning gentlemen, it's a nice day out there".
I wonder, is it me or everybody feels the same.
When I was in the ward I use to hate the way she was waking everybody up.
And now I miss all that.
I must be going bonkers.
And my orchestra… oh my orchestra!!!
I wonder if anybody did take my place.
Imagine a big orchestra like that without a leader.
Bloody chaos I would say.
Where's Anna, the good old tea lady?
Is she running late?
I wonder what time it is.
The sun is up.
Maybe the old lady is sick or something.
I hope not.

She's the most wonderful lady in the world.
She doesn't deserve to get sick.
What if she is really sick and didn't come to work.
She must have called in surely;
I must go to her.
I must go to her house and see her.
I must do my magic again.
Knock-knock on the door and there she was.
The sweetest girl in the word, with the biggest genuine smile;
   "Bon journo Mamma" I said.
   "Good-good morning son" she replied.
She said;
   "Every time you say Mamma to me I feel so good, I think I'm walking on air; I only wish you were my real son I would be the happiest mother on earth".
   "But I am Mamma".
   "You are my real Mamma".
She burst into tears.
   "Oh come now Mamma, you know I don't want you to cry".
She said;
   "I'm sorry but I cry when I'm happy".

She asked me about Christina;
"Did everything go well"?
"Yes, the doctor said she'll be ok in a few days".
She went on;
"I also know of your accident".
"I know you must feel a bit soar now, but don't worry; by tonight all your wounds will be healed".
"I saw it all in my dream last night".
"By tomorrow morning you won't have the slightest mark on you to even remind you of what you went thru".
"Really Mamma"?
"That's good news; you made my day Mamma, thanks".
"I wanted to sound a bit Italian" and said;
"Gracie Dante Mamma, Gracie mille".
Oh that made her day I think.
She gave me the biggest smile yet.
"Now tell me about today, what's going to happen today, I know you know tell me".
"You know I can't do that son" I promised.
"And if I do, it will all end here for me;

"I must go now: she said, "My boys are waiting".
"I know what's going to happen today so I won't wish you a nice day, I'll just say try not to get stressed out doing what you're going to do".
She gives me a gentle hug, kisses both my cheeks and off she went.
Stressed out?
Oh no, another hectic day.
Shit, I thought of taking it easy today.
I was thinking of having no visitors.
Lock the door if necessary.
I looked at the door and realised something.
How comes there's no locks on these doors.
I wonder if all hospital doors are the same.
Come to think of it, it's the only public building in the world without locks.
Yea, no matter what country you're in, the hospitals have no locks on the doors.
Government spending cuts I suppose.
Poor locksmiths;

They must have thought they have a "secure" job.
Ha… I like that, "Secure"… "Locks" There's a laugh.
I mean if I was a locksmith I would Sioux the government.
What do you have against locksmiths…? …"SIR"
This is "Locksmith Discrimination"
Ha… I like that.
Locksmith discrimination!!!
It has a nice ring to it.
I mean there are so many other discriminations in the word; people just either never thought about them or take it for granted and all that.
And why are they called Locksmith?
I wonder where the "smith" came from.
Are all locksmiths called "Smiths"?
And why is it, other professions don't have a smith to go with their job?
I mean a car "seller" is called a dealer.
Why not a "car-smith"
Or a supermarket owner, he should be called "Super-Smith"
Hahaha… Super-Smith…!!!

Oh my, this one sounds even better.
Smith my ass
I think I'll look into that when I go home.
Home…?
Now there's a joke.
One works all year round and can't wait to go places and now I can't wait to go back.
I never thought I would ever say that.
Gestapo walked in together with Kaiser.
The usual good mornings and all that;
Kaiser saw me with the ice bag and said;
  "You've done it again haven't you"?
  "It's true then, you must like pain".
  "Let's have a look"; and she pulls my hand away to see the damage on my chest.
She said;
  "It's not that bad really, it'll be alright in a couple of weeks or so".
  "A couple of week's sister?
I remembered what Anna said to me.

Not if her predictions are something to go by;

"No-no-no… I said by tomorrow morning, all you see here and pointed to my chest will disappear".

"Another one of your miracles."?
I just looked at her and smiled, hoping Anna is rite.

"By the way", Gestapo said;

"Christina sends her love and says thank you; she's a lovely girl".

"She said she wants to come and give you the biggest hug you ever had, as soon as the doctor gives her the all clear; you're her hero".

"Oh that's nice".
Anyway; Kaiser said;

"I must go up to the kids, I'll see you later, and you, Saint Johnny Walker, and pointed her finger at me, take it a bit easy, think of Johnny Walker for a change".

I could only smile and say ok sister, later.

The linen ladies came in and did their job, not able to get their eyes off me while they were

working and of course the usual bla-bla and bla-bla between them. In fact it's the first time it took them so long to just change a bed and dust a little.
The minute they left Gestapo said;
  "What are we going to do with all these cuddly toys"?
  "And I don't mean whatever you see here alone, there's a store room behind the reception counter full of them; well, it became a store room".
  "The decision is yours I just want the room back".
I said;
  "Who do you think will appreciate them more"?
She said;
  "You know the children's wards, yes"?
  "Did you know we have another couple of wards with a lot of children and grown ups together"?
  "They all suffer from leukaemia".
  "What do you say"?
  "Yes, good idea, would you arrange all that please"?
  "I could, only difference is they're all waiting for you;

they're waiting for you to give them, they all know about you and hope to see you".

"Every day they ask the same question; when is Saint Johnny Walker coming"?

"You're their idol".

"I'll go as far as to say some of them lost the will to live; they suffer something terrible and if it wasn't for Saint Johnny Walker we would have lost one or two already".

"You are the reason they're still around, I'm sure of that, the name Saint Johnny Walker is an inspiration to them, a way out, a hope to them".

"They hope for THE miracle".

"If it's ok with you I'll arrange it all after the doctors round, OK"?

"Yes sister, whatever you say".

"If it's for saving someone's life, you know you don't have to ask me".

"In fact, you should demand it".

"Only take in consideration the "hooligans" out there; they're like savages; how are you going to keep them away"?

"You leave that to me".
The doctors came in and the chief said;
"What is it this time"?
"Every time I come to see you it's for a different reason; but what puzzles us is the healing speed; how do you do that, is there a method of some kind"?
"All doctors and professors have a meeting every now and then, ever since you arrived here we have one every day; and you're the subject".
"The last few days we have been discussing your case, or should have said cases, every day a different one; we analyse every day how quickly your injuries heal, and none of us have any answers".
"A lot of questions, yes, but no answers";
"We all agreed on one thing, we need samples of you; samples like blood, bone marrow, etc";
"Would you agree to that"?
"We need to analyse the samples and who knows, maybe what we find will be good for mankind"!!!
I froze for a minute or so.

I said;
"I'll think about it".
"I'll answer you after lunch ok"?
"Thank you he said; now let's see those burns".
When I undid my shirt he said;
"Did you burst the bubbles"?
"Yes I did".
"You do realise by doing that it'll be more painful".
"You'll feel very soar especially when you touch the effected areas".
"I'll arrange a special cream for you".
I said;
"Please doctor, don't bother, it will only slow the healing process".
"My God he said, you're something else"
I said;
"By tomorrow all will be healed you'll see".
"All I need is unlimited supply of ice cubes".
"My God; I wish I had your powers".
The doctor didn't know what or even how to explain to the young

students, how is all this possible.
He just said to them;
　"God took over and he knows a lot more than what we do".
On his way out I could hear him giving lectures to the "kids".
Gestapo replaced the melted ice in the bag and said;
　"I'll be back for you in a while, get ready for your journey".
　"Remember? We said we'll go".
I stopped her and said yes I know.
Fifteen minutes or so later she came back with about a dozen nurses and as many security blokes.
They all had a few teddy bears in their hands and other cuddly toys.
She said;
　"You will go with your wheelchair and we will escort you there".
I sat on my wheels and she started counting the toys.
She wanted to make sure everyone will get at least a toy.
She then placed on my lap two more and we took off.
I felt great again.

I came out of the room and into the corridor.
Oh that feels good!!!
I'm out of that room again.
I felt as if I was given a few minutes freedom from being locked up in prison;
The nurses formed a circle around me and the blokes a circle around them.
I mean I felt more secured than the president of the USA.
We went to the lift area and the nurses used the lift first and when the lift came back we followed.
We were like sardines in a can in that lift.
I couldn't see what button the sister pressed but I could feel we were going up.
The girls were there waiting for us when we came out.
The same formation again as we headed for the first ward.
All the way people were making way and some were actually standing to attention just like in the army, and in disbelief when they realised who I was and with an escort as big as this.

I felt like I was an army general. The only thing missing was the saluting.
We approached the reception and another sister appeared.
Only this one was a real Sister, a nun.
She came to me and said;
 "Hi I'm Sister Margaret, thank you Saint Johnny Walker".
She crossed her self a few times; she closed her eyes and murmured a prayer I think.
 "Thank you… Thank you… Thank you… you don't know what it means to them you being here".
 "They've been waiting for you for days now".
 "They know all about you".
 "I wanted for days now to come and find you, but I said no, God will know when the rite time is, He knows when to send you to us".
 She looked up and said;
 "Thank you for answering my prayers".
She looked at me and said;
 "We never mentioned to them that you can perform miracles; we don't want to build their hopes up in case you…" and she stopped there.

"Well, you know what I mean".
"But I know, inside them they have that hope".
"Even though we asked parents and relatives not to mention what happen in the children's ward for obvious reasons; but I think a few did so, what can I say; I'm sure you will know what to say to them".
She asked me if it's a good idea the… wheelchair.
I thought no, in fact the chair is a very bad idea.
They shouldn't see the wheelchair at all.
After all they mite think he came here to help us, how, he can't help himself.
I quickly got up and said;
"You're rite Sister; hide it behind the reception".
The news that I was there and about to go to them was already, old news;
Some of the parents saw all of us at the reception area and the news was spreading fast.
Suddenly it went quiet, the corridors were empty, not a soul in site.

People just… disappeared.
They went to their loved ones and stood their next to their beds waiting for me I suppose.
I said;
"Well, there's no point in delaying".
The Sister led the way and I followed.
She went into the first ward and to the first bed.
She whispered something to the kid and he was just, well, more like frozen and just looked at me for a few seconds; he stretched his arms wide as if to tell me give me a hug.
This time I froze, didn't know what to do.
There he was, a kid barely ten, with little or no hair on his head, pale-white face, bright big eyes, and a look in his face that was telling me, help me.
I went closer and into his arms.
We hugged and hugged; the kid wouldn't let go.
The only thing that mattered to him was that I came at long last, I was there for him and just wouldn't let go.

Who knows what the kid heard about me.
But I knew, I knew he knew why I was there;
Oh yes he knew I was there to save him;
I mean what do I do now?
I remembered what I did with the other kids.
I tried to give him courage by saying to him it's ok;
everything will be fine, you'll be well again, don't worry, just hang on and all that.
I said;
   "I brought you a little gift, gave him a cuddly toy and said;
   "This is not just any teddy bear".
   "This is Saint Johnny bear".
   "He will protect you".
   "Make sure you keep him with you all the time until the day you go home".
   "And when you go home, take him to your room";
   "If you feel you need him, give him a cuddle; it will make him very happy".
   "Put him to sleep with you and cuddle him all night, OK..."?

This time I wanted a hug, and he was more than willing to respond. The hugging went on until I started feeling some kind of heat between us.
I knew there and then that the kid will be ok soon.
Sister Margaret was on her knees crossing her self and many people did the same.
I said to them;
  "He's going to be ok";
A woman burst into tears and was kissing my feet.
I pulled back and wave my finger to her; NO.
I waved the kid goodbye and onto the next.
Pretty much the same thing only this one was even younger;
I remember this ones name, it was the same as mine Tony, but could not tell him that, he knew me as Saint Johnny Walker.
Sister Margaret was always there next to me on her knees and praying.
I turned to the kid and hugged him tight and I felt my chest burning up as if it was on fire.

I knew he was going to be one of
the first to go home.
After that I started feeling weak.
I felt I needed help if I was to
continue.
I looked at the Sister, she knew,
she knew what I was going thru,
she got up and held my hand.
  "You'll be ok now" she said.
Still holding my hand we went to
the next kid.
The support of the Sister was a
great inspiration to me…
I only needed to hold the forehead
of the kid for a few minutes and I
was feeling the energy travelling
the length of my arm to the kid.
I thought my task was easy, or a
bit easier.
The Sister was a great help.
She was giving me the extra energy
I needed to do my job.
We went on to the next kid and
then the next.
Basically I was following more or
less the same theory.
But the strength in me was getting
weaker and weaker again.
I saw the Sister was about to
faint, and knew why.

She gave it all to me, she was drained out, and she had no energy left in her.
I said to all the people including the ones on their knees praying;
  "We need some help here".
  "Please join hands and help us".
I grabbed hold of a nurse's hand and joined it with the Sister's and every one in there formed a human chain.
I said;
  "Please concentrate in what I'm doing and give generously your love".
  "You will feel the time when I need it most".
  "When you do feel THE moment, I want you to close your eyes and pray".
We went from kid to kid.
It really worked.
The one was giving the other the energy needed and it was passing through to me and from me to the kids.
I felt as if I had an energy generator powering away.
I felt relaxed and did what I had to do with ease.

The human energy generator was working perfectly.
Kids seemed happy enough.
Parents and relatives were even happier.
After all they were participating in whatever I was doing.
Then it was the last kid in the ward.
Only he wasn't a little kid but a big one, he was in his late teens.
He was waiting there patiently for his turn.
He was as pale as a zombie; he was in real trouble and had this look in his face, I mean that look was enough to melt even the hardest of the hardest;
Even his voice was trembling.
The first thing I thought was;
No, I can't give him a cuddly toy;
Surely it would be embarrassing for him.

   I grabbed hold of the nuns hand tight and before I put my right hand on his forehead he said;

   "Don't I get a Saint Johnny bear"?

   "I'm in the hospital nearly all my life".

"I need the bear more than everybody else in here".
"Please give me one too".
Of course I gave him one and said;
"Don't worry you'll be out of here in no time".
"I will make sure of that".
I mean I said that without even thinking; it just came out; as if I was sure I could have succeeded; He was very weak but found the energy to smile.
When I touched his forehead it was as cold as ice.
I tried hard for something but nothing.
Absolutely nothing was happening. The boy was just sitting on his bed looking at me in a weird and desperate way.
He sensed the "emptiness" and said.
"I'm dying yes"?
"There's nothing you can do, I feel it".
And with tears in his eyes said;
"It's ok Saint Johnny Walker; don't feel bad, I knew it for a long time now".
"It's not your fault".

I mean the words this kid used,
and the way he used them!!!
He made me feel awful, yet even
more determine to succeed.
I said;
 "No you're not".
 "You mustn't think like that".
I turned and said to everybody
give me some room.
 "Go back as far as you can".
I asked the nurse to pull the
curtain around the bed so no one
will watch us.
I held his hand and closed my
eyes.
I asked him to do the same.
This went on for a good five
minutes.
Then I put my left hand on his
head and said;
 "Don't open your eyes, keep them
closed".
 "Imagine you're asleep but still
can hear me".
 "Don't move until I tell you".
 "Concentrate on the pain you
have".
 "Keep concentrating on that and
nothing else".
 "Where does it hurt"?
He said;

"All over my body"
"Now I want you to push; push the pain to one part of your body; try hard to concentrate the pain to one corner; keep try hard".
"I want you to hear nothing else, only my voice".
"Keep concentrating".
"Is the pain moving"?
He said "yes".
"Good, where is it now"?
"It's moving to my chest".
"Good".
"Don't move and keep the pain there".
I went out the cubicle and whispered to a nurse;
Give me something to drink quickly.
I felt dehydrated and could not continue.
I signalled everyone for quiet;
They were all just standing and looking puzzled.
She came back with a jar of lemonade and a glass.
She poured and I drank it quickly.
I then signalled again for some quiet and went back in.
I said to the boy;
"Is the pain still there"?

He said "yes".
I said;
  "I want you to lie back slowly".
  "I will lie beside you and I want you to give me the biggest hug you ever gave to anyone".
I lay beside him and we hugged.
We hugged really tight.
I gave it all;
And within seconds it happened.
The heat!!! The energy!!! The force!!!
I don't really know what it was between our bodies.
It was some kind of see thru bright yellowish energy.
But whatever it was, it was hard at work.
Even though I was lying in bed, I could feel my body getting heavier and heavier;
His body was behaving oddly.
I could feel the spasms.
I was holding on to him very tight as if for my dear life.
He was fighting me off, but I was still holding on to him as tight as I could and taking it all.
At some point he screamed, and then went quiet, then the spasms again and more screaming.

He was pushing me, kicking me.
He was more like at war with me.
I was still holding on to him as tight as I could.
This went on for a while.
The spasms he had were so strong, I was having a rough time, I had to use all my strength and whatever energy left in me to hang on to him.
Suddenly he stopped.
He was very calm.
I could actually see the calmness in his face.
I got up and sat beside him.
I looked at him and said;
  "It's OK now Mario, wake up, you're OK".
  "It's all over".
  "You'll be going home soon".
He opened his eyes and just looked at me.
He said;
  "I feel odd, what happened"?
  "What did you do"?
  "I don't feel any pain now".
He was checking his body and double checking.
I remembered I pulled the curtain and said;
  "He's ok now".

I saw the Sister on her knees and praying along with a few other people.
I suddenly felt very weak and wanted to hold on to something.
My head was spinning.
I felt I was twice as heavy.
My legs could not support my body.
I guess I must have fainted.
When I came to I was in my bed with the drip bag over me a tube in my arm and a few wires attached to my chest all connected to this machine;
Oh no, again the same shit?
There were a few doctors, Gestapo, Kaiser, and a few nurses beside my bed, all looking down at me.
  "Welcome back Saint Johnny Walker" someone said.
I think it was Kaiser.
I asked;
  "What happened"?
  "It's OK, you just fainted".
  "Just fainted"?
  "What's this in my arm then if I only fainted".
  "And all these wires, did I had a stroke again"?
The doctor said;
  "It's OK; you're alright now".

"You had us worried for a while but you're ok now".
"How long was I out for"?
"About four hours".
"Four hours"?
I looked at my chest to see if they used electroshock on me again, but didn't see any marks.
I noticed the bubbles were gone too.
I thought they're supposed to go tonight.
That's what mamma Anna said, I think.
"Four hours huh, I murmured".
"Does that mean I missed lunch"?
"Everyone burst out laughing".
"Ha-Ha…" They all looked at each other and laughed.
Kaiser said;
"Yes, he's ok".
I said;
"I'm hungry and thirsty".
"What's in the drip"?
"I hope it's not my lunch".
Suddenly I remembered Mario.
I said;
"How's Mario"
"He's ok, he's resting and that's what you should do too; rest".

"What about all the other kids, are they ok"?
"I can't take them out of my mind".
"They're all ok".
"Don't let that worry you now".
I remembered what Mamma Anna said to me, not to get stressed out. Maybe I should relax a bit.
I asked the doctor;
"What's really in the drip bag"?
He said;
"Energy, and believe you me you need it".
"Don't even think of removing it; you need at least three of those".
The doctor added;
"We don't know what to do with you; you're something else; we don't know what to say to you either; this is all new to us; I for one, I am lost for words";
"We are all fascinated with what you're doing; we cannot explain it but we're working on that".
"We should really have a go at you for "Abusing" your self like this if that's the rite word and on the other hand we're amazed".

"We don't know really what to make out of all this either".

"You could say we're surprised… amazed… puzzled… stunned… fascinated… or all of that put together".

"What you're doing with the patients is like; I don't really know what words to use; we have never ever even read a story like this, never mind live it".

"In medical terms' we don't believe in all this; thinks like this simply don't exist, never happen; but we're seeing it, living it;

"But as scientists we do not accept it".

"Again we took a few samples from you for lab tests".

"We want to find out what makes you "tick" or "click" or, I don't know what";

"What is it that makes you heal so quickly"?

"I mean look at your chest, it's only yesterday you got seriously burned, and today"?

"I mean look at your chest, there's nothing, not even a mark".

"How do you heal other people were medicine fails, and lots and lots more questions".
"You're the talk of every scientist in the country".
"From biologists to psychoanalysers to… you name it".
"I hope you'll reconsider what we asked from you".
"What, become a Guiney pig not on your Nelly mate'.
And suddenly I remembered the kids in the other ward.
I said to Gestapo;
"What about the other kids"?
"I must go to them".
"I'm sure they're waiting for me".
"I mustn't let them down".
She said;
"There's plenty of time to do that".
"Just concentrate on your self for now".
"Believe me, you need the rest".
The doctor also added;
"The condition you're in, you won't be able to stand on your own two feet, let alone go to the kids".

"Let me put it another way for you" he added;

"If you're dead, you're no good to them, so take it easy, there's plenty of time for you to go and see them".

"What I want from you is rest and I mean rest".

"At least a couple of days OK"?

"Yes doc" I replied.

They all left apart from Gestapo, and she said;

"Now you heard what the doctor said, at least a couple of days rest".

I don't know why, but I sensed something weird, something was pushing me towards her, I grabbed her hand as she was fixing the bed a bit and said;

"Be quiet for a minute please".

She looked a bit surprised.

I closed my eyes and squeezed her hand.

I said:

"Who is Jason; I can see him on a wheelchair".

"Who is this kid, he needs my help".

"I must go to him".

"No-No you must bring him to me instead".

"He needs to stay in the hospital for a while after he spends time with me".

I opened my eyes and saw Gestapo in tears.
She told me that Jason was her son and that he was on a wheelchair after an accident at school four years ago.
He had a smashed disc on his spine and he's on a chair ever since.

"There's no hope I'm afraid, we're slowly accepting the fact that the wheelchair is his legs, he still has hopes; at least that's what he's trying to show to me, but I know deep down he's beginning to accept it".
I said;

"I know its school period but I want to have a go; would you trust me"?

"If I succeed it will take him time in here to help him learn how to walk again".
She said;

"Would you do that for him for me"?

She was crying her eyes out; she went confused and didn't know what she was saying.
She said;
  "Would I trust you"?
  "Who in the rite mind will say no"?
  "As for the school, the hell with it, maximum he'll miss a month, or even a year, so what".
  "Oh I can't wait to tell him the good news".
I said;
  "You must understand one thing, there are no guarantees".
  "I cannot promise anything apart from I'll do my best".
She said;
  "Yes…Yes… I know".
But seeing her face I knew she was just saying that.
As far as she was concern her son will walk again.
At that particular moment, I don't think any other possible fact was acceptable to her.
She was that sure of me.
She believed in me.
She asked me;
  "When do you think you can see him"?

I remembered I had to see the other kids today.
I said;
"Tomorrow morning bring him with you when you come for work, ask him to stay with you at the reception until I'm ready; first I will see you and tell you what I need, and then I will give it a go".
She was wiping off her tears and saying "thank you Saint Johnny Walker… thank you".
"Don't thank me yet, I'm not sure I can help in this case; it'll be my first and I don't really know how or even what to do".
Hey sister I said;
"What about my lunch"?
"What did that nice man Giuseppe sent for me today"?
"Yes, yes", she said;
"I'm sorry; I'll go and warm it up for you".
She came back ten minutes later with the biggest pizza I ever saw!!!
"My God sister who's going to eat all that"?

"If I'm lucky I'll eat a quarter, the rest take it to who ever want's it".

"And do me a favour, there's a beer in the fridge, would you"?
She shook her head but could not refuse.
I mean at that particulate minute I could have asked for the world and she would have given it to me.
Oh that pizza was great!!!
Especially when I washed it down with THE golden juice!!!
After I finished it all, I just lay back and tried to relax, well, I was more or less ordered to.
Shit, I remembered I still had something to do for myself.
My teeth;
Shit, with all this going on, I completely forgot, shit.
What I'm I gone do?
I can't go home looking like this.
They'll take the piss out of me.
I'll be the laughing stock.
I quickly pressed the buzzer.
I was pressing it like a mad man.
Gestapo came running.

"What? Are you ok" she asked?
I must have scared the life out of her with all that buzzing.

I said;
 "No I need teeth".
 She laughed.
 "Is that all"?
 "Ha, ha... I thought you were dying or something".
 "Don't do that" she said; "the buzzer is only for emergency".
I said;
 "And what do you think this is"?
 "Never mind all that, just tell me what you are going to do about it".
She said;
 "OK-OK... I'll arrange it for tomorrow, ok"?
 "OK sister tomorrow".
Now then I said;
 "Can we go to the kids"?
She said;
 "No, the doctor said no more excitements today".
 "To hell with him, what does he know"?
 "I'm ready to carry on from where I left it".
 "I have some unfinished business to take care of and I'm running out of time here; arrange my bodyguards again and the nurses; and yes sister do it now".

"And don't give me any arguments".
"And stop looking at me like that, snap out of it".
"Come on now, quickly; I don't have as much time as you think I do".
A bit reluctant at first but I gave her a big shout.
"Halloo; why are you still here"?
"Go… go".
She came back some time later with all those people.
They were waiting for us outside the door.
I said:
"Remove all these wires from me and take this tube out of my hand; I assure you I'm ok".
"All I want is; when we start the round with the kids, make sure I have liquids, and I mean something energetic, something with glucose and lots of it".
I sat on my wheelchair and off we went.
Pretty much the same as before with all these cuddly toys;
All the way I saw something amazing!!!

When people saw me they all started forming a line and holding hands.
Even on the staircase.
When Sister Margaret saw me she crossed her self a few times and before I got out of the chair she knelt before me, kissed my feet and said;
   "You are truly sent here by Jesus Himself".
   "I was praying for you when they took you away on a stretcher, we were all worried".
I pulled the Sister up and whispered in her ear;
   "You mustn't do that".
   "I'm supposed to do that to you, and not the other way round; not to mention it's very embarrassing; you only do that in the church or in front of a cross; after all "You" are wearing the cloth not to me; I'm just a simple ordinary guy".
She said;
   "The doctors here are going wild; they're running tests after tests on the kids you visited; they wouldn't tell us anything; they're still in that ward".

"And from the looks of their faces and the way they're talking to each other, one can understand that something big has happen".

"Only a few of us believe that a few miracles took place this morning".

I stopped her and said;

"I can see you're excited Sister with what happened but, with your permeation, can we begin; I don't have enough time on my hands, I hope you can understand".

She looked a bit puzzled with what I just said and said;

"OK Saint Johnny Walker whatever you say".

She led the way and we all followed.

I noticed the doctors came out of the first ward and followed us.

I suppose they wanted to witness my performance.

As I walked into the ward I saw everybody on their knees looking at me and praying at the same time.

I said to everyone;

"Please don't do that, get up and hold hands";

Sister Margaret was leading the human chain.
This time the doctor's joint in as the Sister demanded.
And from what I've seen, about a dozen of them actually took part.
A nurse said;
"Nearly all the hospital was joining in; you have the support you need from all the people in the hospital, from all six floors people are holding hands and they're with you".
So I grabbed Sister Margaret's hand and approached the first kid.
The usual Saint Johnny bears hugs and all that.
I was placing my hand on the forehead of each kid and was feeling the energy going from the human chain to his body.
After the second kid one of the doctors fainted and soon after a couple more.
In fact, I saw a few people on the floor, all suffering from exhaustion.
By the time I was transferring energy or whatever I was pumping into the last kid's head I heard there were a dozen or so people

that have fainted; all suffering from dehydration.
I was also a bit weak but not weak enough to faint this time thanks to the constant drinking of this special but funny taste lemonade that Gestapo ordered.
It only took about an hour or so to visit all the kids, but I felt really tired, I was exhausted.
All I wanted was to drink, drink and lie down.
I saw Sister Margaret about to faint as well and the nurses were rushing to help her.
I turned to Gestapo and said;
  "Please sister, take me to my room".
But it was no use; she was in a Trans.
I felt I was going too.
I was loosing control of my body.
I only remember people lifting me up from the floor.
I was escorted all the way to my bed by the security boys, Gestapo, nurses and doctors.
Immediately the doctors put me on the drip and wired me to the machine, and I remember a huge mask was coming towards my face.

I was so tired.
I remember I was floating on what seemed to be a cloud, and I was looking down to see where everyone went.
It felt as if I was left in the middle of the dessert only there was no sand around.
The cloud was carrying me further and further away.
I wanted to stop it.
I was trying all sorts of things.
But this flying object had no breaks anywhere to be found.
I realised the only way was for me to jump off.
I looked down and there was nothing.
Just empty space;
It took me a long time thinking whether to jump or not.
All of a sudden I was scared of heights.
I looked up and I saw this massive dark cloud and I was headed straight for it.
I remember thinking if I go into that cloud it will be the end, I will surely get lost in there and there's no way back.
I had to make the decision ASAP.

Take a chance and jump or just take it like a real man wherever this cloud was taking me.
Since I didn't know were I was headed, why take the chance.
I always say, if I don't really know where I'm going, I shouldn't really be in a hurry to get there.
The big cloud was getting closer and closer.
And I did it…!!!
I jumped off the cloud I was on, or my transporter "thing".
And there I was in the air, I was flying, floating in the air, oh I felt great!!!
Holly shit, I can really fly!!!
I spread my arms wide and I was doing all sorts of manoeuvres!!!
So this is what they call free-fall Huh?
Ha… piece a cake!!!
This is fantastic!!!
And only the very last minute I will open my parachute.
Shit, parachute?
I dint have one.
I realized I was in desperate trouble.
I was headed for a major disaster.
Sure death I would say.

I was trying everything I could think of; to… somehow stop the free fall
But the more I was straggling for "survival" the more speed I was picking up.
Suddenly I saw the ground, it was coming up to meet me and it was coming up fast.
Oh shit, I cried out and just as I was going to crush and go into millions of pieces, I felt an explosion inside me.
It was more like an "implosion" than explosion.
I felt the insides of my body were in pieces.
Then a second implosion this time it was bigger, louder.
What the hell is going on?
I thought I actually dropped in the middle of a war zone.
And then an even bigger one, only this time it was a direct hit, it caught me in rite in the chest.
I thought my lungs were blown to smithereens.
I couldn't breathe.
And in my straggle for air I jumped.
I took a few very deep breaths.

I opened my eyes and there he was, the doctor.
He was holding two metal pieces and realised he was electrocuting me again.
The explosions were his doing.
I had a real go at him.
I actually shouted at him and said;
   "Why did you do that; are you trying to kill me"?
I looked at all of them and said.
   "Is this one of your experiments again; I thought experiments are done only on poor animals.
They were all "shocked" at first, but they all had a bit of a smile in their faces.
I said;
   "Do you think this is funny, I for one, I'm not amused".
The doctor with the metal gadgets said;
   "He's back".
He turned to me and said;
   "Saint Johnny Walker; is this going to be a regular thing with you; you're picking up bad habits".
What the hell are you talking about I said.

376

"What habits"?
"I think the sister will fill you in, we have work to do; and they all left.
The sister stayed behind and sat there next to my bed.
"Ok sister, spit it out";
"What happened here"?
"Why was the doctor so rough with me; why was he electrocuting me again"?
"I want the truth; give it to me straight".
Reluctantly and with a lot of tears in her eyes she tolled me the whole story.
Apparently I was "gone" yet again. She said;
"You had no pulse for twelve minutes; in other words you were dead for twelve minutes.
We were all trying hard she added to bring you back to life.
"Bullshit" I said.
"I mean who in the rite mind would believe all that; all these doctors were experimenting on me rite"?
"They realised I'm not just an ordinary bloke and I was the perfect Guiney pig for them rite"?

"You know something she said; you're a very selfish man".
Oops… here comes the Gestapo lecture.
She added;
"You were DEAD whether you accept it or not".
"For twelve minutes you were NOT breathing".
"The doctors were fighting to bring you back; and instead of thanking them you were angry at them".
She got up, checked the blipping machine and on her way out and said;
"I'll be back with your dinner Saint Johnny Walker".
Shit, I'm glad she didn't have a whip with her.
Suddenly I felt guilty.
Maybe she's rite;
Maybe what she said did happen;
If it's true, it's the second time I died;
Holly shit, what if it's true what they say, third time lucky and all that?
That means I only have one life left.

Yes but they also say the cats has nine lives.
Maybe I have nine lives too.
That means I have another seven to go;
Mmm… that's not bad.
I like the second one better.
It's seven more than everyone else!!!
Yes but, what if I don't get to choose?
I know, I'll ask good old Anna in the morning.
She can predict all these things.
Gestapo came back with my dinner.
It was roast beef with potato and greens.
She said;
  "I know you like beer but not tonight; not while you're on drugs".
I asked;
  "Can you remove all these wires from my body"?
  "No" she said; and don't even think about removing them; you will have to sleep with them tonight and that is a strict order from the doctor".
Shit, sleep with all these wires?
I mean I feel like I'm a robot.

I started munching away like mad. As if the last time I saw any kind of food, was donkey's years a go; Even though there was enough food for at least two, I finished it all in no time at all.
Gestapo came back to clean up I suppose.
I asked her;
  "Are you on overtime"?
  "You're here since this morning rite"?
She said;
  "First of all we don't get paid overtime, and yes I'm here since this morning".
  "Why don't you go home, aren't you tired"?
  "Now that I know you're ok I will".
  "Thank you for that and I'm sorry for my behaviour earlier, but I think you better go home".
  "Don't forget we have a big day tomorrow" I said.
She replied;
  "I don't think it's a good idea after what happened today".
  "What did happen"?
She said;

"I'm in a difficult position; what if something happens to you; today we managed to bring you back, what if the same thing happens tomorrow and this time you don't return"?
"Trust me" I said;
"I know the way back; remember you said I was gone; yes?
But I came back, rite?
As for the doctors you said they were fighting to bring me back, that's bullshit".
"I know the way back; it's not the first time, so trust me in what I say; I was on my way back and the doctor was blocking my return with all theses electric shocks; every time he was electrocuting me I was feeling it you know, and every time it was like a bomb exploding in me, and I was hurting something terrible".
"And; if something like that ever happen again, tell the doctor to back off".
"Tell him I said so".
"I know the way back, believe me I do".

"But you have to understand, the way back is a bit long and takes some time".

"And it's not measured in miles or kilometres either".

"I'll try next time to make it back quicker".

I was thinking of my transportation, the cloud, next time I'll just jump and not think about it.

She looked at me in such a way, as if she was trying to picture the journey there and back.

She was lost… puzzled… shocked… stunned… and I don't know what else; in a world of her own.

I think she was trying to imagine what the journey would be like.

She wanted to ask many things, I felt that, but to stop her asking I said;

"I'm a bit tired and want to sleep".

She said;

"I'm not surprised".

What a day!

"I guess I'll see you in the morning sister".

"A Very Good Night Saint Johnny Walker and she bowed to me before leaving".
What?
What the hell was that all about?
I never saw Gestapo doing that before!!!
Mmm... there's hope for her still.
I reached out for my diary.
I started writing the days events.
When it came to my "death" I stopped.
I didn't know how to describe the incident.
I mean how does one describe ones own death?
And what's more, how does one describe the way he or she for that matter came back.
Is it resurrection?
Maybe it's Vampire-ism!!!
Just like all those films.
If people were to read my memos they'll call me a Vampire.
The living dead!!!
I'll have no shadow and two of my teeth will grow.
Shit, I must be watching too much TV.
Oh shit, my teeth.

Tomorrow I must go and see the dentists.
I'm running out of time.
I'm returning home in a couple of days.
Ha… now there's a joke.
My holidays will be over in a couple of days.
Ha… holidays;
Imagine someone buying a ticket from England for a two week holiday in an Italian hospital;
Well, I should look at it from the bright side I suppose;
I didn't pay for it at least;
I felt tired and my eyes were getting heavier.
I was about to turn the lights off when one of the nurses came thru the door and ask me if everything was ok.
She tucked me in, checked the drip thing, looked at the blipping machine I was connected to and said;
  "Goodnight Saint Johnny Walker".
  "And that's from all the hospital staff".
That's nice I said.
  "Good night".

She turned the lights off and closed the door leaving a little gap.
As I was lying there I remembered Gestapo's words.
What a day.
I must take it easy from now on.
I only have Jason to deal with tomorrow.
I mean it's only one kid and that's it.
It should be a piece of cake.
And then it's taking it easy.
This time I'm sure nothing will go wrong.
I mean what else can happen?
I've been thru hell the last few days.
Surely God will feel something for me, and say.
   "Its ok son, you can have a days rest if nothing else".
I mean I think I deserve a days rest to say the least.
After all He said;
   "The seventh day is for rest".
I've been at it now a good ten days.
Yes, I must think positive.
Think of rest and only rest.

Nothing, absolutely nothing will go wrong.
Even though deep down I knew that, all that positive thinking, all that positive attitude, it was all gibberish really, at least in my case, or while I am still in here;
And I didn't need anyone to tell me that;
Ever since my winning this free holiday it's been nothing but disaster after disaster;
I mean I must be the only person in the entire universe who "booked" in a hospital and "managed" to sustain at least one or should say "different" injury every single day in here;
It really makes me wonder if that's not some kind of a record;
Serves me right really;
Ha; free holiday huh?
I mean if that's what one get's… who needs it;
I'll never ever try my luck in winning anything that says "free" ever again;
The minute I go home, I'll order a big poster with the words;
  "Anything that says "free" can seriously damage your health"

I think that would look very nice hanging on my wall;
If anything, just to remind me of all this;
In fact I think not only will decorate my wall nicely but it will be a constant reminder to me "never try to win anything ever again";
And of course, never let me forget what I've been through these two weeks;
Ha… for a man who I must admit, possesses so much, and yet… how little did I know of what was actually waiting for me?
Come to think of it, I even have the "gift" of predicting everyone else's future and yet, I could not foresee my own tomorrow.
I suppose it must be true.
God das work in mysterious ways.
And who can argue with that?

Saint Johnny Walker's
"How to... Become a Saint"

Chapter Twelve
Day Eleven

The next morning I woke up very early yet again.
What a habit to pick up huh
I mean in London I was the opposite.
I just could not get enough sleep, and yet here?
What are these people giving me? This is ridiculous.
I miss my old ways.
Getting out of bed very lazy, opening the front door with pyjamas still on to get the milk, and saying Jesus, its bloody freezing!!!
Oh how I miss all that.
I mean today I woke up, it was still very dark out there, and suddenly I had to go... I wanted to use the loo desperately but couldn't with all these's wires glued on me.
I was still connected to the machine.

I pulled the drip tube out of my arm and started pulling the wires off one by one.
And within seconds the nurse came running in and then another two.
They were holding me down and gluing the wires back on.
They were a bit rough with me and said;
   "No-no-no you mustn't do that".
I was trying to explain to them why, but they wouldn't listen.
I was trying to fight them off.
I started shouting and a doctor appeared.
He said to the girls:
   "Its ok"; and they let go of me.
I said to him;
 "I must go and that I don't need these any more anyway".
He gave me a quick check up with the stethoscope, checked my pulse and said;
   "Ok take them off".
The minute I was free I run to the toilet like I was running the 60 meter dash.
Oh my god, what a relief.
That was indeed a close shave.
Another minute or so and a major disaster would have taken place.

When I came out the doctor was still there.
He said smiling;
   "Are you ok now"?
   "Well, now I am".
I asked him what time it was and he said 5am.
He gave me another check up and said;
   "You're ok; everything looks normal, you don't need these any more and pointed to the wires".
He wrote something on the chart and said;
   "So you are Saint Johnny Walker huh"!!!
   "I wanted to see you and have a chat with you but every time I came to see you, you were fast asleep".
   "You're a fascinating man and a famous one too".
   "I know all about you and what you have been doing since you arrived hear".
   "All those miracles you performed".
I said;
   "I don't feel sleepy and you want to chat; can we at least have some tea"?

He wasted no time and pressed the buzzer.
The nurse came and he ordered two cups, one for himself too.
He looked like he needed one too.
He must have been slipping and I woke him up.
And judging from the way he looked, I think he needed it a lot more than I did.
I thought it's still very early for Anna to come so we'll keep each other company for a while.
The nurse came with the tea very quick.
I sat on my wheelchair facing him.
We had a few sips and the questions were coming in thick and fast.
He was bombarding me from everywhere with his questions.
He wanted to find out how do I do all that I do.
What do I feel when I do it;
What goes through my mind at the time, do I prepare my self before or is it a last second thing;
I mean he wanted to know everything.

Most of the questions were stupid really but I could understand why he was asking them.
He was trying to ask the rite questions but couldn't.
I mean in situations like these, which are the rite question?
If one does not understand something, what kind of a question will he or she put forward?
And let's face it, what really is a miracle?
How does one explain it or even describe it?
Is there a beginning or an end?
Can anybody measure it?
I asked the doctor all these questions, but he was speechless.
He could not answer even one of them.
Now I said;

"Maybe you can understand why I could not give any answers to your questions; and believe me when I tell you, some of the answers you want, I also want".

"Maybe I'll go thru a lifetime searching for them".

"All I can tell you is, ten days ago I was an ordinary bloke that was working in a hotel kitchen and doing what any ordinary person does in his everyday life; I live alone and for companion I have my cat, and don't even know the guy who lives next door to me, and now all this"!!!

"Don't you think I want a few answers"?

"Hell, even my name was changed here".

"And I got so use to my new name, if someone was to call me by my real name I would not answer, I think".

"If this carries on for a while longer, I'll definitely forget my real name; and the worse part people won't accept any other name".

"To everyone here I'm Johnny Walker, and if that's not bad enough, lately I was given a title to go with it".

"Now I'm Saint Johnny Walker".

"So what do you think of that doc"?

"Hell, I came here for a winter break, to soak up some sun and I ended up in here".

"Do you think I'm having fun in here"?

"I am going through at least one disaster a day".

"Or from one disaster to another";

"There isn't a day that goes by in here without "paying" it with some kind of injury";

"I feel as if, if I am to help save a life, I "have" to pay that help with injury first";

"In ten days or so, I have managed to damage and abuse my entire body; and I assure you sir, this is not what I call fun";

"I've even been to hell and back, twice I think".
The guy was just listening to me with a big "Sorry Look" in his face, he was nearly in tears.
I looked out the window and daylight was breaking.
He said;

"It's time for me to go".
He thanked me for all the things I said and totted him and left, still analysing in his mind all what I said.
And to my surprise the Kaiser came in.
I mean this early in the morning?

This could be another one for the record book.
She was just looking at me and shaking her head.
I said smiling;
 "Good morning sister isn't this a lovely day"?
 "Good morning Saint Johnny Walker".
 "You've done it again haven't you"?
I just smile and said;
 "Why so early sister"?
I mean I said that just to avoid the lecture.
She said;
 ?I am filling in for the other sister for a few hours in the morning".
I suppose she meant Gestapo.
She wanted a couple of hours off in the morning to prepare Jason for something big, she wouldn't tell me what but sounded very excited.
 "I think I know why" I said.
 "Would you call her for me, I have something to tell her".
 "Sure I can she said, I'll be back in a minute".

She came back with a telephone set and plugged it in a socket; she dialled and said to her;

"Hi Jeanette, its Helena, Saint Johnny wants a word" and she hands it to me.

"Good morning sister Jeanette" and all that.

"If possible, could you bring with you all the closest relatives you have or at least as many as possible; it will help me and Jason a lot".

"I know it's a last minute thing but if you explain to them they'll understand".

"Take your time I'm not going anywhere".
Kaiser was smiling and said;

"Now I know".

"You are something else Saint Johnny Walker".

"You are truly a Saint".
I said;

"Don't build your hopes up and don't get excided yet, it mite not work, there are no guarantees".

"It doesn't matter what you say, you were sent here on purpose, and you're on a mission here; you confirm that, every day more and more".

"I mean looking back from the day you arrived it's been all miracles and miracles".

"You have made doctors and professors go back to their books".

"I see them every day, they're so puzzled and amazed they don't really know what hit them".

"Nearly all of them are still trying to find logical explanations of what took place in the last ten days".

"They see but still don't believe it was all possible".

"If one was to write all what you have achieved here it will be a best seller I'm sure".

"Sister Jeanette told me of the "journey" you had and how you came back, she told me of the explosions you felt".

"She was on the phone for a good hour last night talking to me; we were both so excided, you must understand that this is all knew to us and as a result we act like little kids".

Good old Anna came in with the tea.
She looked happy and had as usual, the biggest smile in the world.

"Good morning Saint Johnny Walker".

"Good morning Mamma" I replied.

"I see you're doing fine and ready for your next miracle".
Kaiser said;

"I'll be back later, as if she knew I wanted a private conversation with Anna.
I asked Mamma if she knew anything about my nine lives or if the third will be final one.

"She told me not to worry about this at all".
She said;

"The only thing I can tell you is that you'll live to be over eighty and until then you will perform quite a few miracles".

"Sadly you will leave the island in a few days but continue elsewhere".

"God has chosen you because of your pure kindness and good hearted character".
I asked again;

"How many times do I have to face death"?

"I'm not in a position to answer that, but if you do you'll always find a way to come back".

"The only thing I can tell you about your future is that you'll be travelling a lot and do what you do, until one day you will end up in a place of your own; even though one day you will change your title from Saint to something else, become a leading figure in some country and I don't mean England, you will become one of the richest people in the world, and yes, you will hold power, big power; live in a massive house for a while; someone will give you all that, and this someone is very big, big as in president, prime minister, mayor, general, I don't know";

"You will find your self in a country that you will be appreciated and rewarded not only for the gift you have as a healer but for being wise too";

"But, although this is not that far ahead, you will visit a few other countries first, and do what you do";

"The place you will be given all these has a lot of sand with a few fountains and benches all around". someone will offer all that to you as present"; not only because you will save his son but because he will realise that you are the wisest man he's ever known; in fact, you will be the cause of transforming the country from poverty to one of the leading economically rich and stable countries in the world; but, even so, and with all these richness surrounding you; you will eventually leave everything behind you and never look back, only because it is not you; you will carry on travelling and travelling, healing and healing; and after a few years of that, you will eventually end up running a little business in England; a little hotel near the sea; and yes, slow down; and this is where I say enough; let's just leave it there; you know I cannot tell you any more; all I can tell you more is people will come to you without knowing why they're there really".

"People will come to you, and you'll help them but most of them wouldn't know you did".
The place you'll become powerful is not London or England.
"You will keep this big house for ever, even though you will not live in it except the first couple of months or so;
"You will travel the world and visit lots of different countries representing your new or adopted country, and in every one of those countries you will help quite a few people".
"You will find a way to do it without anyone realising it".
"Thank you Mamma, you have made my day" I said.
She left for me the tea and some home made cookies.
She gave me a huge hug and a couple of kisses as usual and left.
Oh those cookies were out of this world!!!
I must ask her for the recipe.
Travel the world huh!!!
Mmm; that sounds exciting!!!

Buy a big house huh!!!
No, not buy, someone will give it to me;
Me, a big house, and a present too…?
Mmm I can just imagine it;
If its big enough maybe I'll turn it into a hotel;
  "The Saint Johnny Walker Hotel"!!!
I like it; it has a nice ring to it.
Then again everybody will know where to find me, and that would not be peaceful living.
No-no; that's a bad idea; maybe under a different name;
Oh I don't care really, I'm sure when the time comes I'll think of something suitable.
The usual thing went on, the linen ladies the cleaners and then the doctors.
Only this time a few more than usual;
I mean there were doctors' students and a few, so called professors.
The usual one million questions but only very few answers.

I must have had a general check up from each one separately.
And from what I gathered, twenty different theories.
Apparently they could not believe a person coming back from the dead could be full of life like I was, and in such a short time, only a few hours after.
As far as they were concerned, a person going thru an ordeal like this will need at least six months or so to recover.
I do understand them in a way, after all, science and miracles don't really see eye to eye.
What I don't understand is all these so called scientists are always trying hard to find answers when they know beforehand that there aren't any; it's really a waist of their so called valuable time
Ha… Talk about masochism!!!
Poor guys, it's as if they're brainwashed to find answers and only answers.
They don't really care about what the end result is, so longest it's scientifically proven.
If it's not?

Well, one can only imagine what they go thru; especially when their computers come out with zilch too.
They drew blood from every finger and every tow of mine for their experiments I suppose.
I felt they were "draining" me out.
Shit, suddenly a terrible thought flashed though my mind;
I know why, I thought; maybe they'll inject themselves with my blood to see if they can perform a miracle or two.
Shit, what if, what I do it's in my blood?
Shit.
What if they succeed?
They will drain me out for sure and use my blood for their own little miracles, and probably, well, surely charge people a fortune as well.
Or maybe charge a few multi billionaires a few million for a "miracle cure" and the poor will be left to die.
Shit that's not fair.
These bastards will do anything for a quick million or two.

No-no… they wouldn't do that.
Well, I don't know really.
Wouldn't they?
We are talking billions maybe here;
In all these films we see, about a discovery, top secret and all that shit, there's at least one that's willing to steel the "product" or the "formula", and sell it to the highest bidder.
What if one of these doctors steels the samples from the lab and uses them to make a quick fortune?
And what if the blood really works?
He's liable to kill me by draining me out.
Come to think of it, no he won't, not if he's clever.
He'll kidnap me, lock me up in a cellar somewhere and draw as much blood as he needs every day.
Shit, I'll never see the light of day until the day I die.
Oh I must put and end to this and rite now.
Somewhat "panicky" with all that thinking I said to all present;

"This is the last time you're taking blood samples from me and I mean it".
And to make sure they knew I meant business I added;

"Do I make my self clear"?
They all looked at me in such a way as if they were saying to me what the hell is gone into you?

"Well gentlemen, and ladies; well, there were a couple of lady doctors there as well.

"Do I make my self clear, this is the very last time you do this and I do mean that";

"I'm very serious about it".

"And one more thing, no more wires, no more oxygen masks, no more electrocutions, I don't want any of that even if you think I'm dead, I'm not breathing or anything similar to all that, just back off, Just leave me be".

"And even if I am "clinically dead" or "brain dead" like you doctors say, I don't want you either to worry or do anything to bring me back; I assure you, I'll be back as soon as I can".

"The last time you nearly blocked my "re-entry" with all the

electroshocks; no more of that, just let me come back the way I know".
 "If you want all that in writing, so be it".
 "I'll sign a paper that says so".
 "Do you all understand me"?
They were all stunned!!!
Just stood there looking at me probably asking themselves what's gone into him all of a sudden, he never talked to us like this before?
I raised my voice a bit and repeated;
 "Do you understand"?
 "I mean do I have the rite or what"?
 "And I will not accept no for an answer".
Well I thought, that's telling them;
Shit, I never spoke to anyone like that before; mmm…
I don't know if they will follow my request or not, but they all left the room somewhat long faced and puzzled as to what brought all that up?

The minute they left I felt so guilty.
After all they're doctors and trying to help me, I think.
Come to think of it, why I'm I in the hospital?
I heal very quickly and without their help, I think so anyway.
Mmm; I'll work on that;
Maybe, just maybe I am rite.
Must look back and analyse everything.
Half an hour or so later Gestapo came in and pretended she was doing things.
I think she was trying to find a way to say that Jason was already here.
I said to her;

"I know Jason is out there and he's anxious; but before you bring him in, I want to make something clear; I promise you I'll do my very best for him so he can walk again but, there are no guarantees of any success, OK"?

"After all, he is more than four years on the wheelchair, it just mite be impossible";

"Sister Jeanette, what I am trying to say is I am also new at

this, I've never came across anything as big";
She said;
"I know, I do understand, but doctors gave up, technology is not that far ahead to do anything else for him, you are his only hope";
"At least it's a hope, and he has nothing to loose and everything to gain";
"OK then";
"1st I want Sister Margaret from upstairs to be here with me".
"2nd before any attempt is made, I want to see all the relatives separately, one at a time".
"3rd most probably I will reject one or more of your relatives for my experiment".
"4th the rejected ones must leave the hospital and I mean as far as possible, at least a mile away".
"5th I want a lot of liquids, anything with a lot of glucose".
"6th when I'm ready for Jason I'll press the buzzer and I want all the relatives in holding hands very and I mean very tight and the first one will hold Sister Margaret's hand".

"She will be leading the chain".

"Then you bring Jason in, undress him leaving him only his shorts and place him in my bed".

"And finally you will hold the last person's hand in the chain with both your hands".

"This might take some time, so two things".

"One, no one and I mean no one will break the chain, even if it's for a second to scratch his or her head".

"And two, no one will come in the room until the whole thing is over; the door must be closed all of this time, no one is to be destructed";

"Give everyone and if necessary force them to drink at least two glasses of that liquid before forming the chain";

"Is there anything that you want me to repeat"?

"No-No No, she said and she went out the door in a flash".
She came back a few minutes later with a couple of big jars with some kind of mixed fruit juice and asked me if I'm ready to start.
I said;

"We'll need a lot more liquids".
"And I mean not only for me".
"Where's Sister Margaret"?
"She's on her way".
"I'll wait for Sister first".
When she arrived she gave me a hug and said;
"Whatever you ask of me, and thank you for what you are about to do".
Bless her heart;
I said;
"Send the first relative in".
A big-ish man came in and stood there looking.
I grabbed hold of his hand and placed my other hand on his forehead;
I said:
"Close your eyes and think only of Jason";
I sensed he was finding the whole thing funny and gave me pretence laughter.
I said;
"Thank you; you may go now, go home.
He looked at me and said;
"What; is this a joke; are you having fun with us; you asked us to come here and we did, some of

us didn't go to our work to be here you know".
He was really upset, well, more like pissed off.
I don't know if it was because I rejected him or for loosing a day's work.
I said;
   "I'm sorry "sir" about that" and since he thought this was a joke I offered to pay, out of my pocket the day's loss;
I think that pissed him off even more;
He was really upset and left in a rage.
I got the feeling if Sister Margaret wasn't present he would have punch me on the nose.
Gestapo came in and said;
   "What happened"?
   "Never mind I said just sent in the next one".
This time it was a lady and I did the same thing.
Same question and the lady answered me.
I felt she was genuinely sorry for Jason being on that chair for so long.
I asked her;

"Do you really believe that, what I'm about to attempt will succeed"?
She said;
"Yes I really believe in you".
I said;
"Would you wait outside until I'm ready to call you in, it mite take some time"?
The answer was;
"Yes, no problem, as long as it takes".
Then the next person and the next; I "interviewed" them all one by one and the only rejected one was the first one.
Gestapo comes in and says;
"I told every one what you asked of us and they're ready".
I said;
"Call them in".
They all came and started holding hands.
Gestapo arranged a few security guards outside the door and I heard her saying to them no one goes in or out and I mean no one, even if it's a doctor.
She wheeled Jason in and started stripping him.

The poor kid was in a world of his own.
He didn't know what to do or how to behave.
He was just following his mother's orders.
She helped him to the bed and all of them were just waiting for me to do what I was supposed to do.
I asked each and every one to have a glass of the juice and that included me as well.
I took my shirt off and apologised for the display to Sister Margaret; after all, she was a nun.
She said;
"It's ok".
I lay next to Jason and said to Sister Margaret;

"I want you to lead the human chain and with the other hand to hold Jason's forehead".

"He will probably fight you off, but you will have to fight back and not to break the connection".

"I want all of you to close your eyes and concentrate in giving your love to Jason".

"All you have to do is think how much you love him and push him with your mind to get up and walk without saying anything, do this with your mind".

"It requires concentration that is all, keep your eyes closed and think of Jason walking";

"At some point you will feel weird and maybe even weak but remember do not break the chain, and don't think of anything else, keep imagining Jason walking again".

We were all set and I said to Jason;

"Keep your eyes closed and concentrate your mind on the broken disc you have".

This time I was doing all the hugging because he was facing away from me, and as time was passing the hug was tighter and tighter.

He started having spasms, his body was shaking and I felt there was a bit of heat between us.

I turned him over, this time facing me.

I placed my hands around him and to the point where the damage was on his spine.

Our bodies were shaking more and more and I suddenly felt a lot of pain travelling through my body.
He was screaming from the pain and the more he screamed the tighter I was holding him.
I felt the pain I had was coming directly from his spine through my arms and into my body.
The pain was unbearable.
I wanted to scream, and at some point I think I did, but I was holding on to him as if for my dear life.
At that time I heard a few of the people also murmuring.
It must have affected them as well.
I could hear the Sister with a few others praying.
The pain was indescribable.
We were both in agony.
He was screaming and screaming.
He was calling for his mother over and over again.
I remember he was screaming for his mother to put an end to this and why did she put him thru all this.
Why did he have to suffer so much?

He was pleading with her to come and put an end to this whole ordeal.
I could only hope the mother will not break and come to his rescue.
I don't really know how long the whole ordeal went on for but it was pure hell.
The pain… the heat… the spasms… the screaming… the agony… you name it, it was there, it was all happening at the same time, suddenly the spasms stopped, so was the screaming.
I looked at him and he was gone, he was out.
I move my hand from his spine and grabbed Sister Margaret's hand, and both our hands were pressing his forehead.
I shouted to all present;
  "Now, give me all your energy, give it to me now".
  "Now is the time Jason needs you".
  "Show him how much you love him".
  "He can feel all of you and he knows you love him".
  "Give it all you've got.

Immediately I felt the energy from the human chain coming to my hand and I was transferring it to Jason.
Suddenly the spasms started again and there was an orange colour light between my hand and Jason's forehead.
The light lasted a few seconds or maybe a minute and it was gone, it vanished, just like that.
I knew then that the ordeal was over.
I did as much as I could.
I simply could not carry on.
There was no more energy to draw from either.
People were exhausted and some of them were on the floor not having enough energy or strength to stand on their own two feet.
I was barely hanging on my self.
It took a few minutes for all of us to catch our breath.
Then I said;
   "That's it, there's nothing else I can do".
Gestapo came closer to me and I said to her;
   "What he needs now is about an hours rest".

"Not to move him from my bed and if someone could help me to my wheelchair";
The sweat was indeed pouring from my body;
I was in real trouble;
I could only move my hands.
I don't know how many people helped but I knew the damage I did to my self was very serious.
I was paralysed from the waist down.
Of course I didn't mention any of this at the time to anyone but I think Gestapo guessed it.
I signalled to her not to say anything.
I saw the people in the room helping each other and offering each other a drink.
I also noticed there were two ladies and a man flat out on the floor, they passed out, they had no more energy left in them.
Gestapo opened the door, called a nurse and said;

"Get me some more juice and lots of it", turned around and said to every one in the room;

"Sit on the floor and rest your backs against the wall.

Two nurses came in with jars full of juice, and two more with glasses.
Every one was having fruit juice, glass after glass, me included. It took about half an hour or so for everyone to somewhat recover. Some wanted to go out and they were looking at me as if to say can we?
I said;
  "You can all go now if you want the work is finished; thank you all for your help".
  "Believe me I said; if it wasn't for all of you being here none of this would have been possible, I thank you all".
They looked at me in a weird way as if they were asking me;
Are you sure we're not needed any more?
  "Best if you go home now and relax, I see you all need it; just go home and rest".
Then I was bombarded with questions.
  "Is he going to be ok"?
  "Is he going to walk again"?
  "Can we see him walk"?

"If he's ok, why is he still asleep"?
"What if something went wrong and he'll never recover"?
All sorts of questions like that.
I mean not enough I was trying hard to hold on to my senses and not faint, I had to deal with all that as well.
I said to all of them;
"Listen everybody, Jason is going to be OK, he just needs the rest, please go home now".
"I promise you he'll walk again in a day or two".
"Trust me; I know what I'm saying".
"And believe me; he will come and visit each and every one of you to thank you personally, and I promise you, he will come on foot".
They all stood up and gave me a round of applause.
I stopped them and said;
"Please don't mention this to anybody, as far as you're all concern nothing happened here".
"And if someone asks a silly question as to what were you all

doing in here, just say we had a meeting".

"Remember, nothing happened, please".

"And don't worry about Jason, he will wake up in a while and he'll go downstairs to learn how to balance his body and by tomorrow he'll walk; maybe with crutches for a while; but definitely, no more wheelchairs".

"I promise you that".

"Please-please-please trust me on that; I know what I'm saying; now go home and remember what I said, nothing happened here".
One by one they all gave me hugs and kisses and left quietly. Gestapo, Sister Margaret and a couple of nurses were still there. They all started cleaning up and the nurses took the glasses away. Gestapo stroke Jason's heir then came to me.
She asked me;

"How do you feel"?
I whispered in her ear;

"I'm a mess".

"I think I'm paralysed".

"I can't feel anything from the waist down".

"Whatever Jason was suffering from and whatever was wrong with his body I transferred it to mine".

"So I don't really have to tell you what or how I feel, you must know".
She was stroking my head and crying.
She was crying like a little kid.
I could see thru her, she was going through hell that minute.
She didn't know what to say or how to behave.
She gave me a hug and immediately I knew what she was thinking.
On the one hand she was happy about Jason and on the other she was really sad that I was going to be stuck on a wheelchair the rest of my life.
I looked at her and said;

"Don't worry, Jason will be ok and to answer the question that's in your mind, no, I will not be on a wheelchair the rest of my life".
She looked and said;

"How did… you… I didn't know you also read minds".

"Can you really do that"?
I said;

"Never mind all that".

"In about twenty minutes Jason will wake up; help him to the wheelchair and take him downstairs to that beautiful girl the physic; tell the girl that he's 100% ready, just ask her to teach him how to balance first and then to attempt the walking; she's a cleaver girl and she'll know what I mean; but before you do that, I, Sister Margaret and you need some lunch".

"And please order some beer".

"Every one in this room needs it".

"We're all a bit dehydrated".

"I'm sure you and the Sister will do me the honour in having lunch with me".

"Would you Sister Margaret"? She was on her knees in the corner facing a cross on the wall praying as usual.
Gestapo said;

"Sure, anything you say".
Anything I say?
Mmm; I wouldn't mind an extra six pack of beers as well please, and don't say no, I'm not taking any

medication; after all we all need some energy".
She smiled and left.
Even though I was really exhausted from all that, I somehow managed not to faint and more important not to die, yet again;
I suppose I'm getting the hang of things or my body is getting use to the punishment.
Sister Margaret finished her prayers and sat on the chair.
She looked really tired and worn out.
I said;
  "Would you do me the honour and have lunch with me"?
She said;
  "It will be a pleasure Saint Johnny Walker, and the honour will be entirely mine".
A few minutes later the food arrived and we were really enjoying every bit of it.
I offered to the two guests of mine a glass of beer and they both looked at me in a funny way.
They both refused; each one for a different reason.
I insisted and said;

"You must, it will give you back some of the energy you lost".
Somewhat reluctant they said ok.
I said to both;
"Sister and sister please; no more of the same please, at least for a while; I feel if I carry on with the same rate I would not be as successful and that's no good to anyone".
"I feel I'm getting weaker and weaker… hence the help I needed from all these people".
They both said;
"Ok Saint Johnny walker"
Jason started moving in bed and was about to wake up.
The mother went to him and was stroking his head.
The kid was lost; he was asking questions and questions.
"Where I'm I"?
"What happened" and all that.
He couldn't remember the ordeal he went through.
All he remembered was the terrible pain he felt.
His mother said to him;
"It's all over now son".
"It won't hurt any more".
"You'll be walking soon".

I asked her to help him to the wheelchair, give him a bite to eat and lots to drink.

"After that you know where to". She did exactly that and while he was drinking he said something funny; well, funny to me at least but brought tears to the mother. He said;

"My foot is itchy".
Sister Margaret and I looked at each other and started laughing. He bent down to scratch it and I said to him;

"Why don't you lift your leg and scratch your foot"?
He was in two minds whether to attempt it and I said;

"Go ahead, you can do it, it's very easy".

"Just lift your leg".
He did, just like that; he put one leg on the other and said to his mother;

"Look mum, look!!!
He was ecstatic...!!!
He could not hide his excitement. He was lifting first the one leg then the other.
The mother and Sister Margaret were crying from joy.

I must admit I shed a few tears my self.
Suddenly I felt really tired and said;
  "Please girls can you help me get on my bed; I need some rest".
  "And I suggest you do the same". They did and I thank them.
I asked Gestapo to put someone out the door so no one will disturb me for at least three hours, and she said ok.
I must have fallen asleep strait away because I don't remember seeing them going.
I woke up late in afternoon.
It was still daylight and I could here a lot of people out in the corridor going about their businesses.
I tried to move my legs but they wouldn't respond, I thought shit, I hope this will not be a permanent thing.
I lifted the covers to see if I could at least move my toes and… oh, what a relief.
I could see them moving, and on both feet.
Yes… I cried out, I was really excited as if it was my very first

time, as if it was the greatest achievement of all times;
I was so happy!!!
If anything it was a start.
I was on my way to recovery.
And knowing how quickly I heal I said to my self;
No need to worry Saint Johnny Walker, you're back!!!
I felt I needed a cup of tea, or a coffee for a change.
I pressed the buzzer and within seconds a nurse came in and said;
  "Yes Saint Johnny Walker what can I do for you"?
I recognised her; she was one of the nurses who brought the fruit juice when all those people were in here.
  "First bring the wheelchair close and put the breaks on".
She did.
  "Now, if you don't mind I would like a cup of coffee and a lot of that fruit juice please".
She asked me if I needed help to sit on the chair and I said; no-no I can manage thank you.
She left and there I was attempting the impossible.

I was trying to get my body off the bed and onto the chair.
I thought it would be a piece of cake.
It was worse than climbing a mountain.
I only had the use of my hands and my brains.
And I had to put them both to work, double quick time.
I don't know really if it's because it was my first time doing this but it took me a good three minutes to complete the task, it was really hard work, and not only physically but mentally as well.
I mean it's so frustrating when you want to move your legs and there's no response, the brain works perfectly and gives the rite order but the legs do not respond, as if they have a mind of their own, as if they're so lazy and they prefer sleeping than working.
When I finally made it to the chair, I could think of nothing else except all those people on wheelchairs.
I think they deserve a medal every single day of their entire lives;

what they must be going through every day is indeed, unreal.
I felt as if I just finished a sixteen hour work day.
I never realised they go through an ordeal like this, and I mean day in day out.
And that is only the getting out of bed; I can only imagine what they go thru the rest of the day.
My God…!!!
These people are heroes in my book.
And the worst part is we, the "normal" people, make their lives even harder in some cases, well… more than some cases in fact.
Oh I wish I was a prime minister or something like that.
I was going to pass a bill in the parliament, introducing to all schools a special class that all students will sit on a wheelchair for an hour and do ordinary every day things.
Maybe the world will learn and have a bit more respect.
If anything, when they see a person on a wheelchair they will know what it feels like, what IS like.

Oh I don't know, even if a member of parliament was all for it, in politics there's always something more important; some stupid issue is always more urgent and bla-bla-bla;
In my opinion all politicians are the same.
They promise you the world and they deliver nothing.
All they care about is the fame and they always get involved in a project that they know nothing about, and why…?
Because their name will be written in the history books;
I mean if one actually takes the time and check each one of the ministers, what they have actually studied and what position they hold, will make anyone laugh really.
And it's the same in all the countries in the world.
I mean we hear a thing like the minister of defence is a doctor or the minister of health is a professor of economics etc-etc…
Halloo…!!!
What does a doctor know about defending a country?

And how on earth the professor of
economics would know how to run
the ministry of health?
And another thing I'll never
understand.
Nearly all these politicians are
of a certain age.
To me, their way of thinking would
be for the next five or ten years
and not twenty or thirty, because
they won't be around any more.
I wonder why we vote for these
"oldies"
Why not vote for someone young
with new ideas who would think
fifty or even sixty years ahead,
or someone on a wheelchair even.
Oh I don't know, maybe, just maybe
it's because we won't have
anything to complain about after.
I mean why there's always a strike
for this or that reason?
It's because some old moron passed
a bill that's only good for the
big sharks, and the excuse is
always the same; "it's good for
the future of our country"
Bullshit I always say, they never
think of the "workers" the simple
people.

Don't they realise that without the workers they're nothing.
After all how can it be good for the country if it's no good for its people?
The nurse came in the room with my coffee and a jar of that famous juice.
That took my mind off things.
I asked her where the sister is and she said she was downstairs with the physiotherapist and Jason.

"She goes and comes every half an hour".

"She's very happy, Jason is walking".

"And it's all thanks to you".

"Nearly all the country's doctors and professors are there as well and you can imagine why". She went on;

"I don't know if you know but the leukaemia wards are nearly empty, nearly all the children went home".

"All parents and relatives want to come and thank you, but we didn't allow them".

"We thought that's what you wanted".

I said;
  "Thank you for telling me that and thank you for stopping them too".
Then she said;
  "But we have another little problem now".
  "We have a room full of mail for you; there must be thousands and thousands of letters for you and every day there's more and more coming".
  "I don't know whose decision is, as to what we do with them".
I said;
  "When the sister comes up ask her to see me please".
The girl asked me if I wouldn't mind if she was to give me a hug before she leaves the room and I asked why?
She said;
  "If I do, then you'll know if I have something wrong with me and cure it".
I laughed and said ok and she wasted no time in doing so.
I squeezed her hard.
I felt her heart beat was pumping harder and harder.

I closed my eyes and saw her future as well.
When I let go she looked at me with a lot of worry in her face and was trembling a bit.
She was really scared of what I was to tell her.
The poor kid was trembling from fear in case I do find something wrong.
I said to her;
 "Relax, its ok, you're in perfect health".
In fact I said;
 "You will get married two years from now to a good person who will love you; his name is Stefano and yes, you will have four children of your own, all boys; you will live to be ninety two and you will have eighteen grand children and twenty four great grand children".
I let go of her and saw many tears in her eyes.
She grabbed my hand and kissed it many times.
She said;
 "I'm engaged to Stefano nearly a year now; so you can imagine why I'm crying".

She must have thanked me a dozen times before she left the room.
Mmm; I can foresee the future as well?
Shit, if I can do that I'll make a fortune.
Mmm; first a healer and now a fortune teller; what next I wonder.
I mean everyone says I have the gift.
Now I discovered a new one.
Maybe I possess a few more and I don't know.
Maybe I can fly or go scuba diving without any oxygen.
Ha… wouldn't that be something.
It wasn't long after when Gestapo and Kaiser came in together.
What went on was indescribable.
Gestapo was hysterical; she was all over me; kissing hugging dancing, you name it she was doing it.
Kaiser was just an on looker but was showing signs of happiness.
Even if she wanted to behave differently she couldn't, there was not enough room for her to do anything.

She was restricted to a huge smile in the corner.
Gestapo was the sole protagonist in the room.
She went bonkers; she was acting like a little kid in a play ground with more than enough toys to choose from.
I must have collected a million kisses from her.
Her face was all lit up from joy. When finally she was a bit calm and tired I would say, she just sat at the edge of my bed, looked at me and said;

"Jason is walking" and immediately burst out crying.
She was really crying her eyes out; tears of joy;
It seems she had doubts whether Jason will actually ever walk again, and now she's seen him walk, well I guess every mother has her own way of celebration.
I could see in her face that she wanted to go and see him again just to make sure it's not a dream.
She was trying to describe every step he was taking all by himself, of course he needs to hold on to

something for his balance but he'll walk properly in a day or two according to the doctors.
Just as you predicted she said to me.
  "How did you know all that"?
  "The doctors said he needs to exercise his muscles a bit and he'll not only walk but run as well".
  "Oh thank you… thank you… thank you".
She went crazy again and the kissing started yet again.
I said to her;
  "Ok sister go to him; go and encourage him, and give him a message from me".
  "Sometime tomorrow afternoon when he feels ready I'll wait for him, I have something I want to tell him but he should come walking and with no assistance from anyone, if he happens to fall on his way here, no one must help him up; he should try all by himself, OK sister"?
She said;
  "Yes, I'll gladly give him the message".

She was off like a tornado, hopping and dancing.
Then it was the Kaisers turn.
She finally was able to put in a word or two.
And she goes;
 "Well, what can I say, what can one say after all I've seen; what can one say about you?
 "Who are you"?
 "Where did you come from"?
 "What are you really"?
 "I for one don't know any more how to address you".
 "Sir… Mr… Saint… Angel… What…"???
 "I mean it still didn't sink into any of us what happened here the last ten days".
 "So much in so little time";
 "Not one of us would believe any of what you did, if we haven't actually witnessed it".
 "We witnessed all your miracles and we're still with a lot of questions".
 "There's no other conversation neither here in the hospital nor in our homes with our families".

"Even my little boy last night at our diner table; he raised his glass and said";
"Here's to Saint Johnny Walker".
"I was stunned, he's only six". I said;
"Never mind all that sister, just think of me as a passing storm that left behind enough rain the land needed and no more";
"Shouldn't you be somewhere in a ward or something, looking after things"?
She said;
"Ha… There's only a few children left upstairs and there's hardly anything wrong with them; the doctors keep them here for more tests".
"I know what the results will be and so do the doctors, but they want to make sure".
"A week ago we were short of staff and now we have people doing practically nothing all day".
"Oh shit I murmured, does that mean some people will loose their jobs"?
"No-no-no… don't you worry about that, there's always more sick people coming in the hospital".

"And besides most of the nurses are on different floors already";

"Oh; I thought for a minute I was responsible for job loses". With all this going on I didn't want to remind Gestapo about the dentist so I asked Kaiser instead. I said to her;

"Since you're not so busy would you take me down to the dentists"? She said;

"The dental surgery is closed in the afternoons but I'll call one of the dentists if he can come in for you".

"After all you're Saint Johnny Walker, who can say no to that name around here".
I said;

"I think sister Jeanette already arranged something maybe you ask her first".

"Leave it to me; I'll see what I can do".
She left for a few minutes and that gave me the chance to check on my own healing progress.
I must get off this wheelchair and walk again.
I moved my toes and they seemed ok, I then moved my legs left and

right, they seemed ok too, so I put one foot down on the floor and then the other.

"So far so good I murmured; now let's see if I can stand up". And of course "Mr knows it all" thru my excitement, I forgot to put the breaks on the wheelchair and yes; I am sure you must have guessed it; the inevitable of course happened.

As I pushed the chair downwards to lift my body up, the chair of course rolled backwards and no matter how much effort I put into steadying it, there was no way of stopping it.

Before I knew it I was on the floor and needless to say I was in deep shit yet again.

I must have landed on my arm and hit my head on the foot rest of the chair.

Within seconds I found my self on the floor, in a pool of blood and with a broken arm.

Oh what pain, I was in agony.

It took some time for Kaiser to come back and when she did, she was actually screaming, she was on

her knees pressing hard on my head wound and screaming for help.
Two nurses came running;
She said;
  "Get the stretcher quickly".
Within seconds I was on a bed with wheels and heading towards first aid, I think.
They stitched me up and then strait to X-rays for my arm and of course it "had" to be broken.
I mean what is it with this hospital?
Or is it me?
It's as if I'm not allowed to go anywhere else.
I must stay here for some reason.
I asked the sister not to take me to that horrible man the plasterer;
I said;
  "Just wrap my arm a bit tight and leave the rest to me".
She looked at me silently and I said;
  "Don't worry I know what I'm saying".
She said;
  "Another one of your miracles I suppose yea"?
I repeated;

"Just wrap it that's all".
She said;
"Ok, I suppose you know best".
Then said;
"Well, are you going to tell me how you managed to do all this damage again"?
I said;
"It's a long story; let's just say I was trying to be cleaver".
All the way back to my room I was thinking.
What is it that's keeping me hear?
There must be something else I have to do here before I leave this hospital;
I mean how else can I or anyone else for that matter explain this?
I was thinking I did enough and had in mind by tomorrow I'll move into a hotel for a couple of days, until my flight home, but this place, this hospital is not ready to release me yet;
I mean haven't I done enough for these people?
I mean I've even been to hell and back twice over.
What more can I do?
I'm tired of all this.

If this is God's doing, let him find someone else for a change.
Why doesn't he give me a break?
It's not fair;
I think I deserve a break.
If this thing carries on I'll go crazy to say the least.
Shit, what if I'll never be able to exit the hospital?
No-no-no… I must think positive.
I was covert from head to toe with a white sheet and could not see anything nor could I move in case I give someone a heart attack.
But the smell of food was piercing thru the sheet.
Oh I could do with some of that and a couple of beers to wash it down with.
Yes, I'll think only of grub and booze.
Oh I miss my local pub, even though sometimes it's a bit on the miserable side, I still miss it.
We finally arrived and there she was none other than Gestapo with my dinner.
Shit, I hope she won't give me another lecture.
Instead she laughed.
She said;

"I'm laughing because I think you're doing it on purpose".

"I think you must like it here and want to stay".

"Or you think we're not convinced yet of your powers and want another exhibition".

"And the third thing that comes to my mind is that you must like pain".

"Apart from being an Angel, are you a masochist too"?

"Forgive me for laughing but I know by tomorrow all these injuries will disappear".

I just smiled, couldn't really answer or say anything; after all, I am looking for the same answer too.

They both lifted me up and sat me on my bed.

I said;

"I want to walk a bit, would you help me"?

Gestapo was the closest to the good arm and she helped me stand. I could only manage a couple of inches with every step.

But I was happy; at least I was on the way to recovery.

This morning I couldn't even move my toes.
Kaiser said;
 "Tomorrow afternoon you have an appointment with the dentist, I hope there's not going to be any more accidents and miss it again".
I was still walking, if one can call this walking and said;
 "Tomorrow I'll walk to the dental surgery, you'll see".
I must admit that walk tired me.
I wanted to find an excuse to sit and the answer was dinner.
I said;
 "My dinner is getting cold; can I sit at the table and eat now"?
 "I'm starving, what is it"?
She said;
 "I don't know let's see".
She took out of the bag this huge, wrapped with foil tray and… aha… carbonara!!!
Oh the aroma as she unwrapped it!!!
And it looked impressive too.
 "Come ladies I said there's enough to feed an army here".
The ladies were a bit shy and said;
 "No, we're not allowed".

"Bullshit" I said; "not allowed"?
I said;
"If you don't join me I will not eat either".
OK, I'll admit it, I was trying to impress and show off a bit.
But as it happens I didn't mind their company at all; after all these two ladies were the only ones I could talk to in this hospital without answering questions all the time.
Reluctantly Kaiser went and got a couple of plastic plates and forks.
We shared it all and started munching away.
I asked the girls if we can all have some beer and again the answer was no.
Of course I insisted and the "no" became "yes", only because they were officially off duty.
I felt a bit guilty when I heard the off duty thing and said;
"I'm sorry, you must be tired and want to go home, and selfish me, still keeping you here, I am really sorry".

They were both very polite and said;
"No-no, it's not you and all that".
I said;
"Whenever you fill like going, don't let me stop you; the only thing I want from you is information".
"How's Jason doing"?
His mother said;
"He was so tired with all that effort he put in today we booked him in a room; he was actually walking on his own but had to hold on to something for his balance; his last walk was eighteen feet"!!!
I said;
"He needs another day with a supervisor and he'll be confident enough to go on his own; then he will start working on his running; I assure you, within a month he will never want to walk, he will want only to run".
"Don't discourage him, let him move the way he wants".
"This will last a little over three months, and then he will ask

you for a bike, don't say no, get him one".
  "But wait until he asks for it".
  "He will use it for a couple of years until he goes to collage".
She asked;
  "How do you know all that?
  "I saw his future, I know".
  "Can you tell me more"?
  "I can tell you he will go to England to study and become a doctor; in fact a very successful and famous one; he will marry a doctor from Scotland and you will have four grand children three girls and a boy".
  "The boy will be the youngest and he will name him Johnny".
The tears were a none stop thing, like a dripping tap.
I don't think a person could be any happier than she was.
She could not stop crying from happiness.
She was kissing my hand and saying "thank you, thank you".
I said to Kaiser;
Better take her out of here before I start crying.
Kaiser also was wiping off her tears and said;

"Before we go shall we help you to your bed"?
I said;
"No, I'll just sit here and concentrate on healing my self, if I need help I'll call for a nurse".

"Goodnight girls and drive safely".

They were about to open the door and Gestapo came back and gave me the biggest hug in the world; she was squeezing and squeezing me.
I couldn't breathe for good minute.
I was signalling Kaiser with my hands for help.
She pulled her off me.
I said;

"Goodnight ladies" again and Kaiser was holding her just in case she comes back for another hug.
I got up slowly and dead slow made it to my bed.
I wanted a little more exercise and did a couple of rounds in the room holding on to the wheelchair.
I used the loo and then to my bed.

It was a bit of a struggle but not as bad as I first thought it would be.
I took my dear diary and wrote the days events.
Yes pal, another day is gone, and what a day!!!
And yes, I've done it yet again.
This time it was my head and my arm.
I wonder if there's a part of my body I didn't manage to abuse.
Who is punishing me and why?
Maybe if I say I'll stay here then things may change.
And there's me thinking I'll book a hotel room for a couple of days.
Ha… that's another of my stupid jokes.
I must get it through my thick head I'll never see the sun again; I mean what was I thinking?
And then it hit me.
Yes, I found the answer.
Why didn't I think of it before?
I mean the answer was there in front of me and could not see it, how stupid of me.
The roof…!!!
Yes the roof…!!!

I'll get all the sunshine I want and need.
And no one will disturb me what!!!
I'll be out of any hooligan's reach too.
First thing in the morning I'll ask the girls if they'll take me to the roof.
What if they refuse?
No, they wouldn't do that.
I mean why would they?
I remember one of them saying, "Who can say no to Saint Johnny Walker"?
No-no… They wouldn't dare refuse.
Oh that made me happy.
I mean the idea alone is worth more than million pounds.
Who else would think of an idea like this?
Getting a suntan at a hospital roof;
I mean if that's not an idea I don't know what is;
I'll ask Gestapo to lock me up there and throw away the key.
Oh I'm great I am…!!!
Now I could go to sleep and dream of tomorrow.
Naked on the roof…!!!
Ha…!!!

I don't think anyone has ever done this before;
Hell, I don't think anyone has even thought of it either;
Oh I can't wait.
I turned the lights out and lay back.
What a day!!!
And what an idea!!!
Surely tomorrow will definitely be a wonderful day.
I mean what can possibly go wrong?
I'll be on the roof and no one will know.
I'll get at least a suntan out of all this.
Maybe God will give me a break after all;
Wow!!!
Get a suntan on the roof of a hospital; I still can't believe I thought of that;
And there is no way, and I mean no way anything will or could even, go wrong;
No way;
Hahaha… How little did I know;

Saint Johnny Walker's
"How to… Become a Saint"

Chapter Thirteen
Day twelve

I must have really needed the sleep something terrible because, I was awaken by Mamma Anna with my tea and cookies, and her sweet little voice saying;
 "Good morning Saint Johnny Walker".
I said;
 "Good morning Mamma" and she gave me the usual hug and a couple of kisses on both cheeks.
For those who are surrounded with "real" love could understand this true and unique feeling, and when I say "real" I mean the love that comes out of someone's heart naturally, no pretence of any kind;
I mean is there a nicer way to wake up or is there?
I sat on the bed sipping away and full of smiles looking at the old lady trying hard to please me straitening the covers over my

legs, picking up bits and pieces from the floor, rearranging a few cuddly toys and at the same time giving me the look as if she was asking me in a silent way if there was anything else she could do for me.
I said;
   "Thank you Mamma, you're so good, you're spoiling me".
She just smiled and gave me another hug and a few more kisses and said;
   "Thank you son for giving me a few more years and that there's a surprise for you in about half an hour or so, rite after the doctors round".
I asked her about my day, "would it be quiet for a change or one of the same".
And on her way out she said;
   "Do you really believe that you were sent here to have a quiet day"?
 Oh shit, shit and shit again;
And I was looking forward for a "sunbath" all day on the roof.
Shit man, shit…!!!
Surprise huh, now what the hell can that be…???

I must be having a visitor, probably one of those big sharks again.
That's all I need.
I'll pretend I'm sick or something, I don't fancy seeing anyone like that, they're all the same, full of pretence smile and show off; probably bring with him a team of TV reporters as well.
I know; I'll lock myself in the toilet and never come out.
I quickly got up and surprise-surprise.
I could walk properly again.
I was a normal person again, hurray…!!!
Only my arm still hurts a bit.
I must concentrate on that.
I used the loo and then brushed my teeth.
The minute I came out, the cleaning ladies came in along with the linen ladies.
It took them just three minutes to do their work but they wouldn't go, they were messing around pretending they're working and looking at me constantly.
I could see in their faces that they wanted answers to all those

questions they wouldn't dare for some reason ask me.
After a few minutes of looking at that, I just had enough of "the look" and said;
  "Come on ladies, out… out".
I mean I had to shed whatever Italian I've learned and said;
 "Basta… Basta" I think that means enough.
I mean this is ridiculous, how long can one sit there and take that?
Being stared at and I do mean constantly by four pairs of eyes, it's not really a nice way to start one's day, is it?
They disappeared in two seconds.
I wish Anna would come back with some more tea.
Instead, the doctors came thru the door;
And there were quite a number of them too.
I felt as if all the hospital's doctors were in my room.
The usual "good morning Saint Johnny Walker";
  "How are we today"?
  "I see you had a little accident yet again".

Oh don't rub it in mate, please.
  "I feel fine doctor and there's nothing wrong any more with me, I think it's time I check myself out".
  "If not today by tomorrow the latest";
He said;
  "You're in a bit of a hurry all of a sudden, why"?
I said;
  "There's nothing you can do for me any more, you patched me up, fixed a few parts of me that needed fixing and I thank you for that, but now I feel there's nothing else for you to fix, nothing wrong with me any more".
  "Nevertheless according to the injuries you sustained you must stay here for a few weeks more".
  "We want to be sure before we release you";
"Halloo"…!!!
"Doctors"…!!!
"Look at me"!!!
I got up from my wheelchair and started hopping and dancing.
  "Do you thing a sick person would or could do that"?

"The only thing that's keeping me here is the dental sergeant and nothing else".
"I think I have the rite to sign my self out yes"?
He and every one of the "bunch" were stunned.
It's the first time from the day I arrived here that I actually talked as firm as that.
"OK" he said;
"If that's what you really want, but I would advice you to stay a few days more at least, just to be sure".
"Ok" I said;
"Only because I need the dentist";
He took my blood pressure and a lot of bla-bla with the rest of the bunch;
If you ask me it was all gibberish.
I mean it's the same thing over and over again, every morning he repeats himself to the students.
"Here we have an accident victim who had signs of broken this and broken that and the x-rays showed this, and we did that and we put him on… etc… etc…"

I mean I ask you, if that's not gibberish, I don't know what gibberish is.
And I actually saw a few students repeating his exact words as he was telling them, in a silent way of course and were trying hard not to laugh;
I did allow him to finish what he started and he said to some students;
  "You're not taking any notes I see".
I mean what notes?
The guys knew it all by heart.
He looked a bit upset.
I don't know if it was because I spoke to him a bit firmly or because the "kids" didn't write anything down, whatever they were supposed to write.
He turned around and left without even a goodbye or something, which was unusual.
Oups… what have I done?
I created an enemy, I think.
The minute they left I got back into my bed.
I was still thinking who this visitor is?

I mean what other surprise can it be apart from a visitor?
I can't even sneak out and hide.
If I go out there they'll lynch me.
I wonder if the doctor was pissed off with me and wanted revenge, he could have my "bodyguards" outside my door dismissed just like that.
Shit, I wonder if they're still there.
I must find out.
I got out of the bed and went to the door.
Well; I'm glad I was dressed up.
As I opened the door to look for the guards, only an inch or two, and the surprise I was waiting for was there in the corridor coming towards me.
It was Gestapo, Kaiser, a few nurses and about a million kids with their parents.
All holding lit candles and headed straight towards me.
Oh shit, I panicked;
I didn't know what to do.
Are all these people coming for me?
Who are they?

I could only recognise one or two kids from a few days ago from upstairs, the ones with no hair.
I thought they were all cured and went home; what are they doing back here?
Shit, there must be millions of them.
There's no point in sitting up in my bed, life will be difficult, better if I sit on my wheelchair.
I only just made it to the chair when the door opened.
The first to come in was Kaiser and Gestapo.
And within seconds the room was filled with kids, all holding a lit candle.
The room was too small for all of them and the door was left opened.
There must have been a lot of them out in the corridor.
And to my surprise they started singing Jingle Bells…!!!
What!!!
I was absolutely and totally stunned!!!
Jingle Bells?
It's only November for Christ sake.

Their Xmas must be earlier than ours.
Maybe Santa visits Mediterranean countries first then goes to England.
I mean I was really enjoying the whole thing.
I was really touched;
It brought a few tears to my eyes.
When they finished singing, one by one the kids were blowing their candles off and reaching for a hug.
They were all saying "thank you Saint Johnny Walker".
I felt my heart was melting every time a kid was thanking me.
Their actual words were.
   "Gracie Mille San Johnny Walker"
Some of the little ones were actually sitting on my lap and hugging me ever so tight.
Then it was the parents.
One by one they were coming in, thanking me and all of them left an envelope containing a card and money.
I said to Kaiser;
   "I don't want any money from these people".
   "Add it to the fund".

She laughed and said;
 "All these people gave a lot of money for the hospital fund, this is something for you".
The kissing and hugging was a non stop.
I was glad I was in a sitting position; otherwise I was going to collapse.
All these people…!!!
I mean how?
I don't remember helping so many?
Where did the rest come from?
This went on and on.
At some point I said to Gestapo.
 "How many more is there"?
She had a look out the door and said;
 "The queue is quite long, so I don't know".
 "Can't you do something"?
She laughed and said;
 "Not really; unless you faint, and don't even think of doing that".
 "Some of these people came from very far just to pay their respects and thank you personally".
I asked her;
 "Can we at least have a break"?

She whispered in my ear;
  "It will be lunch time soon".
And it went on and on.
And the queue was getting bigger and bigger.
There was no end.
Parents, grand parents, great grand parents, all sorts of relatives, friends, family friends, a friend of a friend, you name it.
I was asking my self all sorts of questions.
How many relatives for every child?
Isn't it enough the parents only for a thank you?
And the friend, or the family friend, or the friend of a friend, what the hell are they doing here?
It must be curiosity.
I mean there's no other explanation.
I mean a friend of a friend?
Come on!!!
What other explanation is there?
I looked towards my bed and it was covered with envelopes.
There was a mountain of them and were actually falling on the floor.

I mean it was bad enough half the room was taken by all those cuddly toys and now this.
The smell of food was in the air and Kaiser took it upon her to put an end to this "ordeal"
She started saying to everyone, "enough for today, it's time for his medication, he needs a rest now, please go home now", and that was that.
She came back in and I said;
   "Thank you sister, I think you saved my life".
She looked at me, smiled and said;
   "That's funny, I thought that was your job, and both sisters laughed.
I said to both;
   "What are we going to do with all that", and pointed to my bed.
Gestapo laughed and said;
   "You think that's bad"?
   "Did you know there's a roomful of these and it's all locked up, all of them have your name on them".
   "Maybe one day we'll help you read a few of them, as for the rest I don't know what you're going to do with them".

468

"Let me go and get your lunch first".
I decided to open one or two and asked Kaiser if she would do the same.
I picked one and there were three twenty pound notes inside and a letter saying;
"Dear Saint Johnny Walker, thank you for giving my nephew a chance to live a normal life";
"You see my wife and I don't have any children of our own and Andreas is my only nephew";
"We see him as our own";
"I know sixty pounds is probably a drop in the ocean for some, but for me and my wife is more than little".
"We also gave for the hospital twice as much".
"We feel we owe you much-much and much more; in fact we'll never be able to repay for what you've done for us";
"We know you came to our country to help us, and know you'll be going soon to another country to do the same; all that requires money, it will make us happy

knowing you've accepted this small contribution from us";
  "God bless you and may He give you strength to carry on;
  "You're always in our thoughts and in our prayers";
  "Saint Johnny Walker, thank you thank you thank you".
  Signed Gianni xxx Maria xxx Andrea xxx
Well…!!!
I mean what one can say to all that?
And it's not even their own child.
And where did he get the English money from?
Kaiser said;
  "This one is pretty much the same and here you have five twenty pound notes" Kaiser said;
We opened a few more and there were money in every one.
There was one that had a cheque for a thousand pounds!!!
Another one from a grand mother with five dollars;
I mean I started shedding tears.
I couldn't carry on opening letters, I was really crying like a baby with what I saw.
I was really "moved"

470

All these people trusted me with probably every penny they had or could afford for my expenses around the world with the hope I will carry on doing what I do.
It was like sponsoring me and urging me to carry on.
I don't seem to have a choice now.
I must carry on.
There must be a small fortune here.
I mean we only opened about a dozen envelopes and there was nearly two thousand pounds already in the drawer.
Shit, I will need a week or so to read them all and answer them.
Oh no I checked the ones I opened and realised there was no address on any of them, how was I suppose to thank them?
Kaiser said;
　"People don't need for you to thank them, they know already".
　"They trust in you".
　"They know you'll do the rite thing".
　"You will use the money to go where you're needed most, just like when we needed you here, and you came".

And she added;

"God Bless you Saint Johnny Walker"!!!

"Yes sister but there's a lot of money here; surely I won't need as much just for travelling".

"I can't accept any of this money".
She said;

"You will know when the rite time comes what to do with the rest".
Gestapo came back with lunch.
She said;

"I brought extra for all of us".

"We're having lunch together, and then help you open a few letters and then we're visiting to the dentist".

"Although the dental surgery is open to the public only in the mornings, he said he'll come back after lunch especially for you".

"He was happy when I mentioned your name".

"He's a very pleasant guy and a bit of a joker".

"He adores joking all the time".
He said;

"AHA… I will be in the history books";

472

"I treated a Saint and not just a Saint".
"Saint Johnny Walker no less" Gestapo prepared the table and we all sat around.
And what a feast!!!
It was a bit of everything.
"A Greek meze what"!!!
About twenty different little dishes;
Wow!!!
I said.
"Even if one is not hungry, just seeing all that wouldn't resist diving in".
And the temptation is even greater if there are a couple of cans of beer on the table.
We wasted no time and got stuck into it.
We were eating and eating but no way to finish it all.
Then another surprise;
Jason came in, walking of course, he was with walking sticks, he looked so happy.
He came straight to me and gave me a hug that lasted a good five minutes.
He just wouldn't le go.

He was all "thank you"… and "thank you"… and crying his eyes out.
As for the mother, she was in a worse condition.
She was murmuring something like "I still don't believe it; my son is walking"; and of course the water works;
She was looking up, crossing herself and repeating over and over again, "thank you God".
And I was saying over and over to the kid;
   "Its ok Jason; don't mention it, enough".
I guess he wanted to show me his appreciation the poor kid.
Finally he let go of me and sat down.
He asked me if there's anything he could do to repay for the use of his legs?
I said;
   "Yes, you can help in finishing all this "Gastronomic Pandesia" and pointed to the table; then help open a few letters".
The kid must have been hungry because he was really enjoying it, just like the rest of us.

Then we all started opening and opening letter after letter.
There was no way I could read each and every one of them;
I would have needed a month of Sundays to go through them all.
An hour or so later two nurses came to the room with four more big black bags full of more letters and said;
  "There's another ten of these at the reception".
Oh my God!!!
I said to the two sisters;
  "Ladies, you will have to help me with all theses".
Kaiser said;
  "I'll bring another two nurses from upstairs OK"?
  "Yes, thank you sister".
She went and ten minutes later she came back with two more girls.
She introduces them to me;
  "This is Marina".
I said;
  "Hi, shook her hand and said thanks for coming".
  "And this is Jasmine".
  "Hi jasmine, thanks for coming and shook her hand".

Suddenly something hit me in the brains.
I held her hand really tight closed my eyes and said;
 "I see a house, there's an old lady sitting by the fire place, Katrina, there's an old man in bed, Juliano?
 "I see a baby and a little girl, Julia"?
I opened my eyes and said to the girl, "you know them"?
She said;
 "It's my grand parents and my two little girls".
 "Why"?
 "What is wrong"?
She panicked and started shouting "my babies, what is wrong with my babies"?
I said;
 "Call them immediately, tell them to get out of the house quickly and call the fire brigade".
 "The house is on fire".
She just went hysterical, she was screaming and then at some point she fainted.

Kaiser rushed out of the room and Gestapo and the other nurse were trying to bring her around.
When she came to, she was saying in a panicky way;
 "My babies my babies"
I said to Gestapo;
 "Can someone drive her home"?
 "She shouldn't drive in this condition".
 "No problem she said I'll drive her".
And off they went.
Kaiser came back and said;
 "I called her house and said to the grand mother to get everyone out of the house then called the fire brigade".
The rest of us carried on with the letters.
All three of them Kaiser, Marina the nurse and little Jason were a bit nervous thinking of the fire and the people in the house;
They were very worried.
They were discussing amongst them whether they came out OK.
I said;
 "Don't worry, everything is ok".
 "No one will be hurt".

"And the firemen will manage to save the house too".

"The only damage will be the kitchen".

Marina asked me how I knew all theses things.

I said;

"I just saw it all when she shook my hand".

"The grand father went to lie down in his bed, the grandmother fell asleep on the rocking chair in the living room, the baby was in the pram and the little girl was just playing with her dolls on the floor".

"The granny forgot to turn off the gas cooker, the oil cot fire and it spread to the cupboards".

"And by the time the firemen will get there the kitchen will be, well, not destroyed but in real mess".

"But they'll all manage to come out no problem".

"So relax guys".

"Trust me, I know".

They were somewhat at ease, but I could sense the worry was there still.

About an hour and a half past and there they were.
They came back and surprise-surprise.
Jasmine was giving me kisses and kisses.
 "How did you know and all that"; It happened exactly as I said it did.
They were all looking at me in a weird way, as if they were like… scared from me.
I felt brotherly love around me and yet I sensed the fear in them as well.
And I noticed they were trying to avoid any kind of contact with my hand every time I was reaching for another letter.
And I think I knew why.
Just in case they will here me saying there's another thing wrong with their family or something like that.
Gestapo said;
 "It's time for the joker, you know, the dentist".
 "Get ready; I'll be back in a minute".
She came back with the two guards and a stretcher bed.

"Are you ready Saint Johnny Walker"?
As usual I was covered with the white sheet from head to toe pretending I was a stiff.
When we arrived there and Gestapo pulled the sheet off me, I saw the dentist holding a battery operated toy drill and immediately he turned it on and said;
   "AHA… Now it's my turn".
   "Now I know why they call you the joker" I said;
I suppose he wanted to live up to his name.
After the X-rays and a general check up he said;
   "I'll arrange a temporary set for you and I'll have them ready by tomorrow".
I thanked him and we left the same way we came, pretending I was a corpse.
When we went back to the room I saw a few more volunteers there to help with the letters, two more nurses and a doctor.
They were piling up the money and throwing away the empty envelopes.

I noticed there was another pile with cheques and another with dollars.
At least my bed was cleared from all those letters.
But the bags were coming in four at a time.
Every time a new envelope was opened the amount was announced and one of the nurses was actually writing it down on the back of an empty envelope and from what I saw she was on her fifth envelop.
I didn't know whether keeping a record of the amount was for me or from keeping anyone getting any funny ideas.
This went on until dinner time when Kaiser said;
 "Come everybody, duty calls".
She looked at me and said;
 "Enough for today";
 "We'll carry on tomorrow".
And one by one they were leaving the room.
Jasmine was hugging me and kissing my hand and repeating a few times "thank you thank you".
Kaiser said;

"I have to go up for my rounds, so I'll say goodnight and I'll see you tomorrow";
She bows, kisses my hand and leaves.
I said to Gestapo;
"This is ridicules and very embarrassing".
"It has to stop".
"No matter how many times I said to people not to kiss my hand, they still do it".
"What must I say to them to end this"?
She said;
"People respect you and look at you as a person representing God no less".
"A real live Angel"!!!
"This is what we do in our country".
"You're like an icon in the church, only difference is that you're alive and what's more you're a miracle worker".
"You're a healer"!!!
"To every one of us you're Saint Johnny Walker"!!!
"Kissing your hand or your feet for us is a sign or respect".

"But it's very embarrassing for me".

"I mean there's Sister Margaret for example, she kisses my hand, and it should have been the other way round".

"Or you saw for yourself a few grandmothers did the same thing, if anything I should have shown a bit more respect towards them, the age difference for example".
She said;
"You have to understand they don't look at the age, as far as they know you're an Angel, you're sent here by God Himself and there's absolutely nothing you do or say that will change all that".

"You're in their hearts and they pray for you every day for God to keep you well and do His work".

"And yes; that includes me too by the way".

"You're the "chosen one".

"Anyway I'll go and get your dinner, I'll be back in fifteen" and off she went.
Good, that will give me enough time for a quick shower.
And within ten minutes I came out fresh.

The five minutes more that took Gestapo to come back, gave me the chance to think quietly and with no interruptions.
And the first thing that came to my mind was the damages in jasmine's grandmother's house.
I wonder if they can afford to repair all that.
How could they?
I must find out.
I'll ask Gestapo, she seems to know everything.
She came in a minute later and I asked her a few things.
I said;

"Tell me about jasmine, can she afford to repair all the damages from the fire"?

"No I don't think so she said; it will probably take them a few years to pay for all that".

"She lost her husband when she was six months pregnant".

"She can't even afford a baby sitter while she's at work".

"She has no parents either".

"The only help she gets is from her brother who works on a fishing boat and as you can imagine is not really that big a help".

I said;
　"I want you to do a few things for me".
　"First find out the full names and dates of birth of the children".
　"2nd get me the yellow pages for this town".
　"3rd Find out the address of the damaged house";
　"And 4th do not say anything to her".
I noticed a smile in her as she shook her head as if she knew what was I planning.
She said;
　"You will have to dine by yourself tonight".
　"I've got to go home and see to Jason".
　"It's his first night home "without wheels" and… well I'm sure you can understand".
She went to the reception and brought the yellow pages.
She said;
　"I know what you're thinking and I'll help you with the search tomorrow".
　"I must go now; Jason is waiting for me downstairs".

The smell of fish and chips was all over the room and I could not wait any longer.
I unwrapped and didn't even use a fork.
Straight in with my fingers;
That took me back home for a minute when we buy from the local chip shop a take away and before we reach home it's all gone, and instead of going home we head straight to the local pub.
Pub?
Shit, I wonder, is there any left in the fridge?
Quickly I checked the fridge and… oh yes, what a relief.
I still had a couple of cans in there.
And they were nice and cool.
They didn't last that long though.
I finished everything in no time at all.
Beer, fish and all the chips;
I was happy.
I was relaxed.
I went through the yellow pages and marked a few ads.
It was still very early for bed so I turned the TV on.

And of course, nothing but a lot of rubbish as usual;
I felt lonely and there was no one to talk to.
Shit, this is worse than prison, at least there they allow you to go out the cell for a walk, I think.
I can't even go out the door here.
I'll open a few letters to pas my time.
I opened the first one;
There were two five hundred dollar notes in.
And the note said;
   "Dear Saint Johnny Walker"
   "I have so much to thank you for and I don't know from where to begin, I can not even find the rite words to express whatever I really want to say".
Expressing gratitude, gratefulness or even a simple thank you in black and white I thought it would be easier than in person; I am the mother of little Isabella, remember? The four year old you saved from sure death, who by the way she really sends her love and wanted me to say she'll never go to sleep ever again without Saint

Johnny the teddy bear you gave her".

"She also asked me if there's such a thing as sending kisses through letters".

"She doesn't know how many is one billion and I don't know from where she heard it, but when I said yes, she said make sure mommy he knows I sent him one billion kisses, and when she said that she actually spread her arms as wide as she could".

"She also mentions you in her prayers every night".

"My husband and I tried to come and thank you in person but it was impossible".

"The one thousand dollar is not all from us; it's from all the people in our village, we only gave fifty".

"I know the fifty dollar is by no way near what we wanted to send to you towards your travelling expenses but times are a bit hard".

"Thank you… thank you… thank you…"
And the rest of the page was full of   XXXXXXXXXXXXXXXXXXXX

That brought a few tears in my eyes.
Shit, if I'm going to get emotional every time, I mite as well quit.
I looked at the drawer where they put all that money and murmured; there's an idea, count the money.
The nurse must be a tidy girl because she arranged dollars pounds and checks all separately.
And it was all written down how much of each.
I looked at her notes and it said;
 "Dollars, twenty-four thousand and something…"
 "GBP, fifty one thousand and something…"
 "Italian Lire I don't know how many billion"
 And cheques, sixteen thousand and something;
 OH-MY-GOD… there's a bloody fortune here.
As for the Italian Lire, well, I just could not work out the amount; it had so many zeros;
I can't accept all that.
And there's a lot more in the room behind the reception.

I immediately started thinking, millions of questions;
My mind was working overtime;
I found my self answering my own questions;
Shit, what the hell I'm I going to do with all this money?
I think I'll retire!!!
Maybe I'll buy the flat I'm staying in.
No, I can't do that, the money does not belong to me.
People trusted me with their contributions with one thing in mind.
I must do the rite thing here.
I must prove I am a trustworthy person.
I'll do what people want me to do.
Yes that's it;
I'll travel the world and do what people want and trusted me to do.
I remembered what Anna the tea lady said.
  "You will travel the world and help people that need you and some won't know you did".
What name she'll I use?
If I go by the Saint Johnny Walker everyone will know.
I'll just use my old name;

I mean who will even suspect.
Yes, that's what I'll do.
Oh shit, I just remembered something.
I went over to my things and checked the date on my ticket.
Shit, I am booked to fly tomorrow evening.
Shit, I won't be able to make it.
I still have the dentist, and I must manage somehow to put all this money in a bank or something.
I don't want to carry all that cash with me;
Mmm; maybe that's not such a bad idea;
What if they stop me at the airport and see all that cash?
They'll think I nicked it from somewhere for sure;
And if that happens, I'll end up behind bars;
Surely they would not believe a story like…
   "People just gave it to me"
Ha… good idea my ass;
Shit, I'm going to miss the schedule flight.
I wonder if I can change the date on the ticket.
I must call tomorrow and find out.

Time passed and I felt tired.
I had no more beer in the fridge so, best if I turn in;
I got into my bed and started writing the days events in my diary.
Hi there pal;
Another day gone;
And what a day it has been, full of excitements.
Yet another miracle as the people here calls it.
Poor Jasmine, she must have gone to hell and back.
I must do something for her.
I simply must do something in return for all the kindness I was shown here.
That's it then pal, our so called holiday is nearly over.
Funny how time flies when you're having fun huh?
Ha… having fun, isn't that a joke!!!
Twelve days in a sunny island and yet I managed to "hide" my self in a hospital.
I wonder if I ever decide to write the story down; will there be anyone out there who would believe me?

And what will I call it?
  "Two weeks in the sun, without the sun"
Or maybe "free winter holiday"
Or maybe even, "how to become a saint"
Mmm; that really sounds good;
Oh I don't know really, if what Mamma Anna said is true, I wouldn't have the time;
Maybe in twenty or thirty years from now, when I'll no longer be able to "Perform" any more;
I'm glad I write all these events down every day, at least it will keep me busy when I retire and maybe, just maybe I'll find the courage to put it all in black and white;
Oh I'm so tired.
What a day!!!
Come to think of it, the only thing that didn't happen was;
I didn't hurt my self today in any way.
Isn't that a surprise?
Ha-ha, one could describe this day as, a "day off"
Tomorrow will be an even easier day.

I've only got a couple of things to do and that's that.
I turned the lights out and lay back thinking.
A couple of things that's all.
It must be a good and a quiet day tomorrow.
After all, it is my last day here and I certainly don't want anything "untoward" to happen yet again;
It must be a quiet and above all, injury free day;
Hahaha…
Little did I know what was on the agenda for me?
Instead, the next day or should say my last day on this so called "paradise island" turned out to be the worse day of my so called "holiday" here yet.
Ha; I still cannot believe I have spent my "entire" winter holiday in a hospital;

Saint Johnny Walker's "How to... Become a Saint"

Chapter Fourteen
Day Thirteen

For some reason I woke up in the middle of the night and no matter how hard I tried, just couldn't go back to sleep.
So I decided since it's my last day here to get up, have a shower and a shave.
But when it came to the shaving part I changed my mind.
I decided to leave the beard I have grown and just trim it a bit;
I'm a new person now, so I'll change my image as well, after all, I'm Saint Johnny Walker now, I must "look" the part, be more... distinguish and all that.
Mmm... new look huh?
A new me;
Maybe that's not such a bad idea;
I'll quit my job and do what people want me to do;
Just travel the world, hell I can afford it now.
And what's more, I have a mission now.

Shit, I'll become one of those missionaries.
Ha… a missionary, me!!!
Shit that sounds terrible.
I mean I'm not even religious.
I'm glad I don't have to preach.
Oh I wish Anna was here with some tea.
I know; I'll ask the girl at the reception.
Last time I did that, I scared the shit out of her poor girl.
I'll pres the buzzer so I won't scare her.
It took less than ten seconds for her to appear and said;
  "Saint Johnny Walker, what are you doing out of bed at this time in the morning"?
I asked the time and for some tea if she would be kind enough.
She said;
  "It is four am and I will gladly make some tea for you"
I said;
 "If you don't mind since I was up, to keep you company at the reception for a while".
She agreed to that of course.
I mean who can "ignore" a pair of eyes like that?

The two guards outside they were awake for change and they also came to the reception.
We spend the next hour or so drinking tea and of course the usual bombardment of questions that I could not answer.
It was so quiet and I felt relaxed, it gave me the chance to think a few of the questions before I answered them.
The main questions were;
   "When you passed away, where did you go"?
   "What's it like"?
   "Did you still have feelings"?
   "How did you come back"?
   "Is there a way coming back"?
   "Did you see God"?
   "Did He give you instructions"?
   "How does the soul travel"?
   "Did you actually see heaven"?
   "What is it like"?
I mean even though I couldn't answer these questions I can understand why all that curiosity.
It's the fear of unknown;
The only thing "man" fears the most is the unknown.
All throughout the bombardment I sensed and actually saw it in

their faces; the fear of the unknown.
And the most important answer they wanted to hear was the way back, they were insisting on that.
I was asked that question time and time again.
It was clear why.
I suppose they wanted to know, when their time comes, they won't get lost out there, they'll know the way back beforehand.
I decided enough was enough.
I mean this is no way near a conversation.
This is being cornered and being bombarded from all sides.
I thanked them for the tea and the "conversation" and went back to my room.
It was still dark out there and thought I'll trim a little more my beard, since there was nothing else to do, just to kill time.
I spent the next hour or so "admiring" my self in front of the mirror when I realised it was breaking daylight;
I heard people moving up and down the corridor.
Aha, finally people are awake.

How can people sleep for so long I'll never know;
I mean I was awake a good three hours ago.
Lazy bastards!!!
Oups… I must stop swearing.
Especially now that I am a Saint;
I wonder, all these "Saints" did they ever swore?
I mean before they became Saints, or during?
Mmm… if I ask a priest a question like that, I wonder what the answer will be.
And another thing; how does one really become a Saint?
As far as I know the church declares or awards Sainthood after ones death, I think.
I mean what is the poor guy going to do with the title after death anyway;
That means I will be in the history books as the first living Saint!!!
No, I'm supposed to travel incognito, and do what I'm supposed to do.
I'll travel under my own name.

Then again, how would any church know who I am to award me with the title?
Ha; there goes the history book.
Unless they "discover" me, with by own name;
Then again I won't be called Saint Johnny but Saint Tony.
Actually that doesn't sound so bad.
Maybe I'll even name the hotel I always wanted to buy, "The Saint Tony"
Or even "Flying Tony";
Mmm; I like it!!!
Suddenly the door opened and I heard Kaiser and Gestapo saying "good morning Saint Johnny Walker";
  "The night nurse told us you're awake".
I came out and said;
  "Good morning ladies";
Kaiser said;
  "We came early today especially to help you with your letters, in an hour a few nurses will come to help as well, and with a bit of luck we'll open them all today, then you will decide what you're going to do with all this money"

Gestapo said;

"I suggest you open a bank account here and use credit cards".

"What do you think of the idea"?

"Mmm; Credit cards huh, that is not a bad idea actually".
She went on;

"I have a surprise for you".

"You already have an account".

"I took the liberty and opened it for you";

"I borrowed your passport to do that, I knew you wouldn't have minded".

"I'll be back in a minute" she said and she went out the room.
She came back with all the banks paper work and said;

"There you are, it's all done, all you have to do is go and sign a few forms, deposit the money and collect your credit cards".

"I'll take you there my self just after lunch".
I looked at the paper work and saw a deposit slip with two thousand dollars!!!
I said;

"What's this"?
She said;

"I deposited the money for you and I hope you will accept it without any argument whatsoever".

"After all I owe you a lot more".

"After what you did for us, this is nothing, just a small token of our appreciation, and I want no arguments, period".
Well, for a minute there I forgot who I was dealing with, I forgot her name was Gestapo.
I said;

"Yes, ok sister, thank you".

"No-no-no, the thanks is for you, for everything and let's just leave it there".
As we sat around the table and opened a few letters, the door opened and Anna came in, and with her sweet voice said;

"Good morning everyone I brought you some tea and a few home made cookies".
Sweet old Anna, I'm going miss her something terrible;
She came over to me and with her usual hug and kisses whispered something to me;

"You're leaving us tonight but, I'm sorry to say you will go thru

something bad first, but not to worry, you'll soon be free to carry on".
I asked her "what"?
She said;
  "You know I cannot tell you".
Oh shit, not again.
I wonder what it is this time.
I'm not gone get injured again for sure, otherwise she wouldn't have said, "leaving us tonight"
I mean what can it be?
It can't be all that bad surely if I'm not gone get injured.
I mean is there anything worse than injury?
By the time we finished our tea there was a lot more people in the room helping out with the letters.
The doctors came in and paid their respects, had a word with Gestapo, and left.
About an hour or so later the joker came in and said;
  "Your dental cups are ready, so whenever is convenient".
I looked at Gestapo and she knew I wanted to go and do this ASAP.
The usual stretcher comes in and there I was, yet again pretending

I was a stiff with the white sheet covering me from head to toe.
We went down and it only took the joker ten minutes or so to finish his job.
I asked Gestapo to call one of these firms, if they could fix Jasmines kitchen and all that.
She nodded OK.
We went back up and Gestapo went to the reception for phone calls.
She came back to the room and whispered in my ear;
   "They'll send someone around to asses the damage ASAP"
I said thanks and we carried on with the letters.
The money piles were growing by the minute.
The girl in charge was well equipped today; she brought elastic bands and a calculator with her.
She was separating them in thousands them in five thousand piles.
The bags were still coming in; there was no end to them.
My God, I'll be a millionaire in no time with this rate.

An hour or so later Gestapo came and whispered in my ear;
The repairs for jasmines kitchen will cost six thousand dollars.
I took ten thousand dollars from the pile and put six in one envelope and another four in another.
I gave both to Gestapo and said;
  "After I leave from here give these to jasmine, in the one is the repair money and the other is something for her to replace all the little things she lost in the fire and whatever is left ask her to put half of it in the bank for her daughters;
She said;
  "OK; leave it to me".
We carried on with the letters until lunch time.
Gestapo arranged we all have sandwiches and fruit for all in my room.
After our little break Gestapo said;
  "We have about an hour and a half before the bank closes, so what I suggest is; we take all the money we have so far and make a deposit, sign and collect your

credit cards and tomorrow we'll deposit the rest".
I said;
  "I'm flying tonight at 2am".
  "No problem she said; I'll deposit the rest my self for you; there's not that many bags left anyway".
I said;
  "Ok and we started bagging the money".
The stretcher bed came in.
We arranged the money bags in such a way, as if it was a stiff and covered it with a white sheet.
Kaiser produced a wig and a pair of mirror glasses for me.
I looked in the mirror and saw a real hippy.
Ha-ha, Oh I wished my mother could see me now.
I mean I, didn't recognise my self, let alone anybody else.
And we were off; the two bodyguards, Gestapo and me.
Going thru the corridors, people were looking at me in a weird way; probably thinking what the hell is this clown doing here at this day and age?

Doesn't he know the hippy era was in the sixties?
We went to the back exit leading to the car park.
Gestapo said;
  "Wait here, I'll get my car".
It took her less than two minutes and we started loading.
I'm glad it was a big car; we stuffed it, boot and the back seats.
There was room only for me and her, so we left the guards behind.
The bank was only ten minutes away, and she drove straight to the bank's basement parking.
She said;
  "Stay here, I'll ask for some help".
She came back with two guys and two trolleys.
We loaded the bags and quickly went in the building.
A very serious man came to greet us and said;
  "Come in, have a seat and all that".
It was a big room with a big oval table and a lot of chairs around.

We sat at one end and the guys were counting the money in front of us.
It was a long-ish process even though the nurse had everything in order.
They were recounting every bundle over and over again.
Another guy came in.
He introduced himself as the manager.
He asked for my passport and all the other papers and said;
   "Wait here please".
He was a long faced bastard.
   "I don't like him" I whispered to Gestapo.
I asked him if this is going to take long.
He said;
   "Yes I'm afraid; it's a longish procedure".
Gestapo said to me;
   "I have to go back to the hospital".
She gave me a piece of paper with her number and at what extension I could reach her and said;
   "Call me when you're done here and I'll come to pick you up".
OK I said and she left.

The guys finished counting and said;
   "X amount in GB Pounds cash"
   "X in cheques"
   "X in dollars cash and X in cheques"
   "X in Italian lire";
   "Do you agree sir"?
I said;
   "Yea, whatever man";
I mean I looked like a hippy, I mite as well play the part.
The guys gave me the pay in slip with the amount to sign and they gave me the copy.
They took all the money and left the room.
Twenty minutes later my nightmare began.
Four policemen came in the room, and started interrogating me;
I mean it was something terrible. And the worse part was they were asking questions and wouldn't give me a chance to answer them.
They were bombarding me from everywhere, and it wasn't only questions.
With every question there was a push from the copper behind me, and I don't mean a little push.

I felt as if they wanted me to react so they will be covered if violence was to take place.
I think I was "saved" from all of that because of the CCTV.
After a lot of pushing and shouting I felt I had to put an end to this.
I screamed really loud…
　"SHUT-UP"
They did;
I said;
　"I will answer all your questions but one at a time and with no pushing or shouting, please; thank you".
　"After all I said; I'm not a criminal".
And it worked;
They seemed to ease off a bit.
The sergeant was asking;
　"Who are you"?
　"What is your name"?
I answered very calmly.
　"Where did you get all this money from"?
I told him the truth;
　"People gave it to me".
They all started laughing.
Again he asked me the same question;

"Where did you get all this money from"?
I repeated;
"People gave it to me".
I could see from his point of view it didn't really make any sense; I mean who would do such a thing now days;
"For the last time" he said;
"Where did you get it from"?
I said;
"Please, I know you can hear me but you're not really listening to me, I'm not a thief and I did not steal the money, people just gave it to me".
He looked a bit puzzled.
He said;
"If you don't tell me the truth I'll take you in for questioning".
I said;
"I thought that's what you're doing now, if you take me in you think you will get a different answer"?
He asked me;
"Why are you wearing a wig"?
I said;
"Why...? Is that against the low in this country"?
I said;

"Can I ask you a question"?
He replied;
"I ask the questions here".
I said;
"Ok, but bear in mind that I'm flying back home in a few hours and I don't really want to miss the flight".
"The only place you're going is called jail" he said.
"For the last time, who are you"?
"Where did you get all this money from"?
"There's a different name on the cheques, so where did you get them from"?
I said;
"Some of the cheques are anonymous and some have the name Saint Johnny Walker".
"I am Saint Johnny Walker".
Oh he became really furious.
He said;
"That's it; you're coming with us".
They handcuffed me and I asked if I could make a phone call, everything will be crystal clear. Two of the guys were a bit on the rough side.

My hands were tied behind my back and these two tough guys were more like lifting me up from my arms than simply escorting me to the car.
And they behaved the same in the car all the way to the police station.
I just ignored them.
When we arrived at the station they took me straight into a room and the questions were none stop again.
I mean questions like;
   "Who is your accomplice"?
   "Did you kill someone and took the money"?
   "Did you rob a bank"?
   "Are you money laundering"?
   "Are you working for someone else"?
   "Who are you working for"?
   "What's his name"?
   "Do you work for the mafia"?
And of course, the guy behind me was having a ball.
With every question there was a rough push, a smack on my head, and sometimes both.

I was at their mercy, they could have killed me for all I know and no one would ever know.
After all, there were no cameras in there.
In other words I was in deep shit.
The only thing I said was;
  "I want to make a phone call".
But the answer was no.
Well they didn't exactly say no but they didn't say yes either.
So I decided to play dome.
I just kept quiet and let them enjoy their work.
I mean they wouldn't accept the truth anyway.
Even though in my mind I wanted revenge, I really wanted to kill them all, I was raging mad with them, and my anger was growing with every blow I was receiving.
But I was saying to my self its ok; you can deal with this, stay calm; if I am to be here and go through what I am going through that means God wants me here for some reason; after all, I was in a foreign country, my Italian was poor and they're wearing the uniform, who would the judge believe, me, or the uniform?

I thought only in films they do these things.
But was I wrong.
I don't really know how long this ordeal went on for but it felt like a life time.
And the more silent I was the more I was getting beat up.
I was even thinking if the word "Carabiniery" means torturer
I tried to take my mind elsewhere during this ordeal of mine so I won't go mad, but the beating was so frequent I simply didn't have time to think of anything else.
Eventually they realized they were going nowhere and they dragged me down the stairs and into a cell with three others.
I looked at them and realised they must have gone through the same ordeal as me because they looked hurt.
In fact one of them was in a real bad shape.
I saw a bit of blood on his hand and said;
   "Let me see that".
He looked at me and said;
   "Are you a doctor"?
I said;

"Something like that".
I moved his hand from his wound and placed mine.
And within a minute or so it healed.
I felt something else was wrong with the guy, something really wrong with his health.
I asked him;
"Why you are here"?
He was trying hard to find where the wound was.
He looked at me and said;
"I'm a sick man and don't have long to live".
"We are three brothers and we did a robbery that went wrong".
I said to him;
"I want you all to trust me for a minute OK"?
They all just stood there and looked at me in a weird way.
"I said trust me, we don't have a lot of time".
I said to the two brothers;
"I will hug your brother and I want you to hug both of us; I will try and do something and I really want your help; please trust me on this".

"Salvatore needs you, he needs your help if his gone be ok".
Their expression was as if they were asking themselves how I knew his name.
I just hugged the guy and said;
"Come and hug us both; I want you all to think of Salvatore's problem; just close your eyes and think only that".
And within seconds it happened, the heat and the bright light was between us all.
The more we were squeezing the more Salvatore and I was in agony.
The pain was really bad.
But it lasted only a few minutes.
When I let go of him, I saw the two brothers looking at their clothes, they thought they were on fire.
They were somewhat puzzled, lost really.
They just could not believe what just took place.
As for Salvatore, well, he was in a trance, he was lost in a world of his own.
I said to him;
"You're OK now; you're not dying and no more robberies, OK"?

"In fact I said to all three";
"You will get a job in a vineyard somewhere, for about five years and you will end up buying it from the owner; one of you will become a priest, and the other two will get married after that and have a big family of your own".
"One of you will have four girls and the other five boys".
All three realised that something great just happened here.
They were on their knees and praying.
They looked at me and I saw a change in their faces.
As if they were saying sorry for what we did.
The only thing they asked me was;
"Who are you"?
I said;
"That doesn't matter".
The two policemen came and said to the boys;
"Come; out".
And that's the last I saw of them.
But I didn't worry about them.
I saw their future.
They'll be fine.
About half an hour later the coppers came and took me out of

the cell and back to the same room.
And the same story over and over again.
Same questions all over again.
Finally I was allowed a phone call.
I called Gestapo of course and said I was in a police station.
She said;
   "Let me speak to them, and I handed the phone to the sergeant".
I could hear her screaming at him.
A few minutes later she was there with Kaiser and a couple of doctors.
They came in the room to see if I was ok and Kaiser said;
   "Don't worry, we'll see to it".
They all went out and I suppose they explained the situation.
The coppers came and apologised and I said it's OK, even though I really wanted to ring their necks.
I mean what kind of people are these?
Do they get trained to behave like this?
Gestapo asked me if I was ill treated, and I said no.

I didn't want to go through all that again.
She asked me about the credit cards and if everything ok with the bank.
I said;
  "No, they didn't give me any credit cards and it's the bank manager that put me here".
  "He must have called the police".
She said;
  "Come we'll go there and finish this thing".
  "I know they gave you a rough time in here".
  "Our police are famous for their so called interrogation".
  "It must have been a nightmare for you".
  "I can only imagine what you went thru".
She demanded from the coppers to call the bank so they'll open the back door and let us in.
It was obvious that the banks were closed for the public at this time.
They did I suppose and we were actually escorted there.

520

The manager himself came to let us in and all the way to his office he was apologising and trying to clear his so called position sort of speak for the whole incident. What an ass… I ought to kick his behind.
And even though he knew he was in the wrong, he was playing with words, and all these delay that "we" were causing is highly irregular and that "he" was doing us a favour.
I mean what an asshole!!!
Oh I really, really wanted to kick his butt.
I just could not help nor control myself any longer.
I said;
  "Now you listen to me you moron";
  "Maybe is best to charge me for your so called extra time you're putting in".
  "Maybe that way I won't feel guilty".
  "And just maybe it will put a smile in your miserable f****** face".

"I wonder if you treat your own family the same way as your customers".

"I'm sure after a hard days work you must be exhausted".

"I feel sorry for you".
I could see through him, he was raging mad with what I said.
He got up from his chair and said;
"I don't have to listen to all this".
I just turned and said;
Whether you like it or not I'll say what I want to say to you, you're not fit to manage here; you're more a dictator than a manager and whoever put you in that position must have been really desperate, or need his head examined; I am sure if he knew how you treat people he'll probably want to shoot you himself".

"And don't think that this is over and done with after I'm gone; I'm not finished with you yet; be sure, I'll take it even further".
I think he was embarrassed, he was blushing.
He didn't know how to hide his face.

He got up, took the forms and left the room.
The assistant manager came in and did the rest.
The assistant was very polite and with a smile.
He brought me the credit cards, thanked us all and he escorted us to the door.
As for the asshole the manager, he just vanished.
He didn't even have the decency to come and see us out.
A real asshole!!!
How do people like him get a position like that, I'll never know.
I can't do anything now, but when I go home I'll arrange to relocate the account and put in a "good" word for him.
I can't believe the guy; in fact the word ass… is too good a word for him;
Well; no thanks to him; at least I got to see what is like to be behind bars.
I wore my wig again and we went back to the hospital.

We went straight to my room and saw the people were still working on the letters.
The nurse said;
  "We're down to the last bag".
I asked for some coffee if possible and one of the nurses said I'll go and make some.
One of the doctors said;
  "We can all do with some of that".
  "I think we all need it after what we went through".
  "I also needed a lot of fresh juice".
I felt a bit week and dehydrated.
I looked at Kaiser and immediately she knew what and how I was feeling.
She brought me the chair to sit and a litre of juice.
She said;
  "I know that look".
  "You were at it again weren't you"?
I just smiled a bit.
She said;
  "Who was it this time"?
  "Was it one of the policemen"?
I said;

"Never mind sister, forget it, what I need is to change my shirt please".
Gestapo opened my suitcase and brought me one.
They all saw the bloodstains on my sleeve and panicked.
The doctors came and examine my arm.
They realised it wasn't mine and Kaiser said;
"I knew it; you performed one of your miracles again".
I must have needed the juice something terrible because I finished the whole litre in no time at all.
My head was still hurting from the blows I received and asked for an aspirin or something.
They gave me a couple of pills and sat back holding my head.
The coffee came and I was beginning to relax.
I can't even remember finishing the coffee.
I fell asleep on the wheelchair.
I woke up half an hour later and Kaiser said;
"Even the drugs have no effect on him".

"Look doctor, he's awake". Gestapo said;

"We know your flight is at 3am so we gave you something to sleep for six hours".

"It looks like it didn't affect you at all".

"Anyway here is the list of how much more money we have here; I'll take it home with me tonight and tomorrow I'll make a deposit for you".

"As for that bank manager I'll call the head offices and have a word with them about today's incident".

I asked the two sisters what are they going to do with all those cuddly toys and they said;

"We'll give them to some kid's charity at Xmas.

"We'll say it's from Saint Johnny Walker".

"The children will love them". I said;

"Thank you sisters";

"Thank you for everything". Kaiser said;

"Are you joking"?

"We are supposed to thank you".

"Did you forget already what you have done here"?
Gestapo was actually in tears.
I asked why?
And she said;
"You're flying tonight and we won't see you again, ever.
I said ever?
"Don't ever say ever".
"Ever is a very long time".
"You never know, I just mite surprise you one day".
And just then Jason walked in.
He was with only one walking stick.
He came over to me and gave me a big hug.
He was overcome by emotion, the water works were turned on and he was repeatedly saying "thank you Saint Johnny Walker; I'll never, ever forget you".
"You gave me my life back".
There was no stopping him; he was crying his eyes out.
I had to find a way to stop that and said;
"Take one of this cuddly toys home with you; I know you're not a little kid but trust me on this;

talk to it every night and tell him your every day problems".

"And if one day you ever need me and I mean really need me… tell the bear and I'll know, trust me I'll know;

"Choose one and let me hold it for a minute".

I could see in his face, at that moment he was the happiest boy in the word.

He said;

"Really; can I get one for me"?

I said yes.

"I promise you I'll look after it for the rest of my life".

He chose a middle size one and gave it to me.

I held it close to my heart and said;

"There; now he's part of me".

"If ever you're in need to talk to me just cuddle the bear and talk to it, I'll hear you, I'll be listening, then you will know, you will make the rite decision, whatever your problem is" and handed it over to him.

Mother and son were in a competition after that, which will shed the most tears.

Then I had another visitor, Jasmine.
She just finished her shift and came to say goodbye.
Again hugs and kisses and of course the water works.
She said;
  "I want to give you a little something to remind you that you saved my family" and she takes off the chain with a little cross and puts it around my neck.
I said;
  "I can't accept this".
And she said yes you can;
  "I only wish it was something bigger, and the hugging went on and on".
I also asked her to take a couple of teddies and repeated more or less the same words to her as I did to Jason.
Then Anna the tea lady came thru the door.
As if she was waiting for Jasmine to finish and it was her turn.
And to my surprise she went on her knees crawling towards me.
She stopped in front of my feet and kissed them.
I was really embarrassed.

I helped her up and said;
"No Mamma, you shouldn't have done that".
"You're three times my age and if anything, I should have done that".
She also gave me a chain with a little cross and said;
"You are a great man, God chose you because of your kindness; I thank Him every day for sending you here and prey he'll keep you well to do His job".
I mean there were four women, a boy and two doctors in the room and every one of them was crying, and I mean crying…!!!
I could not hold on any more, I started too.
Shit, I can't even remember the last time I cried.
I had to put an end to it.
I said;
"What's the time"?
"I am starving".
"Is there anything to eat in this place or do I order a take away?"
For a minute there, I saw a bit of laughter.

The next thing I saw was a bit of a panic.
Dinner they were saying; as they all looked at each other.
Panic stations all around as they all wanted to go and get me something.
I said;
   "Ladies… ladies… I was only joking".
Funny how things turn out;
The guy from the restaurant that was sending food for me twice a day, just walked thru the door.
He was a middle age guy; one could describe him as "typical Italian" and said with his typical Italian accent;
   "Ciao ragatsi…" or something like that;
   "I am Giuseppe De Stefano" and a massive smile appeared in his face!!!
He looked at me and said;
   "You must be Saint Johnny Walker e…," and kneels in front of me, crossed him self and kissed my hand.
He said;
   "I want to thank you for saving all those little Italian children;

one of them was my sister's daughter".
I said;
"Thank you for all the wonderful meals you sent".
"Ah… that issss a nothing e…"
"For me issss e the very least I could do to repay for e… what you did e…"
"But tonight…e I knew it issss e your last night here e… and I prepared e… something special for you e… and all your friends here too e"…"!!!
He turns around and opens the door.
Three waiters came in with their food trolleys.
Kaiser, Gestapo and Jasmine went out and brought another table and some chairs;
We all sat down and the waiters started the display.
What a feast!!!
I mean a real feast…!!!
There was lobster, big grilled prawns, grilled salmon, smoked salmon, two kinds of salad, four different kind of pasta, greens, garlic bread, and I don't know what else.

532

Two bottles of white wine and yes… chilled.
I mean what a site!!!
Three tables put together full of everything!!!
I think even her Majesty our Queen, God bless her would have been jealous of.
We were all faced with a dilemma.
Who will start first and from where?
The display was so… perfect; one would think it's a pity really to spoil it.
I think Giuseppe realised what's happening and he sat down next to me and made the first move.
Of course we all followed.
The waiters poured some wine in our glasses and Giuseppe raised his and said in this wonderful Italian accent of his.
"Here's to Saint Johnny Walker e…"
"I hope he will live to be two hundred years old…e and perform e two hundred million miracles e…"
  "Salute"!!!
And every one said "salute"!!!
Then he gives me his business card and said;

"E… if ever you come back to our island I want you to contact me e"?

"I will come personally e my self e to pick you up…e from the Aero-Porto e…"?

"And you will stay at e my villa e…"?

"I will…eee arrange a car and a driver for you and you can stay for…e as long as you wish…e".
With all this Italo-English sentences I'm not really sure if I even spelled them right, but I'm doing my best here; so don't blame me if a word doesn't really sound as it should, but I'm sure you get the point anyway";
And he went on;

"My villa issss e on the east…e side of the island and issss…e on the beach, I'm sure you will like it there e…"?
Well, I must say it was the best thing I've heard since I've been out of prison.
I thanked him for his kindness and said;

"Maybe I'll take you up on that… E…"

The guy didn't really understand what I meant by taking you up and said;
"Up…!!! E… you prefer montania…? E… no problem…e…"
"I have a small palazzo in montania and it is all vineyards around, maybe you see how we make e wine also e… yes…"?
I said;
"Well we'll see".
"Thank you for your kind offer".
What a last night I was having.
I was enjoying every minute of it. And from what I saw in all of them around me, I wasn't the only one, they were all happy and laughing for a change.
But as we all know; all good things must come to an end sometime;
The time came where we had to say our goodbyes.
Giuseppe gave me a big hug and said;
"E… I'm a gone wait for your telephono…e call e…?"
The waiters picked everything up, cleaned the tables and left.

Jasmine did the same with tears in her eyes and then it was good old Anna.
She hugged me and just wouldn't let go.
She was crying her eyes out; she knew it was the last time she was ever going to lay eyes on me.
I knew she was trying to express her love and thankfulness.
So I just stood there hugging her back.
Eventually Jason said something and she let go.
He also did the same thing and they all started crying yet again.
I signalled Gestapo and gently she pulled Jason off me.
Jason held Anna's hand and said to her;
   "Come Mamma we go down together".
They were both sending me kisses on the way out.
And I was left with the two sisters.
We sat down and chatted a bit.
Kaiser was asking if I had any plans for the future.
I said

"Well, everything in my life now has indeed changed".

"I mean I had my job as a chef in a London hotel and the plan was to go back after my holiday".

"Some holiday this turned out to be Huh?"

"Now it seems that's out the window".

"Even if I want to go back, I cannot, people trusted me with their money and I cannot let them down".

"Now I have a different job to do".

"I still have to go back there and work for a while until they get a replacement".

"After all they were good with me, and it's not really a nice thing to just leave".

A few of the nurses came to say goodbye, then a few others.

And then one by one more doctors; Some of them reminded me about the offer they gave me about me becoming a Guiney pig.

They never give up do they?

Well I don't blame them for trying really; after all they're scientists.

That gave the two sisters something to laugh about.
When suddenly we heard a lot of arguing outside the room and a little girl walk thru the door.
She couldn't have been more than six.
She came straight to me, stood there looking at me for a couple of seconds, opened her arms wide for me so I'll cuddle her.
I did of course;
She was squeezing me as hard as she could.
I looked at the two sisters to see if they knew the little girl and both of them shook their heads.
Gestapo went to the door to see and the parents were there.
They wanted to come in but the security boys wouldn't allow them.
She said to the boys;
  "It's ok" and they walked in.
The couple introduced themselves as the parents.
The father was Italian and mother English.
The girl was still there squeezing and would not let go.

I indicated with my finger to the parents to sit down in the corner and be quiet.
After a good ten minutes of squeezing each other with the girl, I knew what the problem was.
I closed my eyes and saw the whole thing, what the parents are going through.
I knew every little detail about the entire family.
A well off family with a good size business;
The fathers name was Mario, the mothers Debbie, and the little one was Francesca.
I also knew they tried doctors and doctors.
And they all said;
   "The problem was psychological".
Psychologists and psychotherapists also tried but nothing.
I mean how could they find what was wrong, they didn't know the story of what actually happened to the little one;
Someone apparently scared the little girl at school and she never spoke since.
That was a year ago.
And that someone was the teacher.

They were playing a game and the teacher got dressed as a monster. The girl opened the door where the monster was supposed to be hiding and… the shock turned out to be too much for her.
The teacher never said anything to anyone about the incident either. The girl trusted me because the mother heard about me and said to her that I was father Christmases' little brother.
And I came especially for her. After a few minutes more hugging, I said to the little one;

"Francesca, Father Xmas sent me here with a gift for you, would you like to see it"?

"Even though the parents knew all about me, they were indeed somewhat shocked when they heard me calling their daughter by her name;
The little one pulled back, looked at me and nodded yes.

"Ok, I lifted her up in my arms and took her to the corner where the teddy's were and asked her";

"Which one would you like"?

She pointed at a brown one, about the same size as she was and I said;
"Oh Cleaver girl, how did you know that was the one he sent for you"?
"And you know what father Xmas said"?
She shook her head.
He said;
"This bear is a special bear".
"It's a magical bear".
"It makes all the monsters go away".
"Look around the room; do you see any monsters here"?
Again she shook her head.
"You see, monsters are afraid of the magical bear and they go away, far away to another country".
"No more monsters here now, they're all gone".
The girl gave me a huge smile. It was clear that the fear of monsters being around was gone. She was convinced that there were none left.
And I said;
"Father Xmas also said the poor bear has no name yet, everybody has a name yes"?

"You're Francesca yes"?
"Mommy's name is Debbie yes"?
"Papa's name is Mario".
I mean the parents were in shock when I mentioned their names.
"Mmm... let's see now".
"What shall we call this magical bear"?
"The girl grabbed the bear from my hand and said;
"His name is Mr Brown"!!!
I heard both the parents crying out "AH" and they were wiping the tears from their eyes.
"What a beautiful name for a bear".
"I'll tell you a little secret".
"Father Xmas said to me";
"If Francesca will guess rite I will bring her more presents at Xmas".
"You see, father Xmas knew his name was Mr Brown but he wanted to see if you could guess it".
"Would you like to take Mr.Brown home"?
She said;
"Yes and I will sleep with him and cuddle him".
"Because you're a good and cleaver girl father Xmas will come

again and bring you more presents".
"Would you like that"?
She said "yes"!!!
"All you have to do is when you go home take mommy's and daddy's hand and you all seat at the table; all of you will write on a piece of paper what presents you want and put the paper under your pillow".
"Mommy and daddy will do the same".
I saw both of them nodding as I looked at them.
"Father Xmas will come and take it and because you're a cleaver girl, he'll bring you whatever you have written".
I whispered in Francesca's ear;
"Look at mommy and daddy, they're both crying".
"And you know why"?
She whispered back, "NO".
"Why don't you go and ask them".
She went to the mother and said;
"Why are you crying mommy"?
The mother just said;
"Nothing darling, I just remembered the bear I had when I was a little girl".

"And where is it now? The little one asked;
"Oh, I lost it darling".
"I'm not going to loose mine".
"What was his name mommy"?
"Mine was also Mr Brown".
"Now the monsters will never come back, yes mommy"?
"Yes darling, never".
The girl run to me again and said;
"Tell father Xmas thank you from me and tell him I love him very much".
She gives me a hug and a kiss and run to her father holding her bear.
The mother came over to me and said;
"I don't know how to thank you, you were our last hope".
"It must be true what they say, you are an Angel".
And the usual hugs and kisses.
She also whispered in my ear;
"How did you know our names"?
I whispered back;
"Father Xmas told me" and smiled.
I simply said;
"What I did was my duty and nothing else".

A psychotherapist could have done this if only he knew what the problem was, the teacher scaring little children.
Someone should have a word with her.
She was saying over and over "thank you, thank you so much".
I said;
   "Go home now, your troubles are over, and remember before you put her to bed, do the thing with the writing, the gift list for father Xmas".
   "She will want to sleep with the teddy, let her, there's no harm in that and as long as it takes".
   "She will know when's the rite time to let go of the teddy.
   "Go home now and be merry with your family".
I collected yet another hug then she kissed my hand and said;
   "Thank you Saint Johnny Walker".
   "She took Francesca from her husband and she went out.
The husband came over to me, kneeled, crossed himself, kissed my hand and said a simple thank you and left.

The two sisters were in tears yet again.
Gestapo said;
 "It really amazes me your coolness when you perform; you make people feel easy after every miracle".
 "You are truly an Angel and I feel I'm one of the luckiest people on earth; I've had the pleasure of crossing your path".
 "I don't think I'll ever, ever forget you".
 "You are the reason I went back to church".
 "For what you did for me at least, I will be for ever grateful".
Time passed very quickly and the girls were getting more and more uneasy.
They knew it was almost time for me to go, and they were packing and repacking my suitcase; well, rack suck really;
I mean looking at them made me really sad.
I hate goodbyes.
I will miss the old girls; we had our moments here in this old hospital.

Oh how I wanted to tell them how I named them both.
Gestapo and Kaiser;
I wonder what the reaction will be.
No, I better not, just in case.
Kaiser said;
  "The joker, you know, the dentist will be driving you to the airport and we're coming along to see you off, ok"?
  "Oh that's nice, thank you".
Kaiser then grabbed me and gave me a longish hug.
  "Oh I wish you could stay here with us".
Then it was Gestapo's turn, she gave me an even longer one.
It was nearing eleven and my flight was scheduled for three am, the joker came and took my bags.
It was really quiet out there, no one in the corridors and most of the patients were sleeping.
That's good, at least I won't have to wear the wig and I won't get lynched.
We went straight to the car park.
We just about fitted in this mini Fiat.

We were headed for the airport and the joker said to the girls seating at the back;
   "If you push the front seats, we'll go faster".
I suppose that must be an Italian joke.
Poor guy, he was trying.
Before long we arrived there and the two girls were in tears again.
I said;
   "Don't do that please, I want to remember you with a smile and not with tears".
Poor girls, they were trying to smile but I could see it was no use really.
We went to the counter and checked myself in.
Even though I still had a couple of hours to spare I said to them;
   "It's best if I go thru and look around the duty free shops".
They said ok and as I expected, the goodbye hugs and kisses I collected were, well one could easily describe as one of hysterical proportions.
They were crying and saying don't go, stay here, you can stay with us and all that.

I mean, grown up girls behaving like that!!!
But they knew that, that was not going to happen.
The goodbyes took more than half an hour.
They simply would not let go, as if their dear life was depended on that.
They finally did, only because I promised them I'll come back for a visit one day, soon.
I finally went thru the check point and I looked back for a final wave.
I saw them standing there waving goodbye at me and wiping tears off still.
I must admit, it made feel good and sad at the same time.
Good because I knew it was genuine friendship and sadness that I was leaving them behind.
But I was strong enough to wipe my tears off and carry on.
After all, I said to my self;
   "I have a job to do, a mission to carry out and what a mission"!!!
I sat at the café and had a coffee, I looked at the departure

monitor and our scheduled flight was on time for a change, no delays.
I went around the duty free and bought an after shave for my friend who lives next door to me.
After all he was looking after my cat; I had to get him something as a thank you gesture.
And it wasn't long after that, they were announcing my flight.
I went thru to gate seven and fifteen minutes later we were on board.
I sat next to an elderly woman in her late sixties.
We were about to take off and this lady was hanging on to my arm and she was trembling.
She said;
  "Do you mind"?
I said;
  "No, no problem".
It was clear that the old lady was scared of flying.
She was holding on to me really tight.
I knew everything about her.
This must be my other so called "gift"

I get to know everything there is to know about the person holding me tight.
She was from Birmingham and her name was Maureen.
She visited her daughter and now she was flying back home.
I said;
   "It's ok Mrs Monkton, there's nothing to fear".
   "You're perfectly safe".
She looked at me in a weird way as if to say how on earth you know my name?
When the plane finally reached its height and everything was ok, she did ask.
   "How did you know my name young man"?
I just said;
   "I've read it on your boarding pass".
She still gave me that weird look, only this time as if "how dare you" or something.
Funny thing though, there was a time that we hit turbulence and I do mean turbulence.
Everybody on board was really scared and holding on to each other, I thought she was liable to

rip my arm off from fear, but no, she was as calm as anything, as if nothing was happening.
As if it was a different person sitting next to me.
We were served drinks and a meal.
And then she went to sleep.
It gave me a chance to write the days events in my diary.
Hi there pal.
It's me SJW.
You'll never guess where we are!!!
We're thirty four thousand feet up in the sky!!!
And yes, it's late.
That means another day gone, and what a day.
What an unbelievable day!!!
Today I have seen everything.
I have even spent time in prison!!!
I always wondered what it feels like being behind bars.
Well, now I know and I don't really like it.
I mean I spent only an hour or so in there, I can only imagine what a heavy prisoner feels, how does time pass day in day out and for years on end.
Heaven forbid.

And then the three brothers in prison, oh they'll be alright, they'll only get probation and community service.
And then it was little Francesca, the little angel.
I mean the innocent and genuine love she showed towards me; it was unreal.
I shall never forget that happy face holding the teddy.
That picture will always stay with me.
And I must not forget the joker.
I wonder if anybody really laughs with his jokes.
Well bless his heart, he's trying.
And of course there are the two sisters, Gestapo and Kaiser.
I mean what one can say about these two.
Devoted to their job, to their families, good sense of humour, great to be with, dynamic as bodyguards;
Come to think of it, I'm not sure the names I gave them are appropriate.
I mean there I was thinking the worse about them and they turned out to be the opposite.

It goes to show you, what the hell do I know in judging people.
I once heard from a wise person the phrase;
   "Never judge a book by its cover";
Now I know what he meant;
And of course there was Anna, the tea lady with the biggest smile in the word;
Good old Anna…!!!
Oh I miss them all already.
I wish I could go back and hug them all once more.
Well I hope my travelling will take me back to that island.
But I must carry on; I still have a lot of work to do.
My mission has just begun.
There are a lot of people out there that need my help and I must, simply must go to them.
I'm on board an aeroplane now headed for home.
Maybe my adventure or rather "My First Mission" will begin from there.
Who knows?
I'm tired now and want to sleep for an hour or so before landing.

Only think I can hope is with these adventures or missions will be injury free;
Signing off now;
Saint Johnny Walker;
Oups...
Wrong name, or is it?
I put my diary away and closed my eyes.
But I couldn't sleep.
I knew something was wrong, something was about to happen.
And funny enough, well, it wasn't funny at all really, but suddenly we had something like a tremor, the plane was shaking badly and the sign fasten your seatbelt came on.
The shaking was getting stronger and stronger.
The oxygen masks dropped and people started screaming.
I looked around and everybody was breathing heavily with the masks in their faces.
Then the unthinkable, the plane took a dive.
Everybody was trying to push with their feet their bodies as far back as possible.

Every one was trying to put any way they could the breaks on, but nothing "works" in situations like these.
In other words we were going down.
Screaming and panic…!!!
Panic and screaming…!!!
That was the only thing people could do.
We could only hope the pilot will keep his cool and not to panic as well and think of something.
But this is where I have to end this story.
I mean steady on.
If I start telling you what happed and how who and what, this book will never end.
Simply, there will be no end.
I'm really, really sorry.
And it's not really my fault either.
It's these publishers.
They charged me a fortune as it is.
So imagine if I carry on with the story.
And another thing I noticed about them; and that is they never joke about money; I assure you of that.

So, now that you've read my book,
I'm sure you'll say.
Saint?
Angel?
What a lot of "rubbish", or "pull
the other one".
But ask yourself, what if I am an
Angel or a Saint;
What if I am telling the truth?
And maybe I really have this
"gift"
Or maybe you're confused and don't
know what to make out of all this;
The truth is, I really am, and I
still perform; though not as
frequent as I would like or rather
could; for some reason I do not
"produce" enough energy any more;
I think God is trying to tell me
"its time to retire";
I'm now what they call a middle
age man; but with all that I've
been through, throughout these
last thirty years, made me feel
more on the "old" side than the
"middle"
Many a year passed since my first
"Healing adventure"
Even my beard that I'm still
wearing has a mind of its own,
it's gone silver-ish;

I am a British citizen but not only;
In fact, I did "collect" over the years a number of nationalities
For obvious reasons I cannot reveal my real name, only because I'll never be aloud to live a normal life.
And yes, I still travel a lot, but never plan my trips.
I pick destinations only through instinct; although I prefer calling it "Guidant's"
My only "goal" is to help those who really need.
And every trip I take, I always use the return ticket back to England or at least I try to.
So for those of you who want to "give up" I have one thing to say to you;
   "Don't give up on life, not just yet".
   "Probably, in a place where you least expects it, you just mite see me there";
   "And believe me, there's a lot more about me".
   "I have discovered through the years that I possess a few more

"Gifts" but let's leave it at that for now".
And if you're wondering, yes, I'm still swearing.
For the moment, I can only wish you… Good Luck with whatever you do in your life.
But remember two very important things;
   "A little respect for people on wheelchairs and… plant a tree whenever and wherever possible".
It only remains for me to thank you for buying this book.
Consider it as money "well" spent.
I love you all.

    Saint Johnny Walker.
★★★

And a little PS: Or an "after-logos" if you prefer;
★★★

The story continues in my next book, titled…
Saint Johnny Walker's "My First Mission"
If you really thought the book you have just read was good, or not bad, wait till you read the next one; it WILL blow your socks off!!!

I guarantee that;
Inside I explain what happened to "our plane going down" how I became a casino owner without knowing it, lots of sex with an entire family, and I mean "orgies" with mother, grandmother and grand daughters;
And if you think that is bad enough, wait till you read that I also slept with nuns and not one at a time either;
I even "describe" in detail the entire night(s) of true passion with them;
Maybe some of you might find this a bit "up normal" or "disgusting" or whatever "label" you care to put there, but it did happen and since I am a "Saint" I cannot lie to you;
Hell, someone even said to me;
  "You should be ashamed of your self"
See what do you think?
One thing I assure you;
I never set out to do these… things, they just… happened;
Read all about it, I'm sure you'll agree with me in calling it fascinating!!!

It has everything one could "not" imagine in it!!!
Expected and unexpected…!!!
I am sure you also noticed, the "lingo" I use in my books; is one of plain simple ordinary English that is actually spoken by everyone, Brit or no Brit;
English that everyone can understand, without any of the so called "fancy" words;
I would love to hear your comments;
And yes; please do be honest;
Or as some people might say "give it to me straight"
As I said;
Feel free to drop me a line here:
   saintjohnnywalker@hotmail.com
Don't miss out the next "episode",
     or you will miss out;
And like my email suggests, it's really **(((HOT)))**
Don't miss it;
SJW

PPS:
I feel I must issue a **warning** here;
   If you're a "heart" sufferer or any other related illnesses or

consider your self "weak" or even think that this book "mite" have an affect on you and I do mean your health;
Do **<u>not</u>** and I repeat **DO NOT** even attempt to buy this book
Simply because…
It's a **(((Real killer)))**
And yes, or rather no, I will not be around to help you out;

www.ingramcontent.com/pod-product-compliance
Ingram Content Group UK Ltd.
Pitfield, Milton Keynes, MK11 3LW, UK
UKHW041259180426
11947UKWH00008B/563